D1526871

UNIONS IN A CONTRARY WORLD
The Future of the Australian
Trade Union Movement

Australia once had extremely high levels of trade union participation, yet since the 1970s the number of union members has been falling dramatically. This book gives the clearest picture yet of why people do or do not belong to unions and, in a sophisticated way, examines the reasons for union decline. Uniquely, it considers both the macro and micro levels, looking at the structure of the economy and the labour market, the relations between unions and employees, the ideological dispositions people have towards unionism, the role of the state and the political and industrial strategies of unions and employers. The author highlights the importance of structural and strategic changes in determining the direction of union membership. This book makes a major contribution to our understanding of union decline, and its implications, and presents a range of strategies for reversing this downturn.

DAVID PEETZ is Head of the School of Industrial Relations at Griffith University, Brisbane, where he is also a member of the Centre for Research in Employment and Work. He spent over five years in the Senior Executive Service of the Australian Public Service in the Department of Industrial Relations, and earlier advised the Minister for Employment and Industrial Relations on fiscal policy. A consultant for the International Labour Organisation in Thailand, Malaysia and China, he has co-edited two books: *Wealth, Poverty and Survival: Australia in the World* (1983) and *Workplace Bargaining in the International Context* (1993). He has also published widely in professional journals.

RESHAPING AUSTRALIAN INSTITUTIONS

Series editors: Geoffrey Brennan and Francis G. Castles, Research School of Social Sciences, Australian National University.

Published in association with the Research School of Social Sciences, Australian National University.

This program of publications arises from the School's initiative in sponsoring a fundamental rethinking of Australia's key institutions before the centenary of Federation in 2001.

Published in this program will be the work of scholars from the Australian National University and elsewhere who are researching and writing on the institutions of the nation. The scope of the program includes the institutions of public governance, intergovernmental relations, Aboriginal Australia, gender, population, the environment, the economy, business, the labour market, the welfare state, the city, education, the media, criminal justice and the Constitution.

Brian Galligan *A Federal Republic*
  0 521 37354 9 hardback   0 521 37746 3 paperback
Patrick Troy (ed.) *Australian Cities*
  0 521 48197 X hardback   0 521 48437 5 paperback
Ian Marsh *Beyond the Two Party System*
  0 521 46223 1 hardback   0 521 46779 9 paperback
Elim Papadakis *Environmental Politics and Institutional Change*
  0 521 55407 1 hardback   0 521 55631 7 paperback
Chilla Bulbeck *Living Feminism*
  0 521 46042 5 hardback   0 521 46596 6 paperback
John Uhr *Deliberative Democracy in Australia*
  0 521 62458 4 hardback   0 521 62465 7 paperback
Mitchell Dean and Barry Hindess (eds) *Governing Australia*
  0 521 58357 8 hardback   0 521 58671 2 paperback
Nicolas Peterson and Will Sanders (eds) *Citizenship and Indigenous Australians*
  0 521 62195 X hardback   0 521 62736 2 paperback
Martin Painter *Collaborative Federalism*
  0 521 59071 X hardback
Julianne Schultz *Reviving the Fourth Estate*
  0 521 62042 2 hardback   0 521 62970 5 paperback

To the memory of my father, Sidney Sierges Peetz,

and for the future of my son, Nicholas Brander-Peetz

UNIONS IN A CONTRARY WORLD

The Future of the
Australian Trade Union Movement

DAVID PEETZ

CAMBRIDGE
UNIVERSITY PRESS

PUBLISHED BY THE PRESS SYNDICATE OF THE UNIVERSITY OF CAMBRIDGE
The Pitt Building, Trumpington Street, Cambridge, United Kingdom

CAMBRIDGE UNIVERSITY PRESS
The Edinburgh Building, Cambridge CB2 2RU, UK   http://www.cup.cam.ac.uk
40 West 20th Street, New York, NY 10011–4211, USA   http://www.cup.org
10 Stamford Road, Oakleigh, Melbourne 3166, Australia

First published 1998

Printed in Australia by Brown Prior Anderson

Typeset in New Baskerville 10/12 pt

A catalogue record for this book is available from the British Library

Library of Congress Cataloguing in Publication data
Peetz, David, 1957–   .
Unions in a contrary world: the future of the Australian trade
union movement/David Peetz.
p.   cm. – (Reshaping Australian institutions)
Includes bibliographical references and index.
ISBN 0-521-63055-X (alk. paper).
ISBN 0-521-63950-6 (pbk.: alk. paper).

1. Trade-unions – Australia – History. 2. Trade-unions – Australia –
Forecasting. 3. Labor movement – Australia – History. 4. Labor
movement – Australia – Forecasting. I. Title. II. Series.
HD6892.P44   1998
331.86'11'00994–dc21   98–7189

National Library of Australia Cataloguing in Publication data
Peetz, David, 1957–   .
Unions in a contrary world: the future of the Australian
trade union movement.

Bibliography.
Includes index.
ISBN 0 521 63055 X.
ISBN 0 521 63950 6 (pbk.).

1. Trade-unions – Australia. 2. Trade-unions – Australia –
Membership. 3. Trade-unions – Australia – History. 4. Collective
labor agreements – Australia. I. Title.
(Series: Reshaping Australian institutions).
331.87320994

ISBN 0 521 63055 X hardback
ISBN 0 521 63950 6 paperback

Contents

List of Figures

List of Tables

Note: In tables, 'N' denotes sample size.

Acknowledgments

My warmest thanks go to a number of people who assisted me in this venture. Steve Frenkel provided capable and insightful guidance, support and comments. Murray Goot generously allowed me access to raw data from his forthcoming book on public opinion and industrial relations and provided thorough comments. A number of other people also provided me with various forms of assistance, including Michael Alexander, Robin Archer, Sarah Bachelard, Mary Brander, Ingrid Brunner, Frank Castles, Bruce Chapman, Bradon Ellem, Chris Fisher, Roy Green, Ian Henderson, Linda Kendell, Iain Ross, Lynne Tacy and Margaret Ward.

My special thanks go to the managers, union delegates and employees whose cooperation was essential in enabling the research on which this book is founded to proceed. I would also like to acknowledge the work of past and present research staff in the Department of Industrial Relations (now the Department of Workplace Relations and Small Business), including John Buchanan, Ron Callus, Mark Cully, Linton Duffin, Miles Goodwin, Alison Morehead, Alison Preston, Peter Riedel, Mark Short, Mairi Steele and Kerry Stephen, whose work generated several of the databases used in this book. Having said this, those who carried out the original collection and analysis of the data for the various surveys used here bear no responsibility for the further analysis or interpretation of them.

Finally, my thanks go to my wife, Mary Brander, a food writer extraordinaire, and to my son, Nicholas, for their tolerance, patience and support.

DAVID PEETZ

Abbreviations

ABS	Australian Bureau of Statistics
ACAC	Australian Conciliation and Arbitration Commission
ACTU	Australian Council of Trade Unions
AES	Australian Election Survey
AIRC	Australian Industrial Relations Commission
ALP	Australian Labor Party
ANOP	Australian National Opinion Polls
ANZSIC	Australian and New Zealand Standard Industry Classification
APAS	Australian Political Attitudes Survey
ASCO	Australian Standard Classification of Occupations
ASIC	Australian Standard Industry Classification
AWA	Australian Workplace Agreement
AWIRS	Australian Workplace Industrial Relations Survey
BCA	Business Council of Australia
CRA	Conzinc Riotinto Australia
DEET	Department of Employment, Education and Training
DIR	Department of Industrial Relations
GST	Goods and Services Tax
HTM	Heylen Research Centre and Teesdale Mueli and Co.
IMA	Issues in Multicultural Australia (survey)
ISIC	International Standards Industry Classification
ISSS	International Social Science Survey
LCS	Labour Council Survey
LFS	Labour Force Survey
NSSS	National Social Science Survey
OECD	Organisation for Economic Cooperation and Development
SEE	Survey of Employees and Earnings
SEMSE	Survey of Employees in Metropolitan Sydney Establishments
TDC	Trade Development Council
WBS	Workplace Bargaining Survey

CHAPTER 1

Patterns and Issues in Union Decline

Through the 1980s and into the 1990s union membership, as a share of the Australian workforce, has been falling. In the space of two decades from 1976 to 1996, union density (the proportion of employees belonging to a union) dropped by two-fifths. The union movement, in a country which had once enjoyed the highest density in the world, is facing a crisis of membership.

While union density is not the same as union strength, it is none-theless one of the most important factors that affects a union move-ment's power. From overseas experience, particularly that of the United States, it appears that declining union density may raise major problems of legitimacy for the union movement as a whole. It can be used as a weapon by employer groups and others to argue that the 'privileges' afforded unions, and denied the majority of the workforce, should be withdrawn. Declining union membership may lead to cutbacks in staff and resources in unions and thereby to reductions in the union organising effort and in services provided to members. Success (or failure) in recruiting union members may influence the attitudes and actions of employees and employers and encourage success (or failure) elsewhere (Rose & Chaison 1992; O'Neill 1971; Western 1993b).

Whether the syndrome of self-perpetuating, deep decline evident in the United States will be repeated in Australia is difficult to predict, but it highlights the importance of understanding the reasons for union decline and the factors that work to reverse this trend. The questions addressed in this book are: *what* are the factors that may make Aus-tralian union membership rise and fall, and *how* and *why* have they influenced union membership? A number of key factors potentially affecting union membership are considered: the structure of the economy and the labour market; the relations between unions and

1

employees; ideological dispositions (or 'sympathy') towards unionism; the behaviour of management towards employees and unions; the role of the state; and the political and industrial strategies of unions.

Union membership, it will be argued, is a function of an array of interacting forces operating at the level of the individual, the workplace, the enterprise and the national and international economy. Most studies, which have focused either on the macro level or on the micro level, but rarely on both, have provided only a partial, and sometimes misleading, picture. Indeed, to disentangle and dissect *all* these influences would require, amongst other things, a thorough analysis of the determinants and processes of union and employer strategies, the political economy of the state, and historical and emerging technological, structural and social change. Such a comprehensive task is beyond the scope of this book. Instead the book focuses on those matters that can be determined within the resources available to a single researcher, while still providing the basis for a broad view of union membership. The methodology pursued draws upon a number of quantitative and qualitative techniques. Inevitably, there are many questions left unanswered, and many others raised by the findings.

This analysis is set in the framework provided by a 'change-response' model of union membership. In this model, changes in union membership depend upon the way in which various parties, but most importantly unions, respond to changes in the environment or in the behaviour of one or more participants in the industrial relations system. At the micro level, union membership is analysed as a function of the factors influencing, in different ways, union reach (the supply of union services) and employees' propensities to join and remain in unions (the demand for union services).

The factors that affect union reach and propensity in turn are argued to be influenced by such matters as the character of the relations between unions and employees, between management and employees and between management and unions as determinants of union membership. The influences on union joining may be quite different from those on union exit (the act of leaving a union). Moreover, factors that increase union membership through encouraging union joining may, in other circumstances, also reduce union membership through encouraging union exit. Apathy towards union-related matters also has an effect on union membership.

The book examines the patterns whereby some jobs are unionised and some are non-union, while the union status of others is dependent on individual choice. The behaviours of employers and unions that determine union reach are argued to be influenced by the political, legislative and economic environment deriving, in part at least, from the strategic decisions taken by the major participants. It is argued, though, that in the end, it is the actions and responses of unions that determine the effect that change in the industrial relations system has upon union membership.

The dominant feature of the institutional environment during the period 1983–96 was the prices and incomes Accord, a bilateral incomes policy agreed between the former Australian Labor Party (ALP) Federal Government and the Australian Council of Trade Unions, involving agreement on wage increases and wage fixing arrangements, and varying elements of economic, social and industrial policy (ALP/ACTU 1983; Stilwell 1986; Carney 1988; Singleton 1992).[1] The Accord has at times been blamed for the decline in union density over that period (Kenyon & Lewis 1992; Bodman 1996). The role of the Accord as a strategic decision of the labour movement is therefore one of the matters given attention in this book.

The decline in Australian union density in the past two decades, it will be argued, is principally due to three factors. The first is a substantial amount of structural change in the labour market. But while this was important in the 1980s, explaining maybe half of the decline that took place then, it does not explain the marked deterioration in the level of union membership in the 1990s. The second, and critical factor, is an institutional break or 'paradigm shift' in the factors determining union membership, which mostly reflects a change in strategies by employers and governments towards unions, notably in their approaches to compulsory unionism. This institutional break also involves efforts by employers and governments to decollectivise employment relations. The third factor is the failure of some unions to provide the infrastructure or act with sufficient vigour or cohesion to prevent employer strategies from leading to a decline in union reach and membership. Indeed, it is argued that the part of the decline in density that is 'explained' by employer actions is in turn due to union performance at the workplace level in response to management agendas for change. However, the factors influencing change in union density are not constant over time. At various times the main forces for change may be legislative, political, ideological or structural, or relate to union or employer strategy, the level of unemployment or the outcomes of major disputes.

Union Density: Trends and Sources 1976–97

For the period from 1976, there are two official and at times seemingly conflicting sources of data: the long-standing Australian Bureau of Statistics (ABS) collection, *Trade Union Statistics*, based on data supplied by unions in an annual census dating back to the early part of the century (hereafter referred to as the 'union census'); and the more recent ABS household survey, usually published as *Trade Union Members*, based on a survey supplementary to the monthly labour force survey (LFS), undertaken on ten occasions from 1976 (hereafter referred to as the 'members survey'). These sources provide quite different estimates of union membership at around the same period, arising from the differences in concepts, scope and methodologies underlying the two sets of data. Neither is clearly preferable to the other for all purposes, though the scope for inaccuracy in the members survey is less than in the union census. The union census follows the approach used in most other countries for collecting data on union membership. However, the ABS considers that the members survey is the appropriate source for measuring union membership, as the prime focus of the union census – which, sadly, the ABS has discontinued – is the number of unions and their size as measured by financial membership. For data prior to 1976 the union census is the only available source.[2]

Figure 1.1 shows the changes in union membership since 1976 in the two ABS series. The break in the union census series in 1985 follows the ABS decision to begin collecting data on financial members, a subset of 'all' members. The figure shows that union membership was either stable, or rose gradually, until 1990. By contrast, there was a sharp decline in union membership during the second half of the Accord.

Figure 1.1   Trade union membership 1976–97

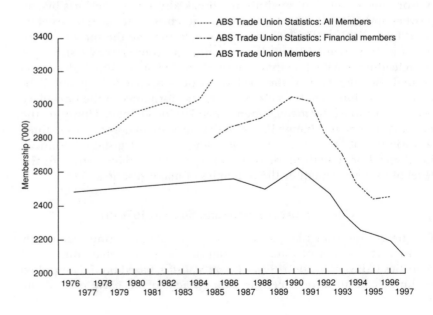

Figure 1.2 Union density 1976–97

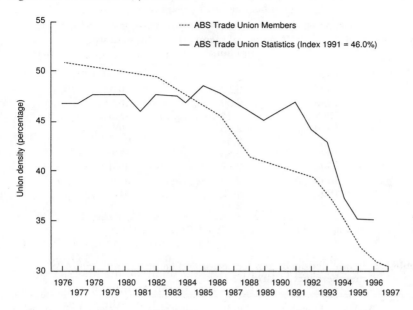

Figure 1.2 displays union density estimates over the period as published by the ABS in these two series. The members survey showed density declining in each successive survey, with a brief acceleration of decline occurring between 1986 and 1988 and another acceleration of decline after 1992. The union census showed union density as increasing between 1976 and 1982, falling slightly in 1986 and 1988, but stable to 1990, falling again in 1992 and each year until 1995, and levelling in 1996. (The density estimates for the union census are presented as an index, with the series linked to form a consistent series at 1985 and 1990.) The census consistently showed union density as being higher than in the members survey, though the gap has diminished markedly since 1992.

Table 1.1 contains the aggregate data from the members survey while table 1.2 shows some disaggregated trends. With just two or three exceptions, each year when density has been measured it has declined for each group, regardless of gender, sector or employment status.

The Decline of Australian Unions in the International Context

Australia's pattern of declining union density is not repeated throughout the western world. Cross-national data inadequacies and inconsistencies make point-of-time comparisons hazardous, but several

Table 1.1 Union membership and density, ABS
members survey, 1976–97

	Number of members (million)	Union density (%)
1976	2.51	51.0
1982	2.57	49.5
1986	2.59	45.6
1988	2.54	41.6
1990	2.66	40.5
1992	2.51	39.6
1993	2.38	37.6
1994	2.28	35.0
1995	2.25	32.7
1996	2.19	31.1
1997	2.11	30.3

Source: ABS Cat. Nos. 6325.0, 6342.0, 6203.0.

Table 1.2 Union density by gender, sector and employment status, ABS
members survey, 1976–97

	Males (%)	Females (%)	Public (%)	Private (%)	Casual (%)	Permanent (%)
1976	54.3	41.8	–	–	–	–
1982	53.4	43.2	72.9	38.6	–	–
1986	50.1	39.1	70.6	34.5	21.0	50.8
1988	46.3	35.0	67.7	31.5	19.7	46.6
1990	45.0	34.6	66.8	30.8	18.8	45.7
1992	43.4	34.8	67.1	29.4	17.2	46.0
1993	40.9	33.5	64.4	27.5	15.9	43.7
1994	39.1	22.9	62.3	26.0	14.7	41.3
1995	35.7	29.1	56.4	25.1	13.9	39.4
1996	33.5	28.1	55.4	24.0	13.1	37.4
1997	33.0	26.9	54.7	23.3	13.8	36.0

Source: ABS Cat. Nos. 6325.0, 6342.0, 6203.0.

observations on broad trends can be made. Several countries experienced substantial declines in union density during the 1980s, but the
size of the decline and their preceding experience varied substantially:
in the US, France, Japan, Spain and (to a lesser extent) Austria, density
fell markedly through the 1970s and 1980s; in the Netherlands and
Switzerland density had been stable in the 1970s but fell in the 1980s;
and in the UK, Turkey, Ireland, Belgium and Denmark, density fell in
the 1980s after having risen in the 1970s (in the last three, the rise more

than offsetting the subsequent decline). By contrast, union density in the 1980s was fairly stable in Canada, Germany and Norway, mostly after rises in the 1970s; density rose in both the 1970s and 1980s in Sweden, Iceland and Finland (Visser 1991:101; OECD 1994:184), though it appears to have fallen in Sweden in the 1990s (Western 1993b:29). Despite the difficulties involved in making direct comparisons, it appears that, while union density has been declining in several countries, it has not been a long-standing, ubiquitous phenomenon. Australia's decline has been one of the largest. In 1985 Australia had higher union density than both Canada and Italy amongst the G7 nations;[3] by 1995 it was below both.

A particularly interesting aspect of the international studies is what they say about the influence that centralisation in wage fixing or union organisation has on union membership. A common belief in Australia is that centralised decision making in wages policy has been responsible for a large part of the decline in union membership and density. The corollary, that this should apply in other countries with similar levels of centralisation, has not been fulfilled. Beaumont, Thomson and Gregory (1980, cited in Beaumont 1987) found a negative correlation between single employer bargaining and union density. Blanchflower and Freeman (1992) compared changes in density according to three alternative taxonomies of corporatism or centralism, and found that 'unions did better in centralised wage-setting systems in the 1970s and 1980s'. Freeman's (1990) econometric analysis indicated that variations in macroeconomic conditions did not explain this result. He argued that in countries with centralised systems the incentive for employers to organise against unions is weaker than it is under decentralised systems such as those in the UK, US and Japan. Indeed, when national employer organisations negotiate with union peak bodies, it is in their interests to encourage constituent firms to unionise and 'assure they pay the going rate' (Freeman 1990; see also OECD 1994:180; Beaumont 1987:190).

In part, Freeman's results were influenced by the fact that several countries with union-administered unemployment insurance systems (Ghent systems) also have centralised wage-fixing arrangements. However, Western (1993a) controlled for the effect of Ghent systems, and still found that, other things being equal, the most centralised union movements had union density 30 percentage points higher than the most decentralised union movements. He argued that centralised unionism was associated with centralised wage bargaining (Western 1993a:269; also Cameron 1984:168), and identified three reasons why centralised union movements performed better: decentralised union movements 'typically waste resources on jurisdictional disputes'; corporatist bargaining typically exposes unions to macroeconomic decision making and enables them to protect and direct resources to organised industries; and employers have little incentive to resist unions when all must pay the 'union wage' (Western 1993a:269).

Similarly, Visser (1992) found union density was highest in countries with, amongst other things, high coverage for bargaining outcomes (reducing the incentive for employers to suppress unions) and high centralisation (or low fragmentation) in the union movement. A cross-national time-series econometric study by Western (1993b:26) found that decentralisation in wage bargaining raised the probability that union membership would start to decline from 30 per cent to 80 per cent (see also Western 1994).

Hancké argued that 'national arrangements are beneficial ... only in addition to strong locals' (1993:596). He examined seven European countries and concluded that the countries whose union movements performed best were those in which 'a strong local union presence coexists with union control over works councils, committees for health and safety and other institutions of workers' participation in the firm' (ibid:598). His data is important in suggesting that the relationship between centralisation and unionisation may be a conditional one, dependent upon workplace union organisation (see also Archer 1995).

The international pattern does not suggest that the centralisation of wage fixation and union organisation can be blamed for the decline in Australian union membership and density. If anything, centralisation should have enhanced rather than eroded union membership. But the international evidence also suggests a reason that may help explain why the Accord could not prevent the decline in union membership: the importance of strong workplace union organisation. This is one of the issues explored in this book.

A Change-response Model of Union Membership

Most studies of union membership fall into one of two groups: those that focus on the micro level, on the individual's decision to unionise, and those that focus on macro level influences. The macro level studies include: 'business cycle' studies, which focus on the role that changes in variables such as inflation, unemployment and wage growth have on aggregate union membership; 'structural' studies, which focus on the influence that changes in the composition of the labour market have on aggregate union density; and various studies that attempt to estimate the impact of public policy changes on membership. Micro level studies of individual behaviour include: those based on psychological theories, particularly frustration-aggression models; those based on economic models, using utility models; and those based on sociological theories, using models of individuals' ideologies. In addition, there are various case studies of particular unions or industries which focus more on the interactions between employers, unions and employees and the influences these interactions have on membership. Unfortunately, there has been little in the way of attempts to integrate these theories (other than Wheeler and McClendon's efforts to integrate the micro-level approaches to union membership).[4] This book attempts to unify these approaches and levels of analyses into an integrated, multi-level model of union membership.

The model used in this study is referred to as a 'change-response' model of union membership, indicating that union membership is determined by *changes* in the environment or in the strategies of major participants in the industrial relations system, and by the way in which other participants (including unions) *respond* to those changes. Amongst other things, this approach attempts to bridge the gap between models that focus upon individual attitudes or behaviour, exclusive of considerations relating to union and employer behaviour and the wider environment, and models that seek to identify macro-determinants of union membership without testing the underlying assumptions about individual behaviour. It is a model of union membership applicable to a 'mature' union movement (Jackson 1982:170–80) which has already established a well-recognised presence; it does not seek to explain 'the original attainment of membership by unions' (Adams 1977:318), although there would be extensive overlap with a model which sought to do so. This model is devised with the Australian experience in mind, but it is one which could apply to many advanced industrial societies. (A glossary of terms used in this model and throughout this book begins on p. 209.)

Core Concepts

Union membership is influenced by both employee preferences and the extent to which employees are able or required to join a union. So the starting point for this model is the distinction between open jobs and restricted jobs, a distinction not commonly used in the literature for this purpose. A job in which the union status of the occupant is primarily determined by the choice of the occupant, that is by union propensity, is referred to as an *open job*. Where the union status of an employee is determined by the characteristics of the job rather than the choice of the employee, it is referred to as a *restricted job*. In this analysis, two types of restricted jobs are identified: *restricted union jobs* (that is, compulsorily unionised jobs), arising usually from decisions by unions, management and/or tribunals that those jobs should be unionised; and *restricted non-union jobs*, arising from either employer attempts to prevent union-isation or union failure to contact and recruit employees.

Union reach measures the extent to which a job is non-union, optionally unionised, or compulsorily unionised. As illustrated in figure 1.3, when an employee is in a restricted job, their union status is determined by *union reach* (cells 1, 2, 5 and 6). When an employee is in an open job, their membership status is not predetermined by union reach. Rather, it is a result of their *union propensity* – the extent to which they would, if they were free to choose, belong or not belong to a union (cells 3 and 4). The first proposition in this model is the simple idea that the impact of any change in the industrial relations system upon union membership depends upon its effect on union reach (the supply of union membership) and union propensity (the demand for union membership).

Union propensity consists of two distinct elements: the propensity of a non-union or new employee to *join* a union; and the propensity of a

Figure 1.3 Union propensity, reach and membership

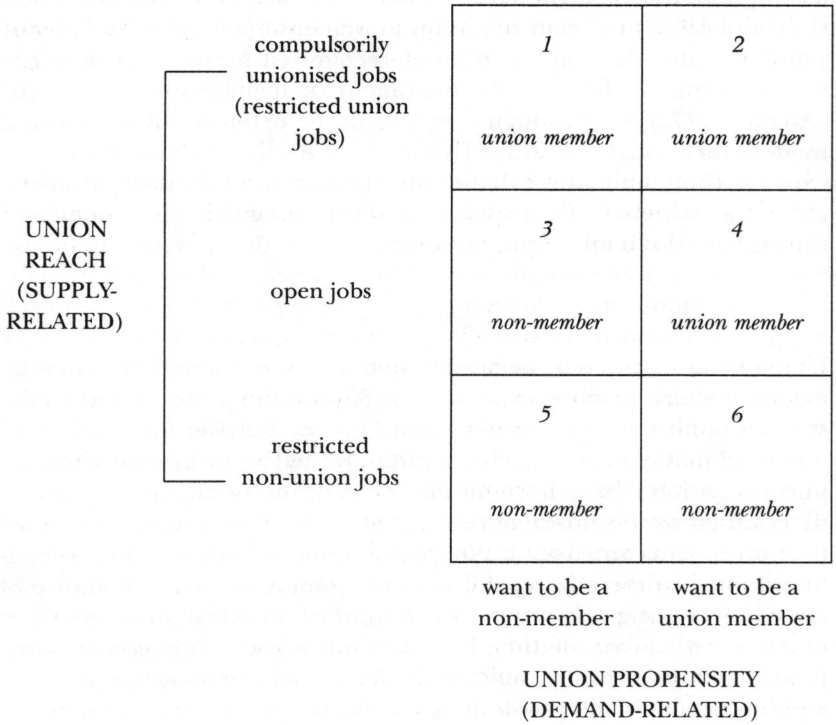

	compulsorily unionised jobs (restricted union jobs)	*1* *union member*	*2* *union member*
UNION REACH (SUPPLY-RELATED)	open jobs	*3* *non-member*	*4* *union member*
	restricted non-union jobs	*5* *non-member*	*6* *non-member*
		want to be a non-member	want to be a union member

UNION PROPENSITY
(DEMAND-RELATED)

union member to either *remain* in the union or, alternatively, *exit* from (leave) the union. Several previous studies have examined the former, and a small number the latter, but examination of both is very rare. Chapters two and three show that quite different factors influence union joining and union exit (or at least they influence them in different ways), because the union has a quite different role in each situation. With regard to joining, union membership is a *prospective* state that the employee will enter if they join the union. Union membership might offer an employee the potential for redress of a present grievance, or a better standard of living, or most importantly union membership might offer a form of *protection* or insurance against future harm.

With regard to the issue of union exit, however, union membership is a *current* state that the employee is experiencing. Employees will still be seeking the continuing protections and benefits unions may claim to offer, and at particular moments they might make decisions about whether or not to remain in their union on the basis of these protections and benefits. These decisions will be based on their workplace experiences for which unions may, at least partly, be held accountable. Unresolved dissatisfactions with work or management, or unsatisfactory resolutions, might have induced some employees to join a union (Wheeler 1985); but they might also induce some employees to leave a union.

Sympathy and Instrumentality

Chapter three also shows that many employees might decide against joining a union for ideological reasons – they might be opposed in principle to trade unionism, or at least to what they perceive to be the ways in which trade unions work. This general ideology people have regarding unionism is referred to as *union sympathy*. It is not, however, independent of actual experience in the workplace – union sympathy increases as employees' negative experiences with their work or employer, or their positive experiences with a union, persuade them of the desirability of, or the need for, unions. But the importance of union sympathy in separately determining union propensity declines once employees have become unionised. Workplace experience, in particular *union instrumentality* – the extent to which employees consider they have benefited from union membership – becomes increasingly important in determining the decision to stay or leave. The longer employees belong to a union, the more they recognise the benefits of union membership (if they have not already left because of some dissatisfaction with the union). Nonetheless, there are still many employees who retain union membership without having achieved any tangible benefits from it, because union membership offers them insurance against future mishap.

The extent to which employees express union instrumentality depends upon a number of attributes of union–employee relations (chapter two). Employees who believe their unions are providing benefit to them will tend to be those who consider that unions deliver protection to their members, are responsive to their members' wishes, possess power at the workplace and act cohesively and cooperatively with each other. Unions exhibiting these characteristics will also promote employee satisfaction with unions.

In order to promote union joining and discourage union exit when employees change jobs, unions need to overcome a phenomenon whose influence is not adequately addressed in the mainstream literature: *union apathy*, a disinterest in union matters and a consequent lack of opinion on union-related issues (Peetz 1997c). Union apathy is influenced by quite different factors to those that influence general political apathy in the wider community. Perhaps this reflects the greater efficacy of collective industrial action over political action in achieving working class objectives. Unions that lack influence and whose structures do not enable them to maintain good contact with employees will have difficulty in overcoming union apathy. Union apathy will be a particular problem amongst casual employees for whom work is less of a central activity (and with whom the union might have difficulty communicating) and, to a lesser extent, amongst younger employees with less experience of work.

Perceptions of union instrumentality, and union membership decisions, might also be influenced by engagement in industrial conflict, although industrial action is typically an infrequent form of interaction. Involvement in disputes will probably reduce union apathy, and if the outcome of a dispute is seen to be beneficial to employees it will enhance union instrumentality and might encourage union joining and discourage union exit (chapter two). Conversely, unsuccessful disputes produce negative union instrumentality and have the potential to discourage union joining and encourage union exit. Some of the most substantial gains or losses in membership of particular unions or groups of unions may arise from successful or unsuccessful major industrial campaigns. However, union sympathy might deteriorate amongst people inconvenienced by industrial action if they have had no direct involvement with that industrial action, especially if the action is not seen as legitimate (chapter three). The impact of (successful) industrial action in facilitating recruitment and retention amongst participants therefore needs to be balanced against its longer-term impact upon union sympathy.

Union Reach

Chapter four shows how union membership is affected by the structure of the economy and the labour market. Union density varies according to workplace size, industry, occupation, employment status and employees' hours of work, so changes in the structure of employment as measured by any of these factors will influence aggregate union density. This is primarily because these structural factors affect the ease with which unions can organise and recruit members and secure union security provisions. These structural factors are also associated with particular stances employers adopt to union membership which in turn determine union reach. Gender differences in density are generally explained by differences in the way union reach varies by occupation and employment status, not by innate gender differences in union propensity.

In the short and medium term, union reach is dependent upon quite different factors to union propensity, but in the long run, union reach is itself influenced by, and influences, union propensity. Unions find it easier to establish compulsory union membership at a workplace or in a firm if there is a high degree of employee support for the union and, conversely, employers find it easier to establish a union-free work environment if support for unions is low (chapter six).

The reverse relationship also applies: union reach can affect union propensity, depending upon the responses of employers or unions. Employers will find it easier to maintain low propensity for union membership by keeping workplaces union-free (chapter two). Whether a non-union employer exhibits benevolent or opportunistic behaviour may influence employees' desire for unionisation.

Compulsory unionism may promote union propensity by exposing employees to the benefits of unionism. But compulsory unionism is also associated with lower incentives for unions to maintain close links with their membership. Some unions may build on the strength that union compulsion reinforces, but others may respond by giving little attention to employees in workplaces with compulsory coverage. The evidence presented in chapter five suggests that, on balance in Australia, union compulsion is associated with lower union responsiveness, protection and participation.

Employer Strategies

Chapters five to seven illustrate the importance for unionisation of the strategies of individual employers regarding unionism. Employer resistance or support for unionisation can, like employees' own union propensity, be affected by ideological and instrumental factors, which in turn are influenced by environmental factors (the extent to which employers are given an incentive to encourage or avoid unions by their legal/institutional and economic environments) and endogenous factors (the nature of union–management relations). They will be more likely to discourage unionisation if union behaviour or the institutional environment enables non-union firms to gain significant cost or productivity advantages over unionised firms. They may discourage it if the economic environment puts a premium on flexibility and this substantially advantages non-union firms over unionised firms. Employers will acquiesce to union presence if the legal/institutional environment requires that bargaining takes place with unions, or requires the establishment of consultative mechanisms at workplace level in which unions are conveniently organised to participate. Employers will encourage unionisation if this gives them an advantage in terms of productivity or flexibility over non-union firms or over firms in which unionisation is neither encouraged nor discouraged. Changes in markets can place increasing pressure upon employers to reduce the power or remove the presence of unions if unions are preventing them from adequately responding to these changes. Employers will be more likely to encourage unionism if they consider unions to be attempting to cooperate in their agenda of workplace change. And they will be more likely to encourage unionism if they have confidence in the union officials with whom they deal – if they trust them to reflect the wishes of the members whom they claim to represent and to keep to their word.

While employer strategy towards *unions* has a major influence on union reach, employer strategy towards *employees* can affect union propensity. Some employers may seek, quite successfully, to pursue 'commitment' strategies with their employees as a means of maintaining non-union status. Others may seek to pursue commitment strategies in conjunction with the workplace unions, that is, to use the union as an element of workplace cooperation. Amongst workplaces that are well unionised, managerial commitment strategies probably have little net impact upon union membership. They may make non-union members less inclined to join, but they will also enhance satisfaction with unions amongst union members. Similarly, bad management and bad jobs will reduce union apathy and encourage some non-union members to join a union – and will certainly assist some non-union workplaces to become unionised. But amongst union members, bad management and bad jobs also reflect poorly upon unions, possibly fostering union exit amongst some members. Some employees will seek union membership as a means of redressing a lack of involvement and participation, but some members will leave a union if it fails to offer any additional say for employees in their work. The management of employees is important but, of itself, is not the critical determinant of union membership.

Union Structures and Strategies

The way in which management employment relations strategies affect union propensity may be influenced by the way in which unions respond to those management strategies; that is, the strategic decisions made by unions at workplace and enterprise level are also influential, an idea that underpins the change-response model. Chapter six shows that, if unions are poorly organised at workplace level, if they lack the presence of a delegate, if they are inactive, if the delegates are not performing satisfactorily in the eyes of their members, then activist management strategies, including those expressed through single-employer bargaining, can make the union redundant. Some management strategies may redress some of the problems that encouraged membership in the first place, and might promote greater trust in the work environment, while the inactive union is unable to demonstrate the need for a continuing role for itself. Managers may adopt such a route for the purpose of circumventing unions. But others, perhaps a greater proportion, will adopt such strategies because that is what they see as being necessary for the survival or prosperity of the enterprise, and they are indifferent to whether the union adapts or dies; their interest is in securing the consent and compliance of the workforce.

Of course, in some cases a union might retain high density precisely because it is inactive at the workplace: it might be the beneficiary of a membership agreement with an employer because the employer sees benefits in having a quiescent union representing its employees. Such short-run benefits, however, should not disguise the long-term vulnerability of a union in these circumstances to severe loss of membership when, due to changes in legislation or employer strategy, that arrangement is finally withdrawn.

The structures of unions therefore play a critical role in enabling an effective union response to the management agenda for change. Active unions demonstrate to members the relevance and importance of continuing union membership and serve as a vaccination against deunionisation. As shown in chapter seven, this might not require that unions engage in workplace-level wage bargaining, but it does require that they engage in workplace- or enterprise-level bargaining of some type, over issues that affect 'the politics of production'. Union structures that are weak at the workplace level will be vulnerable to attack or erosion by employers whose motivations may be malevolent (to unions) or benevolent (to employees). Unions that are not in a position to effectively represent the interests of their members will be deserted by their members and rejected by employers. If management wants and is able to determine wages at the level of the individual within the workplace, unions that do not become part of the wage-bargaining process in the workplace face an uncertain future. And, as shown in chapter two, unions that engage in in-fighting at the workplace, or within a faction-ridden organisational structure, will not retain the loyalty of their existing members and will discourage potential new members from joining.

Unions can be located on a spectrum from *territory-driven* unions to *member-driven* unions. Territory-driven unions' principal orientation is towards securing maximum coverage of members through interactions with employers, tribunals and/or the state. The principal tools of territory-driven unions are compulsory membership agreements or determinations and union preference clauses. Member-driven unions' principal orientation is towards securing maximum coverage and retention of members through interactions with employees. They are alert to and respond to members' wishes and interests. Territory-driven unions may differ from member-driven unions in their internal structures and processes, with territory-driven unions characterised by a focus on extending territorial boundaries, inertia in internal structures, defending incumbency of existing officers, and factional alignments based around internal territories, while lower priority is given to developing workplace communication structures. Member-driven unions give high priority to the workplace, internal democracy, merit principles and circulation of leadership. The degree of reliance on compulsory membership will strongly influence whether a union is territory-driven or member-driven. If there is a major break in the institutional determination of union membership, territory-driven unions are likely to have greater difficulty than member-driven unions in adjusting to a new environment.

Also critical are the strategic decisions taken by unions at workplace level. If, for reasons of prosperity or survival, employees generally support the agenda proposed by management, then unions run a risk if they frivolously seek to derail that agenda. Employees might engage in 'wildcat cooperation' (Streeck 1984) and employers might freeze unions out of the relationship with their members. Unions are more likely to be able to mobilise their members to undertake industrial action if they have demonstrated to their members their goodwill in dealings with management. But employees' agendas rarely coincide exactly with those of management, and often they diverge substantially from them. Employees may not be seeking unions who will pursue unnecessarily conflict-ridden paths, but they are certainly not seeking submissive unions who will yield to the management agenda. That is, to retain and improve their membership unions have to walk the tightrope between conflict and cooperation, by accurately reading and interpreting the mood of their members (chapter two). For this, they need skilled (lay and full-time) negotiators, a fact which stresses the importance of unions' personnel policies and strategies. If unions demonstrate to their members that they are approaching dealings with management in good faith, they will be in a better position to mobilise the workforce to take industrial action when developments necessitate it.

Macro-level Influences

The focus of the model so far has been on the micro-level interactions between employees, unions and management. It is clear from the literature, though, that there are likely to be wider macro-level factors that also influence union membership: the structure and state of the labour market; the nature of product markets; the legislative and political framework; the cultural or ideological environment; the strategies of unions, including the degree of central coordination by union federations; the predominant level at which bargaining occurs; and the policies and strategies of employer associations.

The way in which macro and micro elements interact amongst themselves and between each other in the change-response model is illustrated in figure 1.4. The lower portion of the diagram shows the micro-level interactions that have been discussed so far.

In the upper part of the figure, three principal participants are identified: capital, labour and the state. The *labour movement* (in common shorthand, 'labour') is a term used to encompass the union movement and, where relevant, a labour party. (I use the generic term 'labour party' here to describe such parties as the Australian Labor Party, the New Zealand Labour Party, and the various Social Democratic parties of northern Europe.) The labour parties have originated from within union movements (e.g. Gollan 1960), although their interests, to varying degrees, have diverged thereafter: 'Labor governments are never as consistently responsive as union leaders would like them to be, as unionists at large expect them to be, and as Labor's opponents allege they in fact are' (Martin 1975:106). In relation to capital, most of the key decisions in labour relations are made by managers rather than the owners of capital, when they are not the same people. It is beyond the scope of this book to investigate this distinction any further, and the terms 'employers' and 'managers' are used interchangeably throughout.

The *macro strategic decisions* of labour – of the unions and/or the labour party – can set the framework that, over the long term, is most

Figure 1.4 Union membership in a change-response framework

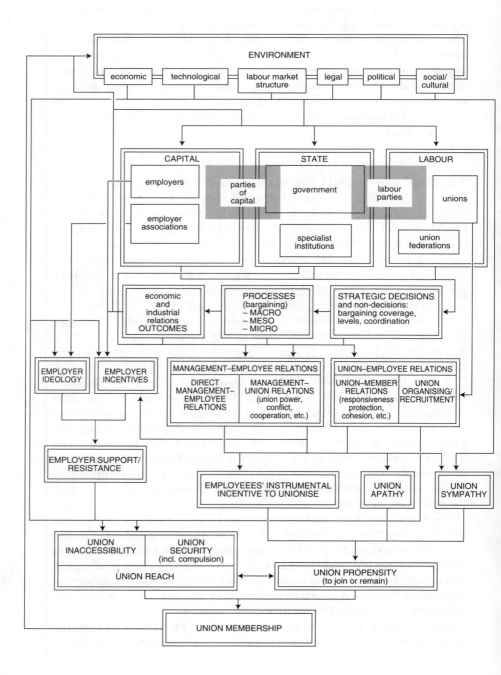

critical to union membership. The decision to adopt a particular macro strategy, in response to a particular change in circumstances, can represent a critical juncture or critical response in the history of a labour movement that determines whether it enters a period of growth, stability or decline (chapter seven). The decisions to establish arbitration systems near the turn of the century were one set of critical responses. The decisions of labour in Australia in the early 1980s regarding incomes policy were another such set.

The importance of these decisions lies in their impact upon many factors including: the coverage of bargaining outcomes; the coordination of bargaining; the protection of union security and of requirements on employers to bargain with unions; the cost, productivity and flexibility advantages of non-union against union firms; and the ideologies and practices of decision makers at the micro level of the union movement. The strategic decisions at the macro level most directly influence employers' decisions on whether to encourage, acquiesce to or resist unionisation and employees' decisions to join or leave unions.

The protection of the union wage (in particular, protecting it from being undermined by non-union employers) is generally more important for union membership than is preventing employees from free-riding on union benefits. This is partly because the individual motivations for union membership go beyond pecuniary benefits to encompass insurance against potential or actual employer maltreatment, something on which it is not easy for non-members to free-ride, and even encompass ideological motivations (chapters two and three). It is also partly because the employer influence upon union reach can be pivotal (chapters five to seven). But protecting the union wage and removing the incentive for employers using cost-minimisation strategies to deunionise is not sufficient to protect union membership. Employers whose strategies focus on productivity enhancement might also adopt individual bargaining strategies that undermine or remove union representation, particularly if collective bargaining with unions is unable to deliver the efficiencies management is seeking in a changing economic environment (chapters six and seven).

A fundamental issue facing labour at the macro level is whether to travel a corporatist or sectional path. Major changes in economic circumstances may create a cleavage which requires a critical response from labour on which path to take (chapter seven). A corporatist path linking the unions, the state and/or employers provides the potential for wide coverage of bargaining outcomes and the generalisation of the union wage, reducing the cost disadvantage of union against non-union labour. It may provide the opportunity to adjust wage-fixing arrangements as economic circumstances change, to take account of

productivity issues and to prevent union firms from facing an increasing productivity and flexibility disadvantage. And it may provide the
opportunity not just to alter the institutions but also the ideologies and
practices of those charged with the micro-level responsibility for bargaining with employers and dealing with employee grievances. For all
these reasons, corporatist strategies offer a potential opportunity for
protection of union membership against the downward pressures
arising from changes in international markets and the determined
pursuit by some employers of employee relations strategies aimed at
increasing employee perceptions of common interest with, and commitment to, the employer, with sometimes negative consequences for
unprepared unions. At the same time, corporatist arrangements need
ultimately to be congruent with employee preferences. Employees may
leave unions if their macro-level objectives and practices are inconsistent with members' own priorities. More importantly, the union
movement and wage system would be unstable if employee views were
too dissonant with union objectives – union leaderships would be over-
thrown, breakaway unions established, industrial action would spread
and eventually the corporatist strategy would disintegrate. Unions under
a corporatist umbrella are threatened both by wildcat cooperation and
wildcat rejectionism. It may even be the case that no 'decision' on bargaining levels or coverage is taken by anyone – rather a 'non-decision'
confines bargaining (as in the US) to the micro level by virtue of the
'social and political values and institutional practices' that 'limit the
scope' of the decision-making process and prevent alternative bargaining levels being considered (Bachrach & Baratz 1962, 1963, 1970). For
example, in Australia, for most of this century, overall bargaining
coverage has not been an issue decided by the parties, as it was
determined by the early development of the award system.

So the factors that determine the nature of the macro strategy
pursued by labour in response to social or economic cleavage also
determine the direction which union membership takes. The structure
of the union movement, the ability of peak bodies to exercise central
control, and the institutional arrangements that operate in the industrial relations system, all have some influence upon the choices made.
Ultimately, though, it is the ideology, experience, intent and leadership
of the labour movement that matter most. The beliefs held by leaders of
union movements, and their insight and ability to anticipate change, are
central to unions' fortunes. To varying degrees union structures and
institutional arrangements may adapt to new strategic paths. Some
structures and arrangements may be so rigid or so far from some ideal
as to preclude particular options (e.g. corporatist paths) being adopted,
but no structures will change unless leadership is shown in forcing
adaptation in response to changing circumstances.

The State and the Environment

The structure of the state will vary substantially between societies. In federal systems (such as Australia, the US and Germany) there are several levels of government. Federalism may severely fragment the state, particularly if government(s) at one level pursue policies contrary to those adopted by government(s) at another level. The principal labour market activity of governments is in setting the legislative framework within which bargaining takes place, but they also have a role as employer, and an important influence on bargaining levels and outcomes through their wages policy. Specialist labour market regulatory institutions are often also created, sometimes to administer and enforce special laws of collective bargaining, less frequently to perform an arbitration function in the settlement of interest disputes (disputes over the terms of a proposed collective agreement). Specialist institutions such as tribunals may have a great deal of autonomy and be prepared to implement policies at variance with those of governments, and therefore have to be treated analytically as distinct from government (Plowman, Deery & Fisher 1981:19). The decisions of the state regarding provisions for union security have an obvious and substantial impact upon union reach and hence membership. The impact of a change in the legal/institutional environment for union reach will depend upon the responses of the parties. Unions that have maintained good contact with their members and demonstrated their ability to offer protection will retain their members in the context of such changes, but those that have become distant from their members will lose them.

These participants (capital, labour and the state) operate within a particular *environment*, which itself is partly endogenous, that is, shaped by the participants themselves. Changes in the environment for industrial relations can also affect union membership, but again the impact depends upon the responses of the participants. Changes in the structure of the economy, away from those sectors that are easily organised towards those which are hard to organise, may lead to a reduction in union reach (chapter four), but fundamentally the size of the effect depends upon the response of the unions. If their recruitment strategies are able to adapt to the requirements of potential members in the new growth areas, then membership will grow. Much depends upon the form of membership expansion unions pursue. If they (continue to) pursue 'market-share' unionism (Willman 1989) – competition in areas of existing, often high-density, membership – then structural shifts in the economy will indeed lead to a decline in union membership. If, on the other hand, unions pursue 'expansionary' unionism, they will seek to attract new members in growing industries with previously low density. The shift in the composition of the labour market from blue- to white-collar occupations during the 1960s and 1970s was not

accompanied by a decline in union membership, precisely because
unions were able to mobilise certain groups of white-collar employees.
There is little that is inevitable about structural change leading to union
decline, unless union responses to that change make it so.

Changes in the business cycle have the capacity to influence unionism, but from the existing literature it appears that only changes in
levels of unemployment appear to have a consistent effect. As unemployment rises, and profits fall, the employer incentive to avoid unions
rises, the capacity to hire non-union labour without penalty increases,
and union instrumentality amongst employees declines. On the other
hand, as shown in chapter two, if unions are able to respond to down-
turns by successfully resisting compulsory layoffs, and demonstrating to
employees that they offer a better form of insurance or job security, then
at the micro level at least some unions may be able to enhance their
membership as a result of rising unemployment.

On the evidence of recent years, as revealed in the literature, other
aspects of the business cycle – changes in inflation and in real and
nominal earnings growth – do not have an obvious, consistent effect and
their impact, if any, on union membership is strongly conditional upon
the way in which unions, employers and the state respond to the particular economic circumstances. Other economic changes not usually
modelled may be more critical. The changing nature of international
markets in the 1980s, the growing exposure of national economies to
international forces, the increasing emphasis upon 'flexibility' in production and outputs, and, in Australia, the crisis in the external account
in the mid-1980s appear to have had an impact on union membership
because of the response that they have induced, most particularly from
employers (chapters five to seven).

Finally, changes in the ideologies of unions, employers and employees
can each influence union membership, by affecting the actions each
pursues and the responses they make to changing circumstances.
Managers who wished to pursue anti-union strategies would have been
encouraged by the apparent victories of some employers who con-
fronted inexpert unions in the recessed economic climate that followed
the external account crisis. Changes in employer ideology can be endogenous to the industrial relations system but they can also arise from
external forces, ranging from rapid economic change to the communist
scare and Labor split of the 1950s and the development of the teaching
of human resource management.

Stability, Change and Response

Generally, the relationships shown in figure 1.4 will be fairly stable;
changes in the overall pattern of union membership are typically fairly

slow. Most of the time the differences made by governments are marginal: the impact of the state is much more a legacy of the past than of the present. But at particular times there may be fundamental institutional breaks or 'paradigm shifts' (Price & Bain 1989) in the relationships governing union membership. These institutional breaks emerge from particularly forceful conjunctions of social and/or economic events and/or powerful alliances among some of the participants. The term 'critical junctures' (Lipset & Rokkan 1967; Collier & Collier 1991) is useful for pointing to the key strategic choices that are made by parties which determine whether an institutional break occurs in the determination of union membership, the characteristics of the shift and how it affects union membership. A critical juncture may arise from a substantial strategic move, perhaps arising from a grand new insight of one or more of the participants; or it may come from some pivotal failure of strategy. Either way, it represents a watershed in political and industrial life that opens up certain directions of change and forecloses others in a way that is likely to shape politics and unionism for years following (Collier & Collier 1991). This concept (discussed again in chapter seven) provides a useful framework for understanding developments in Australia and New Zealand in the early 1980s and the 1990s.

What, then, does a 'change-response' model of union membership suggest is the factor that matters the most? In one sense, the answer is: what matters most is whatever changes and whatever responds. If there is no change, then the system is stable. But if an element of the system does change, the outcomes of the system will change. The way in which those outcomes change will depend upon the way in which participants in the system respond. Ultimately, though, it is union membership that is being considered here, and in that context it is the unions themselves – through their relations with employees and employers and their *responses* to changes in the environment or in the strategies of employers or the state – that have the critical role in whether union membership falls, remains stable or rises in this model. The way in which unions relate to employees is the single most important determinant of union propensity. The way in which unions relate to employers and the way in which they search out and recruit new members are major determinants of union reach. Whatever change occurs in the system, unions are in a position to respond. When structural change occurs in the labour market, the response in terms of union recruitment strategies determines the ultimate importance of the structural effect. When employers adopt particular strategies in response to changes in the macroeconomy, in employer ideology, or any other factor, it is the way in which unions respond to employer behaviour that determines whether union membership falls, remains stable or rises. Yet unions might give the appearance of being unimportant in explaining changes in union membership because they often exhibit a high degree of stability in their relations and fail to respond substantially to changing circumstances. Such non-responses are just as important as any responses they might otherwise have made. No matter how big the changes coming from elsewhere in the system, unions have the ability to respond. They have shown over their history their capacity for response and for making large and sudden gains in membership.

The change-response model attempts to depict the complexity of the relationships involved in determining union membership and therefore requires a research approach incorporating several data sources and techniques. Several individual points of inquiry are possible, but this study attempts to integrate a number of forms and levels of analysis in order to develop a more holistic picture. The cost of this is that none of the techniques is pursued in as much detail as would otherwise be possible and some aspects are given only light treatment. The benefit, however, is that a better, more comprehensive understanding is able to be developed of the mechanisms that determine union membership, the reasons for its decline in Australia and the possibilities for the future.

What techniques of analysis are used? The economic forces that influence the structure of the labour market are considered by examining published and unpublished official data on union membership by use of shift-share analysis, which separately identifies the effect of structural change in employment shares *between* groups, and the effect of *within*-group changes in, for example, union density. At the core of the change-response model is the individual employee, and so data from four surveys of employees are frequently referred to throughout the book. In order to investigate the relationships between the characteristics and behaviour of workplaces or management and union membership, workplace survey data have been analysed, both in their own right and through the matching and analysis of workplace and individual-level data. Finally, the strategies and behaviour of unions, peak union federations and institutions of the state are examined, mostly through a close-pair analysis that compares developments in Australia and New Zealand over the 1970s, 1980s and 1990s and an examination of inter-state variations within Australia in trends in union density. More detail about the research methodologies is contained in the appendix.

The Historical Backdrop: Australian Union Density 1901–76

The focus of this book is on recent years, but it is important to consider the background to recent developments, by examining patterns in the rise and decline in union membership in Australia in the past. There is not a simple history of union membership rising through to the 1970s and falling thereafter. Rather, there have been several periods of rise and decline up until the most recent period of decline that started in the mid-1970s. The main point of this analysis is to show that primary determinants of change in union membership can themselves change over time.

The institutional arrangements enacted at the turn of the century set the framework for arbitration and for the growth of union membership. The origins of arbitration in both Australia and New Zealand date to the industrial defeats of the 1890s as unions battled employers facing substantial pressure to reduce costs in the context of economic depression. Unemployed workers took the jobs of striking unionists and membership of unions had, after two decades of substantial expansion, declined dramatically. Unions sought legislative refuge from further employer onslaughts. In 1894, a New Zealand Liberal Government (with the support of the labour movement) passed the *Conciliation and Arbitration Act*. In the years that followed, tribunal-based arbitration systems or wages boards were introduced in the Australian colonies cum States and, in 1904, in the Australian federal system (Macintyre 1983). This represented the first institutional break or paradigm shift in Australian industrial relations.

It was an explicit objective of the arbitration systems in both countries to encourage the growth of unionism. Moreover, it had a significant impact on employer behaviour, as the generalisation of a union wage through the award system reduced the incentives for employers to oppose union labour. Australian union density, as measured by the union census, rose from 6 per cent in 1901 to 28 per cent in 1911.[5] Although other influences have been identified as leading to the growth of unionisation in some industries (Sheldon 1993), it is clear that substantial union growth followed the establishment of arbitration. For many years Australia had the highest rate of union density in the world (Scherer 1983:170).

Table 1.3 shows union density in the union census from 1911 onwards. Union density rose sharply until 1920. It dipped for a few years and then resumed an upwards path to peak at 58 per cent in 1927. It then fell sharply during the Great Depression, to no more than 43 per cent in 1934.[6] From 1935 union density started to recover some of its lost ground, with growth accelerating during World War II. After falling slightly, from 54 to 51 per cent, immediately after the war, it resumed an upwards path, peaking at 63 per cent in 1953 at the height of the Korean war boom. Thereafter union density declined gradually, to trough at 49 per cent in 1969 and 1970. It rose to 56 per cent by 1975 and remained

UNIONS IN A CONTRARY WORLD

within one or two percentage points of that, on the union census data, for several years.

Rawson (1978) provides a useful historical analysis of the reasons for the rises and falls in union density. The early, rapid growth in unionisation to 1920 was attributable, in no small part, to the continuing impact of the introduction and expansion of federal and state

Table 1.3 Union density 1911–97, ABS union census series

Year	Union density	Year	Union density	Year	Union density
All members (December)		1941	49.9	1973	53.0
		1942	52.6	1974	55.0
1911	27.9	1943	52.5	1975	56.0
1912	38.5	1944	54.2	1976	55.0
1913	41.7	1945	54.2	1977	55.0
1914	45.0	1946	50.8	1978	55.0
1915	44.0	1947	53.4	1979	55.0
1916	47.5	1948	56.0	1980	55.0
1917	48.7	1949	57.0	1981	54.0
1918	49.0	1950	58.0	1982	56.0
1919	50.0	1951	60.0	1983	56.0
1920	53.3	1952	60.0	1984	55.0
1921	51.6	1953	63.0		
1922	50.4	1954	62.0	*Financial members*	
1923	49.1	1955	59.0	*(June) (SEE)*[a]	
1924	49.9	1956	59.0		
1925	53.5	1957	59.0	1985	50.6
1926	55.2	1958	58.0	1986	50.0
1927	58.0	1959	58.0	1987	49.0
1928	57.2	1960	58.0	1988	48.0
1929	56.0	1961	57.0	1989	47.0
1930	52.7	1962	57.0	1990	48.0
1931	45.0	1963	57.0		
1932	44.5	1964	56.0	*Financial members*	
1933	44.4	1965	55.0	*(June) (LFS)*[b]	
1934	42.6	1966	53.0		
1935	43.5	1967	52.0	1990	46.0
1936	44.1	1968	50.0	1991	47.0
1937	45.6	1969	49.0	1992	44.0
1938	46.4	1970	49.0	1993	43.0
1939	47.6	1971	51.0	1994	38.0
1940	47.9	1972	52.0	1995	35.3
				1996	34.7

Source: ABS Cat. No. 6323.0.
a Denominator (number of employees) based on survey of earnings and employees.
b Denominator based on labour force survey.

arbitration. The greater irregularity in changes in union membership after 1920 arose from the fluctuating fortunes of the ALP in the four States that had established arbitration systems. A non-Labor Government in New South Wales removed access to arbitration systems for rural and public sector workers in 1922, leading to a sharp drop in union density in this State. In 1925 a new Labor Government restored their access and reversed the drop in density. A Labor Government in Queensland introduced, in effect, compulsory unionism in 1925, leading to a sharp increase in density there. The return of Labor Governments in South Australia and Western Australia 'was promptly followed by changes in each State's arbitration system and almost as promptly by a growth of union density'. Unionisation was more stable in Victoria and Tasmania, whose wage board systems did not then require the official recognition of unions (Rawson 1978:26).

The major fall in unionisation in the early 1930s resulted from the onset of massive unemployment during the Great Depression. Indeed, unemployment had started to rise in 1928 and 'a series of disastrous strikes helped to shatter the organisation of several trade unions even before the onset of the Depression in 1929'. As unemployment started to ease, unionisation slowly recovered. After this, Rawson attributes much of the change in unionisation to changes in the composition of the workforce. The wartime and early post-war growth of manufacturing, and increasing workplace size, were credited with the growth of union density to 1953. From 1954 to 1971 the growth of white-collar occupations and service industries led to a reduction in union density. A minor but still significant factor was the attitude of governments and public authorities to unionisation. The most notable public policy change was the abolition of compulsory unionism by the Queensland State Industrial Commission in 1966, which saw union density fall from 71 per cent in 1966 to 54 per cent in 1973. The recovery in union density, which occurred in the early to mid-1970s, Rawson indicates was not 'the product of a general increase in union membership but of a major reconstitution of unionism which, after a time lag of some twenty years, ha[d] come to be more in keeping with the workforce of the "post-industrial" era' (ibid:37). An important part of this reconstitution was unions making agreements with employers for compulsory unionism. The growth of unionisation in the public services was, in part, attributable to the presence of Labor governments, especially the Whitlam Federal Government, though public-sector unionisation also grew under conservative State governments (Rawson 1978:27–39).

Rawson's historical explanation of union density over the large part of this century is seminal and well supported by the evidence. However, he attributes probably too great a role to changing composition of the workforce in explaining union growth and decline in the 1950s and 1960s. Shift-share analysis of the effect upon union density of between-industry changes in the composition of employment[7] shows that the growth in union density during World War II was in part attributable to the changing composition of employment associated with the war effort; nearly half of the 6.6 percentage point increase in union density between 1939 and 1944 can be attributed to industry structure effects. However, the impact of changing industry composition was comparatively slight from then on. Structural change between industries explained none of the nine percentage point increase in union density between 1944 and 1953, while over the period from 1953 to 1960, when density declined by five percentage points, changes in the industry composition of employment would have had the reverse effect, tending to raise density, by the order of one-half of a percentage point.

In the second half of the 1960s, when density declined by four points, industrial change probably slightly favoured unions. The magnitude and direction of industrial change did not alter through the early 1970s, yet density grew again by six points from 1970 to 1976. A small part of the growth in the early 1970s can be better explained by shifts between public- and private-sector employment, which had been of no great consequence for union density over the 1950s and 1960s. Growth of public-sector employment accounted for approximately one of the three percentage points of growth in union density from 1972 to 1976.

Despite the growth of white-collar employment, changes in the occupational distribution of employment did not appear to significantly hamper union growth. Indeed, it appeared that between 1964 and 1971, when white-collar employment grew by four percentage points and union density fell by five percentage points, there was little significant downward pressure from occupational change, mainly because the blue-collar decline was concentrated in occupational groups with low density (such as agricultural workers) while the white-collar growth was concentrated in occupational groups that were unionised or, at least, unionisable (professional, technical and clerical workers). Thereafter, the effect of occupational change exerted a slight downward influence on unionisation. Changes in hours of work had a steadier, downwards but also small impact on union density during the 1960s and 1970s: over the period from 1964 to 1976, the growth of part-time work depressed union density by just over one percentage point.

In the light of the generally small magnitude of these effects, and the mutually offsetting nature of some of them, it does not appear that changes in the composition of employment do much to explain the quite substantial upwards and downwards movements in union density over the period from 1950 to 1976. As Rawson points out, the recovery in union membership over the early 1970s probably owes most to the successful union strategy of infiltrating white-collar ranks. The Whitlam Government also assisted union growth. For a while it used the public sector as a pacesetter for the improvement of conditions in the private sector. In particular, the then Minister for Labour, Clyde Cameron, sought to increase annual leave for public servants from three weeks to four weeks, but only for union members. In the end, there was no legal basis for such discrimination, and the increase in leave was awarded to all employees, but the Minister's moves had an immediate and large impact upon unionism in the public sector (Griffin 1983:14). Moreover, upon submission from women's groups, the ACTU and the Whitlam Government, the Conciliation and Arbitration Commission granted equal pay for women, phased in over three years. This probably increased female employees' beliefs that there was some potential gain in joining a union. Between the first, more qualified, equal pay decision in 1969, and December 1975, recorded female union density rose by 12 percentage points (one-third); recorded male density rose 5 points (one-eleventh).

Are there any other explanations for the decline of union density from 1953 through to the end of the 1960s? An important historical factor in the 1950s and 1960s which Rawson discusses (ibid:101–23), but not in the context of declining union membership, was the communist/anti-communist fighting within the union movement, culminating in the split in the Australian Labor Party and the formation of the Democratic Labor Party in the mid-1950s. The effect of this split was to cripple Labor politically, largely preventing it from regaining office until 1972 federally, and until later in several States. It promoted 'market-share' unionism as left- and right-wing unions battled for coverage of already unionised employees. It is also likely that the split and the resultant anti-communist propaganda would have discouraged some employees from obtaining or retaining union membership. It provided an environment that was conducive to employer resistance to unionisation or to agreements regarding union preference for certain unions – although other, right-wing unions may have benefited from preference arrangements aimed at excluding their left-wing opponents. As Rawson (ibid:107) pointed out, in no other Western country except Italy and France did communists become so prominent in trade unions, and in Australia, unlike those countries, unionism was the only sphere in which communists attained prominence. Consequently, anti-communism was intimately associated with anti-unionism in Australia in the 1950s and 1960s, particularly when anti-communist ideology was being propagated by conservative political parties and media.

The decline in union density of about 15 percentage points over the 13 years to 1995 is comparable to, though not as rapid as, the 15-point decline over the seven years into the depths of the Great Depression.

The Depression aside, it was clearly greater than any drop that has occurred in any other comparable period, the next largest being the drop of 10 percentage points over the 12 years from 1957 to 1969. Over the next seven years, to 1976, seven of those 10 percentage points were recovered. From a simple historical perspective, there seems nothing immutable about the continuation of any particular period of decline, including the current one.

In summary, the primary causes of change in union membership alter from time to time. At various times and to varying degrees, the main forces for change in union density have related to: the legislative frameworks at state or federal levels; the political and ideological environment; union and employer strategies; the level of unemployment; the outcomes of major disputes; and structural change in the labour market. The following chapters examine the current determinants of union membership and the reasons for the decline in density over the past two decades and in particular during the 1990s.

CHAPTER 2

Joining and Leaving Unions

This chapter analyses union membership at the level of the individual employee. The data come from four surveys of employee attitudes: the 1990–91 Survey of Employees in Metropolitan Sydney Establishments (SEMSE), undertaken by the author; the 1995 Australian Workplace Industrial Relations Survey (AWIRS95); the 1996 Labor Council Survey (LCS-96); and the 1996 Australian Election Survey (AES) (Jones et al. 1996). These surveys are discussed in more detail in the appendix on research methodology. The first two surveys were restricted to employees in workplaces with 20 or more employees, with SEMSE also being restricted to certain industries and localities; the other two were household surveys with no restrictions on type of workplace or locality. In 1997 a second Labor Council Survey (LCS-97) was, like the first, undertaken by Newspoll; it had far fewer questions but some results are briefly discussed in this and other chapters.

This chapter looks at the reasons people have for belonging or not belonging to a union. The focus is initially on answers to some open-ended questions posed by the surveys, followed by a discussion of union propensity (whether employees prefer to be in a union); the instrumentality of union membership; satisfaction with unions; responsiveness of unions; and aspects of the management-employee relationship.

Union Membership in the Surveys

Before discussing attitudinal data from the employee surveys, we need to know something about union membership in each of the surveys. This is shown in table 2.1. Union density is higher in the workplace-based surveys (SEMSE and AWIRS95) than in the household-based surveys (AES and LCS-96), in part because workplaces with less than

31

20 employees were excluded from the sample and perhaps because managers in some non-union workplaces are less likely to let their employees participate in surveys than managers in unionised workplaces. The latter is especially the case in SEMSE and leads to underestimates of non-members and former members. LCS-96 comes closest to the contemporary ABS union density estimates (33 per cent in the members survey, 35 per cent in the union census).

It appears that a large majority of employees have belonged to a union at some stage in their working lives. The overall union exit rate appears to be something around 50 per cent; that is, around half of the people who once belonged to a union are no longer in a union. The same-workplace union exit rate – the number of people who have left a union at their current workplace, divided by the number of people who were ever in a union at their current workplace – is in the order of one in eight.

Why People Join and Belong to Unions

Why did those currently in a union belong? Their answers to this open-ended question are summarised in table 2.2. Amongst those who answered the question (79 per cent of all union members), over one-third indicated that they belonged to a union because it was compulsory. Although most of these gave no other reason, 37 per cent also indicated (in response to another question) that they would rather belong to a union anyway.

The most commonly stated reasons for belonging to a union concerned the protection and advice the unions offered. Nearly half of those who answered this question referred to unions offering security,

Table 2.1 Union membership characteristics of employee surveys

Source	Proportion belong to a union (union density)		Proportion ever belonged to a union		Union exit rates		Year
	At surveyed workplace (%)	*In any workplace* (%)	*At surveyed workplace* (%)	*In any workplace* (%)	*From surveyed workplace* (%)	*From any workplace* (%)	
SEMSE	66	67	71	83	7	20	1990–91
AWIRS95	50	–	57	–	12	–	1995–96
LCS-96	–	34	–	75	–	55	1996
AES	–	30	–	–	–	–	1996

legal representation, insurance, a fair go, or assistance and advice. This is consistent with numerous overseas studies. For example, protection or insurance was the most commonly cited reason amongst Belgian union members for remaining in the union (Baupain 1992:8). Other studies showing the importance of the insurance concept include those by Van de Vall (1970), Millward (1990:34–5), Gallagher and Strauss (1991), Fundacion Largo Caballero (1988, cited by Wheeler and McClendon 1991) and Waddington and Whitston (1993). Job security has been shown as a motivation in union joining by Goldthorpe et al. (1968) and Lansbury (1978). Several US studies have shown employees to be more likely to vote for a union if they feared employer retribution for supporting a union (Wheeler & McClendon 1991), presumably because many employees sought to unionise as a form of collective insurance. If employees seek union membership as a form of protection or insurance, then as Baupain (1992) pointed out, a perception of union power is an important element in persuading employees that unions will be able to perform this role. Other Australian studies have shown the importance of the insurance motivation: Dufty (1972) found security and protection the reasons for joining amongst 20 per cent of metal workers, while Crockett and Hall (1987) found these to be important motivations amongst graduates.

A smaller proportion in SEMSE referred to motivations representing pecuniary benefits that union representation offered: negotiating and improving conditions and, less commonly, wages. Respondents were not asked a specific question about the types of benefits they had gained from union membership, but an open-ended question along these lines in a pilot survey had found that conditions of employment were mentioned as a benefit approximately three times as often as were wages. The greater importance attached by unionists to conditions other than wages is not unusual. These data are consistent with other evidence that obtaining satisfactory working conditions is a more important motivation for joining unions than obtaining wage increases (Goldthorpe et al. 1968:96–8; Lansbury 1978:144–50; Crockett and Hall 1987:49–68).

A considerable amount of space has been devoted in the union membership literature to the problem of non-union members free-riding on the gains of union members (e.g. Crouch 1982; Cregan & Johnston 1990; Booth 1983, 1991). One response unions make to this problem is the provision of private services. Such services have been credited for a minor or major part of the reason for the maintenance of union membership in Belgium (Baupain 1992:8), Sweden (Hammarström 1992:117–9) and Israel (Ben-Israel & Fisher 1992:95), and the lack of union services has been linked to the fortunes of American and British unionism (Maranto & Fiorito 1987; Booth 1991). Others, however, argue that individualistic services have had little impact on British unionism (Crouch 1982; Waddington & Whitston 1993). The Australian data presented from SEMSE show little evidence of any substantial impact from the provision of private benefits to employees – with one major exception: indemnity insurance offered by a nurses' union appeared to be an important reason for unionism amongst their members. This simply reinforces the point made earlier concerning the importance of insurance as a motivation for union membership. Indeed, the pervasiveness of the insurance motivation really explains why 'free riding' is not a terminal problem for unions, as insurance is not a benefit that is generally available to non-union members.

Table 2.2 Reasons for belonging to a union

Reason for belonging	All current union members (%)		New members (≤12 months) (%)	
Protection, advice, representation	48		47	
– protection, insurance, security		34		33
– advice, information, guidance		4		12
– legal representation, indemnity		8		2
– voice		2		–
Ideological reasons	8		–	
– believe in unions, help the workers		8		–
Pay, conditions	12		7	
– protect, improve, negotiate wages		4		2
– protect, improve, negotiate conditions		9		5
Union reach: compulsion, pressure	38		37	
– compulsory		34		35
– peer pressure, advised to do so		4		2
Other	8		10	
– do a good job		1		–
– other benefits		3		5
– tax deduction		0.4		–
– other		3		5
Critical or reluctant	5	5	5	5
N	486	486	43	43

Source: SEMSE
Population: Union members who gave a reason for belonging to a union
Note: Up to two answers were coded for each respondent. Hence figures sum to more than 100 per cent. Due to rounding, figures in the right-hand columns in each category may not sum to figures in the left-hand column.

Only a small proportion of respondents gave what could be called 'ideological' reasons for belonging ('unions help the workers', 'unity is strength', 'if you accept the benefits of the union you should belong', etc.); this seemed to be considerably less than in some earlier European studies (e.g. Van de Vall 1970; Beynon & Blackburn 1972). These data should not be interpreted as meaning that ideology or union sympathy is unimportant, however. Open-ended questions tell us about the perceptions that employees have of the reasons for belonging to or joining a union, but they do not tell us the full story of the causal relationships affecting joining. Chapter three will investigate the influence of ideology upon union membership and show that ideology has a significant influence on the likelihood of union membership.

The data also enable the investigation of the reasons people might have for joining, as distinct from remaining in, unions. In principle, an employee's original reasons for joining may be quite different to the reasons for remaining, once the employee has belonged for a substantial period. But amongst recent joiners – that is, employees who had belonged to a union for 12 months or less – the reasons given for *belonging* can probably be construed as the reasons they had for *joining*. (These data are shown in the two right-hand columns of table 2.2.)

As it happens, there were few differences between the explanations offered by new joiners and those offered by members of long standing, though new joiners may have been more likely to be motivated by the desire for advice, information and guidance and less likely to have ideological motives. True, the number of new joiners was small, but the pattern does not alter significantly when we double N by including those who have belonged for 24 months or less.

Why People Do Not Belong to Unions

Respondents who were not union members were asked why they were not. If union reach was an important explanation of the membership of unions, it was an even more important explanation for non-membership. Thus while 38 per cent of unionists in SEMSE explained their membership in terms of union reach (table 2.2), 47 per cent of employees who did *not* belong to unions explained their status by referring to union reach, that is, to the availability or non-availability of unions (table 2.3). Most common amongst this class of reasons were explanations related to management or the job: the company was not unionised or the job was not a union job. A small number of respondents referred to management pressure and expressed the fear of dismissal if they joined a union. A significant number gave reasons which suggested that unions had not made adequate contact with them:

they had not been asked to join or they did not know much about the union. Some respondents simply indicated that they did not belong because it was not compulsory (by contrast, presumably, with an earlier job they had held).

Over half of non-union respondents gave reasons related to their attitudes towards unions. Over a quarter of non-members cited the effects or actions of unions: they caused trouble, made excessive demands, or had leaders who only acted in their own interests and did not act in the members' interests. A larger group referred to the ineffectiveness of unions: they were not needed, had no influence, or there was no gain from belonging. And 11 per cent of non-members gave reasons that were ideological in nature – they did not believe in unions.

The data also allowed a distinction to be made between the attitudes of employees who had never belonged to a union, and those who had in the past but no longer did (see the two right-hand columns of table 2.3). Former members and 'non-joiners' do not differ greatly in the extent to which their motivations relate to union reach or to union attitudes. But there are notable differences with regard to the aspects of union reach and union attitudes that may influence their non-membership.

In relation to union reach, employees who had left a union commonly appeared to have done so as a result of moving from a union or open job into a non-union job (or from a union job into an open job), or as a result of encountering management that is anti-union. One cause was promotion into 'staff' areas. A 1983 survey had shown that a number of companies refused to allow certain supervisors or 'staff' to remain in a union (NSW ADB 1983:282). Supervision, in itself, is not the issue. Other SEMSE data showed that, on average, employees who reported that they supervised other employees were no more likely than non-supervisors to be union leavers. In many instances, former union members had moved to non-union workplaces. In LCS-96, some two-fifths of union leavers were in non-union workplaces.

Employees who had never been members, on the other hand, were more likely to cite union failures to contact potential members to inform them about the union and request they join as their reason for non-membership. This reinforced findings by Palmer and McGraw (1990) that many young employees in the industry they studied (travel agencies) had never been approached to join. Overseas studies have also demonstrated a link between inadequate union recruitment and low union reach (Cregan & Johnston 1990; RIALS 1993).

Union attitudes also differed between the two groups. Those who had never been in a union commonly said that they did not need a union. Union leavers rarely said that, but commonly said that unions were

Table 2.3 Reasons for not belonging to a union

	All non-members (%)		Union leavers (%)		Non-joiners (never been in a union) (%)	
Union ineffectiveness	29		30		29	
– no gain, no influence		16		26		9
– don't need them		13		4		21
Union effects and actions	26		27		26	
– unions cause trouble		9		9		9
– don't act in members', my interests		7		7		7
– leaders are self-interested, bludgers		6		9		3
– demands are too high		4		2		7
Ideological reasons	11		6		16	
– don't believe in unions		11		6		16
Other union-related	5		8		2	
– costs too much		2		4		1
– other dislikes of unions		3		6		1
Union reach: management- or job-related reasons	31		40		24	
– not a union company or job		10		11		9
– type of job (supervisor, apprentice, staff, etc.)		11		13		10
– not compulsory this job		9		13		6
– management pressure, would get sack		1		3		–
Union reach: union-related reasons	16		7		24	
– not been asked, mentioned		7		3		10
– don't know about union		3		1		6
– not been here long, not got around to it		6		3		8
Other	1		1		1	
N	214	214	107	107	105	105

Source: SEMSE
Population: Non-members who gave a reason for not belonging to a union
Note: Up to two answers were coded for each respondent. Hence figures sum to more than 100 per cent. Due to rounding, figures in the right-hand columns in each category may not sum to figures in the left-hand column.

ineffectual, had no influence in the workplace or offered no gains to union members. This was a common reason for employees leaving unions when they had *not* changed employers. One-third of those who had left the union at their current workplace referred to union ineffectiveness as the reason for their non-membership, suggesting that union instrumentality may be an important factor in decisions to remain in, or leave, unions.

Union leavers also differed from those who had never belonged in terms of ideological motivations, the former being less likely to give ideological reasons for non-membership. Other data also showed differences in union sympathy between the two groups, with employees who had never been in a union being more likely to agree that Australia would be better off without unions. The 16 per cent of 'non-joiners' who cited ideological motivations for non-membership contrasts starkly with the absence of ideological motivations for membership amongst new joiners. This emphasises the point that negative union sympathy has a particularly important role in preventing unionism.

Union Propensity

The demand for union membership – union propensity – can be measured in two ways. The first involves observing employees 'attitudinal' propensity towards unions – the willingness or unwillingness of employees to join a union – principally by asking them whether, if they were free to choose, they would prefer to belong or not belong to a union. This measures their predisposition towards union membership. The second way involves observing their 'behavioural' propensity – by measuring whether those employees who are free to choose actually join (or fail to join) a union. By definition, behavioural propensity can only be measured amongst employees who are free to choose their union status (that is, those in open jobs). Attitudinal propensity, however, can in principle be measured across all employees and is therefore the meaning generally given in this book to the term 'union propensity'.

There are four surveys that contain measures of employees' attitudinal propensity towards unions. These are summarised in table 2.4. Three of the four surveys, including the largest one (AWIRS95), show that the number of employees who would rather be in a union exceeds the number who would rather not belong. The fourth (the AES) shows numbers approximately equal. The one survey that did not give respondents the explicit option of choosing a neutral response (LCS-96) showed a majority of employees would prefer to be in a union. The other three surveys indicate that between one-fifth and one-third of employees are neutral or undecided on the issue, with LCS-96 suggesting that, when pushed for a response, these 'neutrals' divide fairly evenly or slightly pro-union.

The differences between, on the one hand, the SEMSE results and, on the other hand, the AWIRS95 and AES results are probably not

Table 2.4 Union propensity in four surveys: whether respondents would, if they were free to choose, rather belong than not belong to a trade union

Source	Agree	'Neither agree nor disagree' or 'don't know'	Disagree	Year	N
	(%)	(%)	(%)		
SEMSE	41	32	27	1990–91	942
AWIRS95	38	30	33	1995–96	18863
AES	38	23	39	1996	1211
LCS-96	52	3	45	1996	538

indicative of a change in attitudes over time, but rather reflect the composition of the SEMSE sample, which under-represented non-union workplaces and only referred to award-covered employees in certain industries. To gauge the impact of differences in sample construction, a revised AWIRS95 estimate was made, which was restricted to those industries covered in SEMSE, excluding non-union unstructured workplaces (of which none were represented in SEMSE) and managers (who were essentially excluded from the SEMSE sample). In this reduced sample, 41 per cent of AWIRS95 employees said they would rather be in a union, while 29 per cent said they would not.[1] These results are not significantly different to those from SEMSE five years earlier, in which 41 per cent said they would rather be in a union and 27 per cent said they would not. That is, there is no evidence of significantly declining union propensity over the first half of the 1990s. To find the reasons for declining union membership, we have to look elsewhere – a task that will be taken up in later chapters.

The overall pattern – that more people would prefer to belong than not belong to a trade union – contrasts sharply with actual patterns in union membership, whereby around 1995 there were twice as many non-members as members, including three times as many non-members than members in jobs that were not compulsorily unionised. This dissonance between employees' preferences and their membership status is something that we will return to in chapter five.

Restricted and Open Jobs

Employees whose union status was primarily determined by union reach are referred to as being in *restricted jobs*. Employees whose union status was *not* primarily determined by union reach are referred to as being in *open jobs*. One difficulty in studying this area is in accurately measuring open and restricted jobs. The general approach in this analysis is to identify jobs that appear to be restricted in any way and then treat all remaining jobs as being open. Where full information is not available to identify restricted jobs, this can lead to an overstatement of the number of open jobs. For example, in LCS-96 union density amongst permanent employees in open jobs is similar to union propensity in the same group, but amongst casual employees union density in open jobs is well below union propensity, suggesting that there are problems of union reach for casual employees that could not be identified through the available data. Hence data on the extent of open and restricted jobs need to be treated cautiously.

In SEMSE, employees were defined as being in restricted jobs if they either: indicated (in a closed-choice question) that, to work in their job, they had to belong to a union; were non-union members in a workplace that management considered to be a non-union workplace; were union members who gave reasons related to union reach for their union membership; or were non-members who gave reasons related to union reach for their non-membership. *Restricted union jobs* usually arise from decisions by unions, management and/or tribunals that those jobs should be unionised or that preference should be given to union members; and *restricted non-union jobs* arise from either employer attempts to prevent unionisation or union failure to contact and recruit employees. Employees in restricted jobs accounted for an estimated 49 per cent of employees in the SEMSE sample. Employees in open jobs therefore accounted for an estimated 51 per cent of the SEMSE sample.

In LCS-96 a different method was used to identify open and restricted jobs: here, only 42 per cent of respondents indicated that they were in workplaces with a union presence where they were genuinely free to choose whether or not to belong to a trade union – the best measure in that survey of open jobs.[2] Of the remaining 58 per cent, 11 per cent were in compulsorily unionised jobs (restricted union jobs), 39 per cent were in non-union workplaces and 5 per cent were in jobs at unionised workplaces where the employer would prefer they did not join the union.[3]

By examining union membership in open jobs, the second measure of union propensity, behavioural propensity, can be measured. In SEMSE (a biased sample), 62 per cent of employees in open jobs belonged to a trade union. In LCS-96 46 per cent of employees in open jobs belonged to a union. In AES the figure was 51 per cent, although the denominator (the number of open jobs) is probably overstated in AES, leading to an understatement of union density in open jobs. In terms of magnitudes, these findings are consistent with the attitudinal propensity data: where employees are free to choose and a union is available, around half or so will join a union.

On the face of it, union reach and union propensity each appear to be of broadly similar importance in terms of their effect on union membership. However, it would be incorrect to view union reach and union propensity as being independent of each other. If this were so, it would also follow that, amongst employees in restricted jobs, the probability of union membership would be unaffected by union propensity. This is not the case. Even in what we have termed restricted jobs, employees in SEMSE were more likely to be union members when they prefer union membership. Likewise, in LCS-96, while 34 per cent of employees in restricted jobs who wanted to belong to a union actually belonged, only 11 per cent of employees in restricted jobs who did not want to belong actually belonged to a union.

The explanation is simple. Unions are more likely to be able to achieve compulsory unionism where employees want to belong to unions. Employers are more likely to be able to achieve union-free status in particular workplaces or jobs where the affected employees do not want to belong to unions. Thus union propensity influences union reach. Conversely, employees who have no workplace experience of unions may have low union propensity because of views mainly shaped by negative perceptions of the union movement as a whole. Thus union reach can influence union propensity.

The Role of Union Instrumentality, Satisfaction, and Voice

This section looks at the importance of employee perspectives on the performance of unions on a number of matters directly affecting employees. Several issues are examined, including the importance of union instrumentality in explaining the joining and leaving of unions, the role of employee satisfaction with unions and how this satisfaction has changed, and the influence of union voice.

Union Instrumentality

Union instrumentality – the perceived ability of unions to deliver benefits for members – is the variable that is most consistently related to union support in US studies (Fiorito & Greer 1982; Fiorito et al. 1986; Wheeler & McClendon 1991). Farber (1990) estimated that a substantial part of the decline in demand for unionisation during 1977–84 was attributable to a deterioration in workers' perceptions of union instrumentality. Others have found union instrumentality or effectiveness to be important in cross-sectional studies of pro-union voting, joining and propensity to join (Premack & Hunter 1988; Montgomery 1989) and union satisfaction (Glick et al. 1977; Guest & Dewe 1991).

Union instrumentality in SEMSE was measured by responses to the question 'have you benefited from belonging to a union, or been made worse off by it?'. Of current and former members, 46 per cent replied that they had benefited (12 per cent had benefited a lot, and 34 per cent a little); another 46 per cent said that it had made no difference to them; and 7 per cent replied that they had been made worse off (that is, they perceived negative instrumentality from union membership).[4] Restricting the sample to current members, union instrumentality was a little higher: 50 per cent better off, 45 per cent no difference, and 5 per cent worse off. Union instrumentality increased the longer that members were in a union (even amongst members who would rather not be in a union).

Union propensity in turn was strongly related to union instrumentality. Measured as the proportion of respondents who agreed that they would rather be in a union than not in one, union propensity in SEMSE was 62 per cent amongst those who considered that they had been made better off by union membership, 33 per cent amongst those for whom it had made no difference and 19 per cent amongst those who considered that they had been made worse off.

Union instrumentality was the critical influence upon union exit and hence union density[5] amongst employees in open jobs: the union exit rate was 62 per cent amongst those who considered that they had been made worse off by union membership, compared to 9 per cent amongst those who considered they had been made better off. (There was no relationship amongst employees in restricted jobs.)

A key aspect of union instrumentality is perceived union power at the workplace. In SEMSE, perceptions of union strength were positively associated with union membership in open jobs. Union joining was higher, and union exit lower, when unions were perceived to be stronger (Goot & Peetz 1998). This is consistent with the data discussed earlier showing that one-third of employees who had forsaken union membership at their current workplace referred to union ineffectiveness as the reason for their non-membership.

Another element of union instrumentality was perceived union cohesion – the extent to which unions appeared to be working together rather than fighting with each other. Most employees in SEMSE seemed content with the degree of union cohesion they observed. Only 15 per cent of employees with an opinion agreed that 'unions at this workplace spend a lot of time fighting each other', while 53 per cent disagreed. Where unions were seen as spending a lot of time fighting each other, however, the effects upon unionisation were quite serious. Employees who said unions fought with each other had lower union satisfaction, scored unions lower on responsiveness and protection, and had lower instrumentality and propensity. More importantly, low union cohesion was probably associated with a lower union joining rate and higher union exit rate and definitely associated with lower union density (Peetz 1998). In short, union in-fighting led to lower unionisation.

Union Satisfaction

In overseas studies, satisfaction with a member's union has been shown to be an important determinant of the decision to stay in or leave a union (Klandermans 1986) and in hypothetical or actual behaviour in union ballots in the US (Bigoness & Tosi 1984; Leigh 1986). As Gallagher and Strauss (1991) point out, survey research suggests that the majority of union members are satisfied and desire to maintain their membership (see Wedderburn & Crompton 1972:102; Kochan 1979; Hills 1985; Leigh 1986; Fiorito et al. 1988). This, however, is not a universal situation. Guest and Dewe (1991) found low union satisfaction in their UK electronics case study, as did Simey (1956:128) some 40 years earlier amongst dock workers. Nonetheless, individual union studies in Australia have shown majority member satisfaction with unions representing metal workers (Chaples et al. 1977; Dufty 1972:104) and WA firemen (Dufty 1979:163) while a 1990 national cross-sample had similar findings (Morgan 1992a).

Most studies have either not differentiated between attitudes to workplace union delegates (shop stewards) and union leaders or paid officials, or they have only examined one or the other. Where attitudes to unions at different levels are examined respondents are typically more satisfied with their workplace delegates than with their leaders – that is, more satisfied with the level of the union closest to the respondents (Guest & Dewe 1991:86; Simey 1956).

SEMSE asked about satisfaction with three levels of the union movement. Respondents to SEMSE were most satisfied with the union representatives with whom they had the closest contact – delegates/shop stewards – and least satisfied with the most distant arm of the unions – the ACTU. Satisfaction with paid union officials and leaders was also substantially lower than satisfaction with union delegates, but was slightly better than satisfaction with the ACTU (table 2.5).

Fortunately for unions, satisfaction with delegates appeared to be more important than satisfaction with leaders and officials, or the ACTU, in explaining union density and union exit in SEMSE (table 2.6). As discussed in chapter seven, dissatisfaction with the ACTU did

Table 2.5 Satisfaction with union delegates, officials and leaders and
the ACTU

	Employees			N	Union members			N
	satisfied	neutral	dis-satisfied		satisfied	neutral	dis-satisfied	
	(%)	(%)	(%)		(%)	(%)	(%)	
SEMSE 1990–91								
Union delegates	39	41	20	705	46	35	19	538
Union officials								
and leaders	28	42	30	692	32	37	35	540
ACTU	22	52	26	691	23	50	27	508
AWIRS95								
The services								
unions here								
provide to								
members	39	31	22	10809	42	31	20	9482

Population: All employees with opinions on union delegates/leaders/ACTU
(SEMSE)
Present or former union members at the workplace (AWIRS95)

not necessarily indicate rejection of the corporatist concepts underlying
the ACTU's role in the 1980s. For the rest of this chapter, when discussing union satisfaction it shall be confined to satisfaction with union
delegates, officials and leaders.

On the whole, at the time of SEMSE, dissatisfaction with Australian
unions appeared to have grown. While 10 per cent of members said that
they were now more satisfied with 'unions here' than they were 'a
couple of years ago', 19 per cent said that they were less satisfied; 71 per
cent reported no change. Only 2 per cent of non-members said that they
were more satisfied with unions at the workplace than two years ago;
17 per cent were less satisfied. In SEMSE, employees in open jobs who
said that their satisfaction with unions had declined had a same-
workplace exit rate of 15 per cent, whereas the rate was just 4 per cent
amongst those whose satisfaction had increased.

This trend of deterioration may have slowed or halted by the mid-
1990s. In LCS-97, members were asked how they rated the performance
of their union now compared to twelve months earlier. Responses were
fairly evenly divided: 28 per cent had a 'more positive' view and 31 per
cent a 'more negative' view.

It is also notable that, at the time of AWIRS95, the proportion of
members with an opinion who agreed that they were satisfied with 'the
services unions provide here to members', at 42 per cent, was nearly as

Table 2.6 Union satisfaction, propensity and membership

	Open jobs		N
	Union density (%)	Union exit rate (%)	
Satisfaction with union delegates/shop stewards			
– satisfied	87	6	235
– neither	60	25	300
– dissatisfied	59	30	146
(satisfaction differential)	(+28)	(–24)	
Satisfaction with union officials and leaders			
– satisfied	82	12	207
– neither	62	23	521
– dissatisfied	74	18	220
(satisfaction differential)	(+12)	(–6)	

Source: SEMSE
Population: All employees with opinions on union delegates/leaders
Note: Satisfaction differential = per cent satisfied minus per cent dissatisfied

high as that recorded for satisfaction with union delegates in SEMSE in 1990–91 and substantially higher than that recorded for union officials and leaders. Although the question is worded differently and the samples are different,[6] the comparison provides no indication that satisfaction with unions declined over the first half of the 1990s.

Union Voice: Responsiveness and Protection

'Voice' refers to 'the use of direct communication to bring actual and desired conditions together' (Hirschman 1971). A union is a mechanism for 'providing workers with a means of communicating with management' (Freeman & Medoff 1984:8). SEMSE looked at two aspects of union voice: *union responsiveness* – the extent to which unions are able to accurately reflect and respond to employee preferences on desired conditions – and *union protection* – the extent to which unions are able to act in defence of employees' desired conditions.

Union responsiveness

Jarley, Kuruvilla and Casteel (1990), in a study of workers in Iowa (US) and Sweden, found that members' satisfaction with member–union relations was the most important determinant of overall satisfaction with

their union. It was more important than satisfaction with union performance in terms of improving wages and conditions, job security, and
improving the quality of work itself. Similar results had been obtained
by Fiorito, Gallagher and Fukami (1988) using a national US survey, and
earlier by Glick, Mirvis and Harder (1977). Leicht (1989) also found
union satisfaction to be related to perceptions about internal union
democracy.

Australian case studies of union members in different industries come
up with a range of findings on the extent of union responsiveness,
some suggesting that members view their union as democratic (Dufty
1979:165–6), others suggesting that women, in particular, consider their
union is too distant, undemocratic, and weak in providing information
to its members (Gale 1990:16; Storer & Hargreaves 1976). In one union
study, the most common reasons given by members who wanted to leave
were the lack of communication between officials and members, and
the inefficiency of the union (Johnston 1977:107).

In the 1990–91 SEMSE, union members were remarkably evenly
divided on union responsiveness. Thirty-two per cent of union members
with an opinion agreed that 'generally speaking, unions who have members here do what their members want them to', 33 per cent disagreed
and 34 per cent neither agreed nor disagreed. A more positive finding
came through in LCS-96, which had 62 per cent of union members
agreeing that 'unions at your workplace do what their members want
them to do', and just 27 per cent disagreeing.

The second component of the measure of union responsiveness in
SEMSE assessed whether respondents agreed that 'unions who have
members here really take notice of their members' problems and complaints'; 45 per cent of members with an opinion agreed and 30 per cent
disagreed, with 25 per cent offering a neutral response. This seemingly
positive perception was tempered by more negative views on how
unions' performance had changed. Only 14 per cent of union members thought that unions were more effective than two years earlier
(1988–89) 'in taking notice of employee problems and complaints',
24 per cent believed they were less effective and 62 per cent perceived
no change. Yet, by the time of AWIRS95, 51 per cent of members with an
opinion agreed that 'unions here take notice of members' problems
and complaints', with just 18 per cent disagreeing and 31 per cent
neutral – suggesting that, if anything, union performance had improved
slightly on this front.

The third component of union responsiveness in SEMSE concerned
communication with members. Again, at the time of SEMSE, members
were very evenly divided in their views: 34 per cent of union members

were satisfied with 'the way that unions here keep in contact with employees', 33 per cent were dissatisfied and 33 per cent were neither satisfied nor dissatisfied.

In SEMSE, an index of union responsiveness was constructed ($\propto$ = .76),[7] based on responses to these three questions, and is used in table 2.7. There was a strong relationship between union responsiveness and changes in union satisfaction: in SEMSE, 34 per cent of employees who scored their unions low on the responsiveness scale said they were less satisfied with unions, whereas only 9 per cent of those who scored their unions high on responsiveness said they were less satisfied. Although the other two measures of responsiveness might have suggested an improvement, if anything, in union responsiveness since 1990–91, this was not so regarding the third measure, which, bearing in mind the limitations on comparisons, seemed to suggest little net change. In LCS-96 some 49 per cent of employees agreed that 'unions at your workplace do a poor job in keeping in touch with their members'; 46 per cent disagreed.

Finally, AWIRS95 showed that 29 per cent of present and former union members at the workplace agreed that 'unions here give members a say in how the union operates', and 27 per cent disagreed.

The most negative attitudes towards unions were found in responses to a question on whether most Australian union leaders only looked after themselves. By a majority of two to one (48 per cent to 24 per cent), union members supported this proposition in SEMSE. Thus there was a large difference in employee attitudes between their views of responsiveness of unions at the workplace level and responsiveness of unions at a level remote from the workplace. This pattern of comparatively positive attitudes towards workplace unions and comparatively negative attitudes towards seemingly more remote aspects of union organisation is consistent with the pattern for union satisfaction, already mentioned.

Given the differences in questions and samples and the mixed nature of the findings, we must reserve judgment about the overall direction of changes in union responsiveness since 1990–91. It seems unlikely that there has been either a major deterioration or major improvement over that period – but in order to reverse the membership decline unions would have needed a substantial improvement. The general picture that emerges is that unions were perceived as taking notice of and responding to members' problems and complaints when they heard them but were, as might be expected from territory-driven unions, quite unimpressive at keeping in touch with members in the first place.

Union protection

Unions were judged more favourably for the protection they afforded employees than for their perceived responsiveness. Forty-four per cent of union members with an opinion agreed that 'unions here make sure that their members get a fair go', and only 24 per cent disagreed. Similarly, 49 per cent agreed that 'unions here do a good job in obtaining a safe and comfortable working environment'; just 18 per cent disagreed. The index of union protection ($\propto = .69$), used in table 2.7, is the sum of these two items in SEMSE. These results are important, given the role of protection and security among employees' stated reasons for belonging to unions.

Union protection was also regarded positively in LCS-96: 75 per cent of union members said that unions were 'doing about the right amount' regarding 'the safety and health aspects of your working conditions', and 66 per cent responded that way regarding respondents' 'job security'.

Perhaps the most important aspect of protection is job security. Union density in SEMSE was higher amongst employees in open jobs who believed their job security had declined as a result of job changes (73 per cent) than amongst those who considered it had been enhanced (52 per cent). However, this does not appear to be because job insecurity inherently promotes union membership. In open jobs there was *not* a significant relationship between union joining or exit and either the level of or changes in perceived job security, even though union satisfaction and union responsiveness were positively related to perceptions of improvements in job security. The absence of such relationships suggests that a third variable might be associated both with union membership and perceived job insecurity. In particular, it appears to have more to do with the types of jobs that were most under threat at the time of SEMSE, reflecting the structural changes underway in the labour market. Deteriorations in perceived job security were most marked amongst long-serving union members, and indeed for employees with long tenure with their employer. These also happened to be the employees with the strongest union propensity.

The importance of effective delegate organisation is also reflected in employee attitudes to unions. Matched data from SEMSE and AWIRS90 indicate that union members in workplaces with a high number of members per delegate were more likely to be dissatisfied with the way in which the union keeps in contact with them, to consider their union inferior in terms of union protection, to disagree that unions are strong at their workplace,[8] and to be less satisfied with their union delegates. Moreover, union instrumentality was higher amongst members in workplaces with low member–delegate ratios.

A broadly similar pattern was evident in the AWIRS95 employee survey: employees in workplaces with member–delegate ratios over 30:1 were four to five percentage points less likely than those with lower ratios to agree that unions did a good job in improving members' pay and conditions, took notice of members' problems and complaints, give members a say in how the union operates, or did a good job in representing members when dealing with management, and by a similar margin were less likely to be satisfied with the service unions provide to members.

Predictably, union protection and union responsiveness both influenced union propensity and union membership in open jobs. The relationships are detailed in table 2.7.[9] Union propensity increased when union responsiveness was higher and when union protection was higher. Union protection appeared to be the more powerful influence of the two.

There were sharper differences between the effects of union responsiveness and union protection on union membership and, to a lesser extent, union exit. Union density increased substantially when union protection was higher. Union exit was substantially higher where union protection was lower. Each of the components of the union protection measure was as powerful, or more powerful, an influence on union density as was any of the components of the union responsiveness measure. This highlights again the importance of union protection as a reason for union membership. But perhaps the most important finding was on the responsiveness side: the same-workplace union exit rate was only 1 per cent amongst those who were satisfied with how unions kept in contact with members, but 14 per cent amongst those who were dissatisfied.

As a means of affecting general union propensity and membership, the two aspects of union voice discussed here significantly influence both union instrumentality and union sympathy. Union responsiveness had a relationship with union instrumentality that was twice as strong as its relationship with union sympathy.[10] This is what would be expected, but it also highlights the way in which union sympathy is not exogenous to the system, but is itself influenced by workplace developments.

Management–employee Relations and Union Membership

Employee Participation in Management

The greater involvement of employees in decisions that affect them is one of the pillars of the closer relationship between management and

Table 2.7 Union responsiveness, voice and unionisation

	Union propensity			Open jobs		N
	Positive	Neutral	Negative	Union density	Same-workplace union exit rate	
	(%)	(%)	(%)	(%)	(%)	
Union responsiveness index						
– high responsiveness	61	24	15	79	3	260
– neutral	37	46	17	57	12	117
– low responsiveness	44	23	34	70	14	238
(difference)	(+17)		(−19)	(+9)	(−11)	
Unions here do what members want						
– agree	67	22	11	78	4	191
– neutral	36	41	22	61	11	258
– disagree	42	16	42	65	17	221
(difference)	(+25)		(−31)	(+13)	(−13)	
Unions contact with members						
– satisfied	66	17	16	78	1	209
– neutral	38	39	23	62	10	249
– dissatisfied	47	21	32	69	15	212
(difference)	(+19)		(−16)	(+9)	(−14)	
Unions take notice of members complaints						
– agree	60	19	21	76	6	293
– neutral	30	43	26	50	12	188
– disagree	47	21	32	63	17	210
(difference)	(+13)		(−11)	(+13)	(−11)	
Union protection index						
– high protection	64	21	16	79	6	319
– neutral	34	43	23	53	16	202
– low protection	35	18	48	54	22	147
(difference)	(+29)		(−32)	(+25)	(−16)	
Unions ensure members get a fair go						
– agree	65	20	14	82	5	264
– neutral	36	39	25	58	13	267
– disagree	39	15	46	57	20	149
(difference)	(+26)		(−32)	(+25)	(−15)	
Unions obtain safe, comfortable work environment						
– agree	61	21	19	76	7	307
– neutral	35	40	25	54	14	260
– disagree	41	15	43	56	23	127
(difference)	(+20)		(−24)	(+20)	(−17)	

Source: SEMSE
Population: All employees

employees that modern management strategy purports to be based upon. At the same time, one of the purposes of trade unionism (pursued with varying degrees of enthusiasm by different unions and in different countries) is to increase the voice or control that employees have in relation to their work. So does union success in achieving this objective undermine unionism by reducing employees' propensity to belong, or does it have the reverse effect, by enabling employees to recognise the benefits of union membership?

Several measures of employee participation were utilised in SEMSE. They tended to show a low level of employee involvement. In response to the statement 'employees here do have a lot of say in decisions that affect them in the workplace', 34 per cent of employees with an opinion agreed but 51 per cent disagreed. Employees were also asked to indicate, on a four-point scale, how much say or influence they had regarding what work they did, how they did their work, and the way the workplace was run. The responses to these three items were calculated as an index of current employee involvement ($\alpha = .81$).

There seemed to be a diversity of employee experiences on changes in employee involvement, but only small net increases overall. In SEMSE, 24 per cent of employees indicated that, compared with two years earlier, workers had more say in decisions that affected them, but 19 per cent said that they now had less say. Likewise, in WBS94, 25 per cent of employees said that their 'say in decisions that affect you' had increased, while 18 per cent said it had decreased. However, AWIRS95 suggested a larger improvement: 27 per cent of employees said 'your say in decisions which affect you' had gone up over the last 12 months, but just 11 per cent said it had gone down (though, interestingly, those who thought their say had gone up also reported greater work effort).

In response to questions designed to reveal whether employees wanted more involvement, 59 per cent of SEMSE respondents with an opinion agreed that 'I would like to have more say in how my work is organised'; just 6 per cent disagreed. Some 56 per cent agreed that 'I would work better if management and employees made decisions together on things like how my work is organised'; just 7 per cent disagreed.

Employees who agreed that they had a lot of say in decisions, and those who were satisfied with the information provided to them by management, were more satisfied with their union delegates and union leaders, and rated unions higher in terms of union protection and (especially) union responsiveness. Those who detected an increase in employee influence or an increase in the information provided by employers also rated unions higher in terms of protection and responsiveness. Those who scored themselves highly in terms of their own influence upon the way the workplace was run also rated unions highly on voice and responsiveness. However, perceptions of employee participation did not seem to influence union instrumentality.

Union propensity was higher amongst employees who did *not* consider that employees had a lot of say, who considered that employee say had declined, and who scored themselves low on the current employee involvement index. Amongst the participation-related variables, the most important influence upon union propensity was the desire for greater influence. Union propensity was 51 per cent amongst those who agreed that they would prefer more say in how their work was organised, compared to 36 per cent amongst those who were neutral or disagreed with the statement. Union sympathy was also stronger amongst employees who perceived themselves and their co-workers as having low involvement, and amongst employees who wanted a higher level of involvement.

The impact on union membership, however, was not as dramatic. Amongst employees in open jobs, there were no significant differences in union density between those who rated themselves highly on the employee involvement scale (59 per cent) and those who rated themselves lowly on this scale (61 per cent). Nor were there any differences in density in open jobs between: those who agreed that employees had a lot of say (62 per cent) and those who disagreed (62 per cent); between those who thought employee influence had increased (65 per cent) and those who thought it had decreased (63 per cent); or between those who wanted more say (62 per cent) and those who were neutral or in disagreement (62 per cent).

Union *joining* in open jobs was higher amongst those who scored low on the involvement index (37 per cent) than amongst those who scored in the middle (10 per cent) or high on the index (16 per cent). This index was not separately significant in regression equations explaining union joining. However, another conditional variable – indicating employees who *both* scored low on participation and were satisfied with union delegates – was significant in some equations, as a result of its influence on union sympathy (Peetz 1998).

While there was some evidence that the act of joining a union was linked to low participation (perhaps especially if the union appeared to offer something positive to employees), frustration at declining employment participation also led to some employees leaving their union. In open jobs, the same-workplace union exit rate was slightly higher amongst employees who considered that employee say in decisions had declined over the past two years (16 per cent) than amongst those who said it was stable or had increased (9 per cent). Exit behaviour was significantly higher amongst employees who were dissatisfied with the information provided to them by management (14 per cent) than amongst those who were satisfied (7 per cent). Several of the other measures of employee participation described above had no influence on the union exit rate.

These trends reflect the effect that unions' perceived role in enhancing participation has on union attitudes and membership. Union joining in open jobs in SEMSE was higher amongst employees who showed approval by disagreeing with the statement that 'unions here don't really help employees have a say in their work' (49 per cent) than it was amongst those who agreed with this statement (19 per cent). And, as we would expect, the overall union exit rate was higher amongst those who agreed that unions did not help them have a say (29 per cent) than amongst those who disagreed (16 per cent). Consequently, union density in open jobs was 62 per cent amongst those who thought that unions did not help employees have a say, but 76 per cent amongst those who thought that they helped employees have a say.

In sum, there was some evidence that the act of joining a union was linked to low participation, perhaps especially if the union appeared to offer something positive to employees. There was evidence that frustration at declining employment participation also led to some employees leaving their union. If employees considered that unions did not help employees have a say in their work, they were less likely to stay in the union where they had a choice. Where they did not have a choice – that is, where membership was compulsory – it appeared possible that unions were not as effective in ensuring that members had a say in their work, and were perhaps vulnerable to membership loss if compulsion were to be removed.

Cooperation and Conflict

What of the impact on union membership of union practices regarding cooperation with employers? If the weight of recent rhetoric were to be believed, we have entered an era in which a new mood of cooperation is sweeping Australian workplaces – although the evidence suggests that employees themselves are as likely to perceive cooperation decreasing as increasing (DIR 1995:225). Peetz (1996) has examined the impact of conflict and cooperation on union membership. This study found little evidence of employee rejection of collaboration, or of the objective of improving productive efficiency, as a significant explanation for union membership loss in recent years. This was probably because, for reasons of company survival, employees seek a generally 'cooperative' – but not acquiescent – relationship between their representatives and their employer. Employee perceptions that unions were attempting to cooperate with management were positively related to union membership in open jobs. Employees seeking more cooperative behaviour from their unions are likely to leave (or not join) if unions are not seen as attempting such behaviour, just as unions that are too weak or acquiescent will lose members.

Nonetheless, there was empirical support for the widely believed notion that industrial action has the potential to increase union membership, sometimes quite substantially. Whether there were gains in employee approval of unions, and union membership, was often a question of whether the outcomes of disputes ultimately were to the benefit of employees. It was found that it was possible for both 'cooperation' and industrial action to be not only consistent with union membership growth but also positively correlated with each other, because employees who had favourable attitudes towards their union, arising in part from perceptions of union cooperativeness, were more inclined to support what they considered to be legitimate industrial action organised by their union.

The employee search for 'cooperative' union behaviour was, therefore, not a search for union compliance. They were not looking to unions to simply adopt management's agenda. Indeed, it was found that employees were looking for even more cooperative behaviour from management. The 'cooperation' that employees were willing to offer management depended upon the cooperation that management offered to employees. The key for unions was to know when employees considered that management had gone too far.

Conclusion

This chapter has described a number of analytical constructs that help in examination of the determination of union membership: the distinction between open and restricted jobs; the distinction between union propensity and union reach; and the notions of union joining and union exit. A complex array of influences on union membership was also revealed.

Around half of employees would rather be in a union than not be in one and, when free to choose in a workplace with a union presence, around half of employees belong to a union. Amongst those with a choice, the desire for union protection was an important factor in union joining and membership. The perceived ineffectiveness of unions, or adverse affects that they generated, were important reasons for non-membership.

Union instrumentality was a powerful influence on union retention and exit. Many employees joined a union because they had to. But if they later had the opportunity to return to non-union status (for example, by moving from a restricted to an open job), whether they actually did so depended more upon the benefits that unionism had provided to those employees and their perceptions of other union competencies.

Union responsiveness, protection, cohesion and satisfaction are each positively related to union membership. To varying degrees they each enhance both union instrumentality and union sympathy. As a result they directly promote unionisation in open jobs and, indirectly, facilitate union reach; that is, unions that are seen by their members as being responsive to their priorities, protecting their interests and having influence at the workplace, and behaving in a cohesive manner, create an environment that encourages people to join and to stay. In relation to some of these issues, however, Australian unions perform poorly, suggesting a significant proportion of unions are territory-driven rather than member-driven. Low levels of employee participation encouraged people to join unions, but where unions failed in giving a say to their members they were also more likely to leave unions. Unions which, in principle, resisted cooperative relations with management were more likely to face disapproval from their members and experience greater difficulties with recruitment and retention of members. But the employee search for 'cooperative' union behaviour was not a search for union compliance. Industrial action against management, where it was supported by members and achieved beneficial outcomes, clearly promoted union membership.

Ideological factors appeared to be more influential in determining whether people joined unions than in determining whether they remained in or left unions. The influence of ideological factors will be considered in more detail in the next chapter.

CHAPTER 3

Sympathy for Unions

A number of studies have distinguished between 'ideological' and 'instrumental' reasons for belonging to a union. Researchers have used a range of names with varying degrees of elegance – such as 'enterprise unionateness' and 'social unionateness' or 'instrumental unionism' and 'social unionism' (e.g. Prandy et al. 1974, 1982) – to distinguish between these or similar concepts. In this book, the term 'union sympathy' is used to describe the general, ideological views about unions held by employees, and 'union instrumentality' to describe the extent to which employees consider they will benefit or have benefited from union membership.

Union sympathy and instrumentality may vary between situations and countries (Gallagher & Strauss 1991). Perceptions that unions improve the welfare of *all* workers have been found to provide a substantial independent, altruistic reason for union membership in the US (Fiorito 1992). Some researchers suggest that changes in ideological views of unions can affect union density. Lipset (1986) argues that the success (or failure) of US unions in organising and recruiting is correlated with measures of the public approval of unions. Measures of the general image of unions have revealed image to have a strong influence upon the likelihood of union membership or propensity in the US (Getman et al. 1976; Schriesheim 1978; Youngblood et al. 1984; Deshpande & Fiorito 1989) and Belgium (Gevers 1992). A few Australian studies have shown the importance of ideological views of unions in influencing membership of Australian unions (Christie & Miller 1989:263–8; De Cieri 1991; Christie 1992; Deery & Grimes 1994). However, as Chaison and Rose (1991) point out, international differences in sympathy towards trade unions do not appear to explain international differences in union density (see also Bruce 1989).

Moreover, ideological motivations appeared to be less important than other considerations for union joiners in studies from Belgium (Baupain 1992), the UK (Goldthorpe et al. 1968; Mercer & Weir 1972; Cook et al. 1975; Waddington & Whitston 1993), Spain (Fundacion Largo Caballero 1988, cited in Wheeler & McClendon 1991) and the Netherlands (Van de Vall 1970), although Beynon and Blackburn (1972) concluded that membership motivations for almost half of their British sample were ideological. The balance between ideological and instrumental motivations might also vary between blue- and white-collar workers (e.g. Batstone et al.). Peak unions in a number of industrialised countries consider that decisions to join a union are less influenced by ideology today than in the past (Pankert 1992:156).

This chapter examines the role of union sympathy in explaining union membership. The main issues discussed are the influence of union sympathy on union joining and exit, trends in union sympathy over time and union sympathy in Australia in an international context.

The Relevance of Union Sympathy to Union Membership

The most sweeping question in SEMSE regarding union sympathy asked respondents to agree or disagree with the statement 'Australia would be better off without unions'. Only 25 per cent of respondents with an opinion agreed with this statement, while 53 per cent disagreed. (In this question, as with others reported later, the remainder 'neither agree(d) nor disagree(d)'.) This suggests that, at its broadest level, union sympathy in the SEMSE sample was more positive than negative towards unions. In every industry and occupational group in the survey, there was net disagreement with the view that Australia would be better off without unions. Only in non-union workplaces was there slight net support for the view that Australia would be better off without unions.

Essentially the same question was asked in LCS-96 and AES, and both these studies also showed majority opposition to the notion that Australia would be better off without unions. In AES, only 19 per cent agreed and 54 per cent disagreed. In LCS-96 (where neutral responses were not explicitly sought), 23 per cent agreed and 69 per cent disagreed.

A more specific question on union power, along similar lines to those asked in numerous opinion polls, produced less favourable results. Forty-six per cent of SEMSE respondents with an opinion agreed that 'Australian unions have too much power', while only 25 per cent disagreed. In AES, 57 per cent of employees agreed, and 24 per cent disagreed, with this proposition.

These two items were used in SEMSE to constitute an index of union sympathy ($\propto$ = .73), which is used in some analyses later on. A third question, not included in the index,[1] correlated equally with union sympathy and with satisfaction with union leadership and the ACTU: 50 per cent agreed that most Australian union leaders only look after themselves, and 20 per cent disagreed. While this proposition suggests a very high level of cynicism about union leaders (also reflected in very low 'trust' ratings given union leaders in opinion polls, e.g. Morgan 1992b), this is not necessarily translated into as high a level of cynicism about unions themselves. In LCS-96, 45 per cent of employees disagreed (and 43 per cent agreed) that 'trade unions in Australia don't effectively look after their members' – a poor result, but considerably better than that for union leaders.

Consistent with evidence from overseas studies (Van de Vall 1970; Gallie 1989; de Witte 1989 cited in Hartley 1992), parental union membership influenced union sympathy in SEMSE. Fifty-eight per cent of employees who had a parent who had been a union member disagreed with the notion that Australia would be better off without unions, compared to 47 per cent of other employees. A number of other studies have shown that the existence of union-active or union-sympathetic parents increased the likelihood of pro-union sympathy amongst employees (Brotslaw 1967; Barling et al. 1991; Beaumont & Elliot 1992) and was important in explaining initial decisions to join unions (Baupain 1992).

There is a very strong relationship between union sympathy and general union propensity. As shown in table 3.1, general union propensity was much higher amongst employees with pro-union ideological positions, whether measured by the union sympathy index or by its component parts. While the data in table 3.1 relate to AES, a similar relationship involving the same questions was found in SEMSE, the former being reported because of its larger sample size.

The data also supported other researchers' findings that *political* ideology influenced unionism (Deery & De Cieri 1991; Grimes 1994). In SEMSE there was a correlation between general union propensity and agreement with the statement 'the difference between the rich and the poor in Australia is much too great'. Likewise, in AES employees who wanted to be in a union were more likely: to agree that income and wealth should be redistributed towards ordinary working people, to prefer increased spending on social services over reductions in tax, to disagree that promoting economic growth is more important than distributing income more fairly, to consider that Aboriginal land rights and government assistance to Aborigines have *not* gone too far in recent years, to consider the Queen is not very important to Australia, to support changes to the flag, and to vote Labor.

Table 3.1 Union sympathy and union propensity

	Union propensity (Whether would prefer to belong to a union)				N
	Agree (positive propensity) (%)	Neutral (%)	Disagree (negative propensity) (%)	Total (%)	
Australia would be better off without unions					
– agree	14	8	78	100	224
– neutral	16	39	45	100	331
– disagree	57	22	22	100	649
Australian unions have too much power					
– agree	23	20	57	100	689
– neutral	39	43	18	100	250
– disagree	75	14	11	100	271

Source: AES
Population: All employees

Union sympathy was a critical factor in union joining. The rate of union joining in open jobs was 59 per cent amongst employees with pro-union sympathy, but only 5 per cent amongst those with anti-union sympathy. A statistical analysis (using logistic regression equations: Peetz 1998) shows that union sympathy was by far the most important determinant of union joining. Recall, however, that the open-ended questions on reasons for union membership (chapter two) suggested that the main feature of this relationship is not so much that people predominantly join unions for overtly ideological reasons, but rather that anti-union sympathy is a strong impediment to union joining. Some positive or at least neutral union sympathy may be a prerequisite for voluntary union membership, even though it need not be the stated reason for joining.

If ideological factors strongly influenced union joining, they had a very limited effect on union exit. The rate of union exit in open jobs was 14 per cent amongst past and present union members with a pro-union orientation, and 31 per cent amongst those with an anti-union orientation (table 3.2). This relationship, however, was not significant in many regression equations once other factors – particularly union

Table 3.2 Union exit rates in open jobs by union instrumentality and sympathy

	Aggregate union exit rate (%)	N	Same-workplace union exit rate (%)	N
Union instrumentality				
– benefited from union				
membership	9	166	4	156
– made no difference	25	176	12	150
– made worse off	62	21	44	14
Union sympathy				
– pro-union orientation	14	191	6	175
– neutral	24	69	9	57
– anti-union orientation	31	81	18	68

Source: SEMSE
Population: Past and present members of a union in open jobs: in all work-
              places (columns 1, 2); at their current workplace (columns 3, 4)

instrumentality – were controlled (see Peetz 1998). Union instrumentality had a much more powerful effect on union exit in open jobs than
did union sympathy. Non-ideological factors were much more important
in determining whether employees, once they belonged, would leave a
union. As discussed in chapter two, union leavers were also less likely
than the non-joiners to give ideological responses when explicitly asked
the reasons for their non-membership.

There may be a certain amount of inertia in union membership –
once employees join, they tend to stay until something of significance
happens. For most employees, union sympathy probably does not
undergo major changes in the short to medium term, although it is
influenced by unions at the workplace. Single events can more starkly
change employees' perceptions of whether or not they are benefiting
from union membership, and such events may also lead to union exit.

Union sympathy had a very strong relationship with union membership in open jobs (table 3.3). Employees in open jobs with pro-union
ideological orientations were much more likely to belong to a union
than were those with anti-union orientations. However, a significant
number of employees with anti-union ideological orientations in open
jobs remained union members – a point to which we shall return.

Changes in Union Sympathy

With such strong relationships between union sympathy and union
propensity and membership, it is worth asking whether there have been

Table 3.3 Union sympathy and union membership in open jobs

	Union status			N
	Member	Non-member	Total	
Australia would be better off without unions				
– agree	43	57	100	98
– neutral	46	54	100	95
– disagree	78	22	100	248
Australian unions have too much power				
– agree	53	47	100	187
– neutral	57	43	100	132
– disagree	88	12	100	111
Union sympathy index				
– anti-union orientation	45	55	100	125
– neutral	56	44	100	94
– pro-union orientation	80	20	100	199

Source: SEMSE
Population: Employees in open jobs

changes in union sympathy and whether these may help explain changes in unionisation. Rawson (1983), for one, suggested that the decline in unionism may be associated with the increasing unpopularity of unions. The major difficulty in addressing this question lies in the absence of a consistent series of data on union sympathy. However, a study of questions in opinion polls and social science surveys covering the last half century has pieced together the trends in union sympathy (Peetz 1997d). Five main points emerged.

First, while unions have been considered to be a good thing for the country, on other aspects of union sympathy – whether unions have too much power, whether voters' sympathies are generally for or against strikers, whether there should be tougher laws on unions, attitudes to compulsory unionism – public attitudes have been consistently more negative than positive towards trade unions.

Second, when attitudes towards unions in Australia are compared with those in other countries, Australian unions do not fare well. There are six questions that have been asked in surveys during the 1980s and 1990s enabling 15 comparisons to be made between Australia and another country (Peetz 1997d); in these comparisons Australian unions consistently attract lower sympathy than unions from the other country. This may reflect the influence of arbitration and its impact on the legitimacy of the strike weapon. The arbitration system has consistently held wide public support (APOP 1946, 1955, 1970, 1979, 1984, 1986; McNair 1988), and been more valued by Australians than the right to strike (APOP 1948, 1949, 1960, 1962; Morgan 1977). Probably more so than in other countries, Australians have not recognised the legitimacy of the strike weapon, whereas people elsewhere, operating under purer collective-bargaining frameworks, have not questioned the validity of industrial action or so strongly questioned the legitimacy of union behaviour.

Third, there was a gradual deterioration in union sympathy over the period from the 1940s to the 1960s. For example, when asked in 1951 'Looking back over the history of trade unions in Australia, do you think that the unions have been a good thing for Australia or not?', 80 per cent of Australians said that they thought they had been a good thing (APOP 1951). Support was slightly lower in 1966, when 75 per cent gave a positive response after being asked 'Speaking generally, do you think that unions are a good thing or a bad thing?' (APOP 1966). Attitudes to compulsory unionism also show something about union sympathy: across four polls from 1942 to 1953, an average of 35 per cent of Australians supported compulsory unionism and 52 per cent opposed it (APOP 1942, 1943a, b, 1953); but across four polls from 1956 to 1971, average support was just 28 per cent compared to 66 per cent opposition (APOP 1959, 1966, 1971).

Fourth, there was a more marked deterioration in union sympathy during the early 1970s. By 1974, just 62 per cent said 'a good thing' when asked 'Do you think that, on the whole, unions have been a good thing for Australia or not?' (Morgan Gallup 1974). Between 1971 and 1974, the proportion of Australians who nominated unions as a group that had 'too much power' rose from 49 per cent to 66 per cent (Age Poll 1971, 1974). Between 1969 and 1979 the proportion of people who said that when they heard of a strike, their sympathies were generally against the strikers, rose from 41 per cent to 49 per cent (Aitkin 1977; APAS 1979).

Fifth, during the Accord period there was a gradual recovery in union sympathy. The proportion of people who said that unions were doing either an 'excellent', 'very good' or 'fairly good' job rose from 36 per cent to 50 per cent between 1984 and 1995. The proportion who said their sympathies were generally against strikers fell from 49 per cent in 1979 to 32 per cent in 1995 (Evans 1996). The proportion who felt that unions had too much power fell from 82 per cent in 1984 to 62 per cent in 1996[2] (Kelley et al. 1984, Jones et al. 1996). And the proportion who considered there should be stricter laws about trade unions fell from 74 per cent in 1987 to 59 per cent in 1996 (McAllister & Mughan 1987, 1996).

This last point is crucial when considering the decline in union density in the 1980s and 1990s. Clearly, this decline in Australian union density cannot be explained by declining sympathy towards unions.

To properly assess the role of union sympathy it is necessary to take account of the way in which union joining and exit may be influenced by the interaction between union sympathy and growth in employment. The 1970s, which saw a significant deterioration in union sympathy, were also years in which employment growth was generally slow, as unemployment rose from 1.3 per cent in 1970 to 10.3 per cent in 1983. By contrast, the period from 1983 onwards was one of rapid employment growth. The main way in which union sympathy appears to affect union membership is through its impact on union joining. The era of rapid employment growth from 1983, in which many people either entered the labour force or moved from unemployment into employment, was a period of great potential for union joining. But for several years, at least, union sympathy was low and slow to recover from the battering it took during the 1970s. The failure of unions to pick up new members at this time (between 1982 and 1986 an estimated net 495,500 wage and salary jobs were created, but union membership grew by just 26,300) may therefore have partly reflected low union sympathy.

The decline in union sympathy in the 1970s may also have assisted employers in creating non-union restricted jobs, and in bringing about the end of some compulsory unionism arrangements. Both these objectives could best be achieved over the longer term. The full effect of the reduction of union reach would thus lag well behind any observed changes in union sympathy. That is, some unknown part of the decline in union reach and in unionisation over the 1980s may be due to the low levels of union sympathy that followed after the fall in sympathy over the period until the 1970s. However, the larger part of the decline in union reach probably relates to employer rather than employee motivations.

Unfortunately, it is not possible to attach robust estimates to these hypotheses from the time series data. The cross-sectional data from the employee survey do strongly suggest that, when major changes in union sympathy take place, some impact upon union membership may eventually be expected, depending upon the state of employment growth, but the data do not enlighten us as to the lags involved.

Conclusion

Without question, when choices are unconstrained union sympathy has a strong influence on individual decisions to join unions and a weaker influence on decisions to leave. But sympathy towards unions has, if anything, increased since the early 1980s during the Accord period, at least partly because of the lower level of industrial disputation during the Accord. With rising sympathy, union density should have increased. Instead, it fell.

The low level of union sympathy in Australia probably reflects the low legitimacy afforded industrial action in an arbitration-based system, with unions taking on almost demonic imagery during the industrial conflicts of the early 1970s. Perhaps, over time, as Australian unions adjust to the new legislative environment in which legal legitimacy is given to industrial action during periods of bargaining over agreements, industrial action in this context may also acquire greater political legitimacy. The association of communism and unionism from the 1950s to the 1970s probably also contributed to the longer-term decline in union sympathy that preceded the Accord; the virtual disappearance of this issue may also have contributed to the gradual improvement in union sympathy over the Accord period.

Union sympathy is not only low in absolute terms in Australia but also appears weaker than in several other countries. Certainly, differences in union sympathy between countries do not in themselves explain differences in union density, and are not being put forward here as the most significant factor. Nonetheless, the weak level of union sympathy at a time when employment was growing rapidly in the 1980s made new recruitment into unions more difficult, and would appear to make Australian unions especially vulnerable to the removal of compulsory unionism.

These results do not mean that the arbitration system and awards have been bad for union membership, and that the decline of the award system will be good for unions. The award system has historically been a major advantage to unions because it ensured that the 'union wage' was generalised, minimising the financial incentive for employers to avoid union labour. The problem was that union behaviour appeared inconsistent with the norms of that system. If real award wages fall so low as to create a large union–non-union wage gap, then the damage to union membership from heightened employer resistance may outweigh any longer-term gains from the improved sympathy associated with greater legitimacy.

More importantly, recent changes in union sympathy do not help explain the recent decline in union density. However, the low level of sympathy towards unions, by international standards, is part of the weakness in Australian unions that is exposed by the collapse in compulsory unionism (chapter five). If the improvements in union sympathy during the Accord period could be maintained under a Coalition government, then this could make it easier for unions to turn around the decline in union density. But, as the experience of the Accord years shows, the benefit to unions of growing sympathy is likely to be slowly felt and may not be enough to offset the institutional forces that have been depressing union density over the past two decades.

CHAPTER 4

Structural Change in the Labour Market

There are differences in union density between different industries and occupations; density varies according to the size of the workplace and between the public and private sectors, between full-time and part-time workers, between casual and permanent employees, and between the sexes. Structural change in the labour market might therefore be expected to lead to changes in union density. This chapter examines the influence of these factors on union density, and assesses the extent to which they might be said to be 'structural'.

Industrial and Sectoral Change

In all countries, there are differences in rates of unionisation among different industries. Workers 'are more likely to be union members in manufacturing, transport or public administration than in agriculture, (retail and wholesale) trade or financial services' (Visser 1991:107).

The pattern of industry variation in union density in Australia is comparable to that overseas, but Australia appears to have larger gaps in density between the private and public sectors than many other countries (the average gap in OECD countries being 20 percentage points in 1988). Public-sector unionisation exceeds private-sector unionisation by 55 per cent to 23 per cent in the members survey. Inter-industry variation in union density is greater in the private sector than in the public sector. That is, union density tends to be high amongst public-sector workers irrespective of their industry or employment; in the private sector, union membership is more dependent upon employees' industry.

One important question is whether differences in unionisation rates by industry (and, for that matter, other structural variables such as workplace size and occupation) primarily reflect 'differences in tastes for unionism' (Wooden & Balchin 1992:19) and 'different attitudes towards trade unions and perceptions of the services they offer' (Harris 1993:575), or do they primarily reflect differences in union reach? The answer to this question affects our understanding of the extent to which employment changes between industries are genuinely 'structural' in nature. Where economic change leads directly to an increase in the number of workplaces with non-union jobs, or a decrease in the number of workplaces with restricted union jobs, then the effect can be said to be clearly structural. By contrast, it is not so clear whether the label 'structural' can genuinely be applied to the change if all that is happening is that employees are moving from industries where (because of the types of workers who were attracted to those industries) employees typically had high union propensity to those where their colleagues have typically had low union propensity. This type of movement of workers between industries would tend merely to reduce inter-industry differences in unionism rather than affecting aggregate density, although this is said with two caveats in mind. First, if employees move from environments with pro-union cultures to those with anti-union cultures, aggregate density may decline even if there is no change in union propensity. Second, inter-industry differences in propensity could partly reflect differences in the hazards or unpleasantness of work, in which case movements of workers to industries with low union propensity could fairly be said to have a 'structural' effect on union density.

LCS-96 has been analysed to identify the minimum structural component of inter-industry density differences – that is, the extent to which differences in density reflect differences in union reach or differences in 'taste' or propensity (Goot & Peetz 1998). It was found that, while there was a 30 percentage point density differential between the high-density industries (government administration and infrastructure services) and the low-density industries (hospitality, mining and agriculture, and 'other'), over two-thirds of this differential was explained by differences in the incidence of non-union workplaces. A smaller proportion of the difference could be explained by the different incidence of compulsory unionism. But there were no significant differences between average union propensity in high- and low-density industries, and union propensity did not correlate with the union density of industries. Analysis of SEMSE data similarly revealed that union density of industries was strongly related to union reach, and had a non-significant, negative correlation with the level of union propensity in an industry. The implication is that changes in union density that arise from industrial changes are likely to be mostly, or entirely, 'structural' in nature.

The same is not quite the case for public–private sectoral differences in union density. While the higher level of public-sector union density in LCS-96 and AES primarily resulted from differences in the incidence of non-union workplaces, it also reflected some differences in union propensity. These in turn were partly related to differences in the general ideologies of the employees that were attracted to work in the public and private sectors.

Cross-national differences in industrial structures of the various OECD countries do not make a substantial contribution to explaining the differences in unionisation levels between countries (Visser 1991; Meltz 1990a). However, it is highly plausible that *changes* in industrial structure can lead to, and perhaps explain, changes in unionisation rates within countries. Around the western world, structural change in economies in the 1980s acted to disadvantage unions, as employment grew faster in industries with relatively low union density. In two studies, Visser used shift-share analysis to estimate the impact of structural change in nine European countries during the early and mid-1980s (Visser 1988) and in seven European countries plus North America, Japan and Australia during most of the 1970s and 1980s (Visser 1991). His analyses were undertaken at a broad level of aggregation[1] and so would not identify all the effects of industrial change. In most countries, structural change measured at this level detracted 0.1 to 0.2 percentage points per annum from union density. Visser (1991:114–15) deduced that the analysis 'clearly shows that the change in aggregate unionisation rates resulting from changes in the structure of employment … only accounts for a small part of the decline' in union density. Structural change could not account for the substantial differences between many countries in unions' experiences during the 1970s and 1980s. Furthermore, between countries, there was little correlation between employment shifts and changes in union densities. Changes in aggregate unionisation rates, he concluded, resulted mainly from movements *within*, not between, industries.

A number of nation-specific studies, some of which have used higher degrees of disaggregation (and therefore accuracy) than Visser, have reached broadly similar conclusions. For the UK, Carruth and Disney (1988) have taken a harder line than Visser, estimating that union membership would have been no higher in 1982 if the industry composition of employment had been the same as in 1978. Freeman and Pelletier (1990) estimated that only 0.4 percentage points of the 8.6-point drop in union density during the period 1980–86 could be attributed to industry changes. It may be the case, as Mason and Bain (1993:341) argue, that Disney and Freeman and Pelletier underestimated the impact of structural change in the UK; nonetheless, the bulk of the decline in density could not be attributed to this structural change between industries. And, as others such as Kelly (1990) have pointed out, structural change in the UK economy pre-dated the decline in unionisation.

For the US, Farber (1985, 1990) indicated that structural change was important in explaining union decline prior to the 1970s but accounted for only one-fifth of the decline in union density during the period 1977–84 (see also Mitchell 1983; Dickens & Leonard 1985; Doyle 1985; Visser 1991:115). Arguments by Moore and Newman (1975:444) and Troy (1992, 1993) that structural changes were important in explaining union growth or decline were in the minority. Industry change accounted for only 40 per cent of the recent (small) decline in Canadian unionism (Meltz 1990b), and in the 1970s Canadian density actually increased even though structural change had supposedly disadvantaged unions (Meltz 1985; Visser 1991:115).

What of the role of structural change in Australia? Some measures of the impact of structural change have relied upon the inclusion in time-series econometric equations of proxies to measure the extent to which the industry composition of employment favours unionism: for example, the share of total employment in manufacturing, or employment growth in the sector defined as unionised (e.g. Ashenfelter & Pencavel 1969; Kenyon & Lewis 1991, 1992; Sharpe 1971; Borland & Ouliaris 1989). Although this approach in time-series studies is superior to those which ignore structural effects altogether in Australia (cf. Bain & Elsheikh 1976; Western 1993a), it captures less information than do shift-share techniques and is subject to variation as other variables are included in, or excluded from, the specification of the equation. In Kenyon and Lewis (1991:17), for example, the impact of employment growth upon union-membership growth in the 'unionised' sector was, in one equation, 2.6 times greater than in another equation covering the same period.

For the period from 1976 to 1993, the 12 industry groups[2] have been arranged into three ranked categories, each containing four industries, according to whether they have low, medium or high density.[3] From 1994 onwards the 17 industry divisions have also been grouped along these lines. A break in the series, due to the ABS changing its industry classification system,[4] prevents direct comparisons between 1993 and 1994.

As illustrated in the bottom two lines in figure 4.1, during the first sub-period, 1976–82, employment grew more rapidly in industries with high union density. Indeed, the employment share of industries with low density fell slightly. Since 1982 the situation has been reversed. Employment has grown most rapidly in industries with low density, and fallen slightly in industries with high density. During the first period, union density actually fell in the high-density industries, but it fell only slightly in the medium- and low-density industries. After that, however, density declined in all industry groups, and indeed declined faster in the low-density industries.

The impact of the changing industry structure of employment (at the one-digit level) is shown by the thick continuous line in figure 4.1. When the line goes up, it means that industrial change is favouring unions and acting to raise union density. When the line goes down, it means that industrial change is acting to depress union density. The movement of that line can be compared with the overall movement in union density, shown by the thick broken line as gradually declining from one-half to one-third of employees over the 20-year period covered in the graph.

The upward movement in the thick continuous line shows that, in the period 1976 to 1982, between-industry change favoured unionisation. Yet during this period overall union density declined slightly, reflecting

Figure 4.1 Industrial change and union density

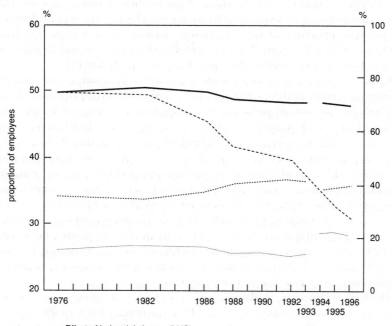

within-industry falls in density (mostly in high-density industries). From 1983–84 onwards,[5] between-industry change and within-industry declines in unionisation have had the same effect: to produce continuing falls in union density. From 1982 to 1992, approximately 16 per cent of the decline in union density can be explained by between-industry employment changes measured at the one-digit ASIC level. (Perhaps quotation marks should be placed around 'explained' because the effect of structural change is not immutable: it may make it easier or more difficult for unions to recruit members and for employers to resist unionisation but, as has been shown by Australia's earlier experience and the more recent experience of several other countries, a consequent fall in union density is not inevitable.)

Data measured at the two-digit ASIC level would allow for greater precision, and data for some years have been obtained. This higher level of disaggregation enables some 37 per cent of the decline in union density between 1982 and 1992 to be explained by between-industry changes in employment at the two-digit level.

Perhaps the most notable aspect of the graph, however, is that there is no indication that the acceleration of the decline in union density from 1992 onwards can be explained by structural change between industries. There is no evidence of any acceleration in structural change, and from 1992 to 1997 only about 2 per cent of the decline in union density can be explained by industrial change (at the one-digit level).

One of the most important aspects of industrial change has been the changing shares of the public and private sectors. From the early 1970s the relative growth of public-sector employment favoured unions as a result of the much higher density in the public sector. But this trend was reversed in the early years of the Hawke Labor Government (see figure 4.2). From 1982 to 1990, some 22 per cent of the decline in union density could be explained by the decline in the relative share of public-sector employment. The decline in public-sector employment eased during the late 1980s, but accelerated again after 1993. While this has made a contribution to the acceleration in the decline in union density, it cannot explain it. Only 18 per cent of the decline in density from 1992 to 1997 was explained by declining public-sector employment. In total, 17 per cent of the decline in union density since 1982 was explicable by public–private sector employment shifts.

Within industries, public-sector employment grew more slowly than private-sector employment.[6] The *combined* effect of changes in the sectoral and industry (single-digit) composition of employment explained 43 per cent of the fall in union density during the period 1982–92, but accounts for a smaller proportion of the decline since 1992.

Figure 4.2 Declining public-sector employment and union density

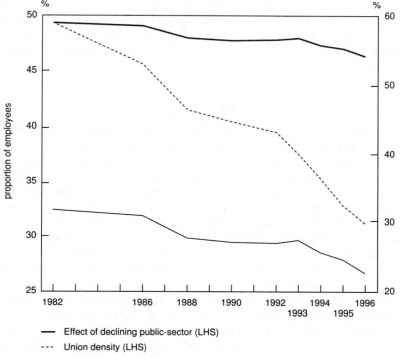

— Effect of declining public-sector (LHS)
--- Union density (LHS)
— Public-sector share of employment (RHS)

There are two ways of measuring the relative decline in the private and public sectors: as a proportion of all employees (that is, in percentage points) or as proportion of union members. Measured in percentage points, the decline in density was greater in the private sector than the public sector up until 1992, but it was greater in the public sector after 1992. When measured as a proportion of union members, density in the private sector fell by nearly four-tenths over the period 1982–95, whereas the decline in the public sector was closer to one-quarter. Which is the more useful way to measure the effect on each group? If membership both rises and falls in roughly equal amounts (over the long run), it is meaningful to measure net changes in membership as a proportion of employees (that is, as percentage points), in much the same way as 'swing' in elections is measured.[7] But if the movement is always one way (downwards) then it is more meaningful to measure decline as a proportion of union members. In this case, neither condition properly applies, but the universally downward trend in the data period being considered suggests that the latter approach (measuring decline as a proportion of union members) is probably the slightly better indicator when using aggregated statistics. By this indicator, the decline in the private sector has been considerably worse than in the public sector.

Occupational Change

The members survey shows that union density is higher amongst blue-collar occupations (40 per cent in 1996) than amongst white-collar occupations (27 per cent). Between white-collar occupations there is also considerable diversity in unionisation, with high union density amongst professionals (35 per cent) and low density amongst managers (16 per cent) and advanced clerical and service workers (13 per cent).

Union density is higher amongst blue-collar (manual) workers than white-collar (non-manual) workers in all but three OECD nations (Visser 1991). The gap between union densities of manual and non-manual employees was larger in Australia than in all but one other OECD nation in the early 1990s.

Occupational differences tend to be less important than sectoral differences: union density of white-collar workers in the public sector (63 per cent in 1992) is much higher than that of blue-collar workers in the private sector (42 per cent in 1992). Inter-occupational variance of density in the public sector is half that in the private sector: employees in the public sector tend to have high unionisation irrespective of occupation, but in the private sector occupation is a more important determinant of union status. Hence in the public sector, some 62 per cent of managers and administrators were unionised; in the private sector, just 9 per cent.

Occupational differences in density reflected differences in both union reach and union propensity. In our surveys, blue-collar workers had higher union density than white-collar workers by a margin of 7 (AES) or 11 (LCS-96) percentage points, the latter being close to the 12 per cent differential recorded by the ABS in 1994. In both surveys blue-collar workers were substantially more likely to be in compulsorily unionised jobs than white-collar workers. In both surveys they also had higher union propensity than white-collar workers. LCS-96 showed these factors to be approximately equal contributors to the occupational gap in density, but the AES suggested that differences in the incidence of compulsory unionism were the more important factor. The findings from SEMSE are closer to those of the AES than of LCS-96. The explanation as to why white-collar workers are less inclined to union membership than blue-collar workers cannot be found in differences in union sympathy (there are virtually no differences) or in their attitudes to union performance at the workplace. But they differed in terms of how much of an advantage they think management has over workers and how satisfied they are with management, and partly (but not entirely) for this reason they differ in terms of their union propensity (Goot & Peetz 1998).

Analysis of occupational change is complicated by the breaks in the ABS series in 1986 and 1995 arising from the adoption of the Australian Standard Classification of Occupations (ASCO) and the Australian and New Zealand Standard Classification of Occupations (ANZSCO) respectively. Hence the best period over which to meaningfully analyse disaggregated occupational effects is 1986–94.

Data based on the old occupational classification revealed that changes in the occupational distribution of employment had a negligible, positive impact on union density in the 1976–82 period. After 1986, occupational change, like industrial change, disadvantaged unions, though at the one-digit level of analysis the impact is not so great as industrial change. From 1986 to 1994, just 11 per cent of the decline in union density is able to be explained by changes in the occupational composition of employment, including just 7 per cent of the decline from 1992 to 1994. This small, negative effect on density is confined to male employees, amongst whom occupational change explained 12 per cent of the decline in density from 1986 to 1994; for female employees, just 2 per cent of the decline in density could be due to occupational change.

Between 1986 and 1996 union density fell by 17 percentage points amongst blue-collar workers and 12 points amongst white-collar workers. This difference probably largely reflects the decline of compulsory unionism, which had previously been more common among blue-collar than white-collar workers, and the fact that union density was higher to begin with amongst blue-collar workers. By 1996, amongst female employees, the gap between union density of blue- and white-collar workers was a mere 4 percentage points (compared to 9 points in 1986), though amongst male employees it was 17 percentage points (19 points in 1986).

Hours of Work and Employment Status

The members survey shows that union membership was substantially higher amongst permanent employees (36 per cent) than amongst casual employees (14 per cent) in 1997. By a lesser margin, it was also higher amongst full-time workers (34 per cent) than amongst part-time workers (21 per cent) in the same year.

Obviously there is considerable overlap between part-time work and casual employment. However, it is casual employment rather than part-time employment that is the key factor in diminishing union membership. In 1996, density amongst permanent part-timers, at 35 per cent, was almost the same as that amongst permanent full-timers, at 36 per cent. Likewise, density amongst casual part-timers (14 per cent) was similar to that amongst casual full-timers (13 per cent). The reason for low density amongst part-time employees is simply that they are more likely than full-time employees to be in casual employment.

As to the reasons for the differential in the densities of casual and permanent employees, LCS-96 showed that two-thirds of the differential could be explained simply by casual employees being much more likely to be employed in a non-union workplace. By contrast, in LCS-96 at least, there were no significant differences in union propensity between casual and permanent employees. Despite this, casuals' 'open density' (the density amongst employees who are in workplaces which have a union presence but whose jobs are not compulsorily unionised) was lower than open density amongst permanents. While this difference was only significant at the 10 per cent level, a comparable pattern was found in SEMSE: fairly similar levels of union propensity between casuals and permanents, but lower open density amongst casuals. This suggests that there are problems with union reach for casuals that go beyond whether or not there is a union at the workplace. Even for the minority of casuals who are at unionised workplaces, their irregular work patterns may make it difficult for unions to make effective contact with them (or unions may not consider it a high priority to recruit or represent casual employees).

Data on both full-time/part-time hours and casual/permanent employment status have not been collected continuously during the members surveys. However, consistent data are available on the former from 1988 to 1997 and on the latter from 1986 to 1997.

Casual employment's share of employment grew substantially, from 19 per cent of total employment in 1988 to 26 per cent in 1996. Since 1988, the growth of casual employment has been more important than industrial change in explaining declining union density: over the nine years from 1988 to 1997, approximately 17 per cent of the decline in union density could be explained by casualisation of the labour force. It explained 25 per cent of the decline in density from 1986 to 1992 but just 12 per cent of the decline from 1992 to 1997.

A slightly smaller proportion is explained by the relative growth in part-time employment. (Because there is so much overlap between the two, and the part-time effect is really a casual effect, we would not expect their combined effect to be above the individual figures quoted above.)

If casualisation of labour is an important element in the most recent decline in union membership, unions have not yet found the strategy to address it. Between 1988 and 1997 union density amongst casual employees fell by 7 percentage points compared to 15 points amongst permanent employees – but this represented a drop of 34 per cent of casual union members, compared to about 29 per cent of permanent union members.

In sum, the increasing casualisation of labour and associated trend to part-time employment explains a significant proportion of the decline in union density, and unions are facing a decline in membership amongst these expanding ranks of casual employees.

Working from Home

Data separately collected by the ABS show union density amongst employees who work from home to be just 4 per cent in 1995 (ABS Cat. No. 6275.0). This is notwithstanding the fact that 31 per cent of them were permanent employees, and 35 per cent usually worked 35 hours or more from home. About 1.8 per cent of employees worked from home in 1995, up from 1.4 per cent in 1989. In three years from 1992, there had been some changes in the composition of home-working employees, with a fall in permanent employment (from 44 per cent to 31 per cent) and a decline in union density (from 7 per cent to 4 per cent). Only one-third of home-workers were employees. The growth of home-work will clearly have a downward effect on union density, but the magnitude of its impact is likely to be small.

Workplace and Firm Size

A number of studies have demonstrated that unionisation varies by firm or workplace size: it is lowest in small workplaces or firms (e.g. Bain & Elsheikh 1976; Hirsch & Berger 1984; Millward & Stevens 1986; Booth 1986; Hundley 1989; Elias 1990; Green 1990; Beaumont & Harris 1991; Visser 1991; Grimes 1994; Turner 1994). This size effect might reflect either supply or demand factors. On the supply side, two factors stand out. First, the cost per member to unions of organising is greater in small workplaces: it takes much less time to organise 500 employees in one workplace than 500 employees in 100 workplaces (Bain & Price 1983). Second, employer attitudes to unions may be more amenable in large firms and workplaces (Beaumont & Rennie 1986; Gallie 1989). On the demand side, it is claimed that employees in small workplaces or firms may be less inclined to unionise because of better employment relations and stronger links and identification with management in small workplaces or firms, in contrast with the more bureaucratic manner in which workers in large firms are managed (Bain & Price 1983:27–8). The evidence in support of this proposition is limited; it suggests that there may be some link between size and attitudes (Lipset et al. 1956) but this link appears to be small or non-significant (Gallie 1989).

For Australia, Harris (1993) and Wooden and Balchin (1992, 1993) showed a strong relationship between firm size and union presence and density, and a positive link between workplace size and union presence using AWIRS90 data. Neither LCS-96 nor AES had data on workplace or firm size. However, SEMSE data indicated that the majority of variation in density across the five workplace size bands was attributable to variations in union reach, and that variations in union density were much greater than variations in union propensity: a 23 percentage point differential in density between workplaces with 50–99 employees and those with 200–499 employees, compared to an 8 point differential in union propensity explaining only one-sixth of the density differential. Lower employee desire for unions therefore did not explain much of the difference in unionisation between large and small workplaces. Nor was there evidence to support the idea that low union density in smaller workplaces could be attributed to greater satisfaction with management (cf. Bain & Price 1983:27–8), as management satisfaction did not vary significantly between size bands once other factors were controlled. However, there is evidence (discussed in chapter six) that management in small firms is less tolerant of unionism.

Data on workplace size were only collected in the members surveys from 1990. The data showed a drop in average workplace size over the 1990–95 period, partly reflecting continuing layoffs in large organisations while new and existing small businesses were experiencing employment growth. From 1990 to 1995, changes in workplace size explained a drop of 0.6 points in union density, accounting for 12 per cent of the decline in that period. However, between 1995 and 1997 the entirety of the 'size effect' accumulated over the preceding five years was wiped out. Workplaces with less than 20 employees, which accounted for 37.5 per cent in 1990, rising to 40 per cent in 1995, fell back to 37.5 per cent in 1997. Trends in workplace size appear to be more cyclical than structural, and so do not explain longer-term union decline.[8]

Density has fallen in all size bands. Measured in percentage points, the fall has been least in the smallest workplaces (6 percentage points over seven years amongst workplaces with less than 10 employees, compared with 11 to 13 points in other size bands). But measured as a proportion of union members, the fall in density has been worst in the smallest size band (38 per cent) and least in the largest size band of workplaces with 100 or more employees (21 per cent).

Gender

The members series shows that union density is higher amongst males (33 per cent) than females (27 per cent). A lower rate of unionisation amongst women is apparent in most OECD countries, with the exception of Sweden, but the gender gap in Australia has been similar to the average gap in other OECD nations (see Visser 1988).

At the start, we should point out that there is no evidence to support the view that women are intrinsically less supportive of unions (a view seemingly reflected, for example, in research commissioned for the ACTU: see ANOP 1989:9, 1992:5). Union sympathy in SEMSE amongst females was no lower than amongst males, nor was it lower amongst female non-unionists than amongst male non-unionists. This was consistent with other surveys of the time: the 1988 Issues in Multicultural Australia survey had also shown no consistent differences between men's and women's union sympathy (Grimes 1994). In 1996, the AES showed no significant differences between the sexes in attitudes to whether unions have too much power or should be regulated more strictly, or whether Australia would be better off without unions. Similarly, LCS-96 showed no gender differences in attitudes to whether Australia would be better off without unions. Women in LCS-96 were, however, *less* likely to agree that unions don't effectively look after their members. There was, in short, virtually no evidence from any of a number of surveys that women were less sympathetic than men towards unions.

With very high occupational segregation of male and female employees in Australia (Karmel & McLachlan 1986; Lewis 1983), we might also expect that gender and occupational patterns in union density could be closely related, an expectation that is met by close analysis of the members survey data. When controlling for differences in the degree to which males and females are in casual employment, the 1992 gap between male and female union density falls from 5.4 percentage points to 3.3 points. When controlling both for differences in casual/permanent employment status and for differences in occupations (measured just at the one-digit level), the male–female gap reduces to slightly over 1 point. If males and females had the same distribution of employment in terms of occupation and casual/permanent employment status, male unionisation would be 32 per cent and female unionisation would be 31 per cent in 1996. Controlling for occupation and employment status consequently left less than one-fifth of the observed difference in unionism by gender unexplained. This broadly fits with overseas evidence: Antos, Chandler and Mellow (1980) and Freeman and Medoff (1984:28) estimated that 50 to 65 per cent of the male–female unionisation gap in the US could be explained by differences in industry and occupation.

Data since 1988 suggest that the gap between the male and female union density has been reducing more rapidly than the structural gap in male and female densities. In 1988 and 1992 the female–male density gaps in the members survey were 11.6 and 8.9 percentage points respectively. Yet the structural gap due to the effects of occupation and employment status fell only slightly, from 7.1 to 6.7 points, explaining just one-seventh of the fall in the gender gap; that is, the portion of gender difference due to other, partly non-structural factors fell from 39 per cent to 24 per cent.

Data issued in publications from the members survey since then do not allow the same degree of structural analysis, but they do show that the gender gap has continued to decline, to just 6.1 percentage points in total. A trend to a smaller male–female gap is even more prominent in data from the union census (which was considerably less reliable for gender research).

So while structural changes explain much of the gender gap in union density, the gap is not reducing as a result of structural changes or reductions in the barriers of occupational segmentation and casualisation of female labour. Two other factors might be responsible. One is the decline in compulsory unionism, which would affect male density more than female density as its incidence amongst males was considerably higher than amongst females in the late 1980s. In 1988, some 35 per cent of men were employed in closed shops, compared to 19 per cent of women (Grimes 1994). Data from LCS-96 and AES suggest that, as compulsory unionism has declined, the differential between male and female levels of compulsory unionism narrowed substantially. This reduction in the gender gap in compulsory unionism could account for a significant proportion of the narrowing of the gender gap in union density.

The decline may also be due to relative improvements in the way in which unions offer services to female members. A number of Australian researchers have referred to the poor performance of unions in serving their female members (Storer & Hargreaves 1976; Manning 1990; Gale 1990) and the lack of interest by male-dominated union structures in women (Ryan & Prendergast 1982). So it would not be surprising if Australian women were historically less likely to want to join or stay in unions than men; but with the publication of strategic union documents such as of *Future Strategies for the Trade Union Movement, Can Unions Survive?* and *Together for Tomorrow* (ACTU 1987, 1991; Berry & Kitchener 1989), and the formation of union policies on women, some improvements in the relative attractiveness of unions to women would be hoped for by unions. More important than the targeting of policies and practices towards the needs of women workers might be differences in the character of unions to which men and women typically belong. Just as unions covering men have relied more heavily on compulsory unionism, so might they tend towards being territory-driven rather than member-driven unions. It is thus quite possible that the member-driven unions to which women have more commonly belonged may be adjusting better to the changing environment and providing better support to their members than the territory-driven unions to which many men belonged.

Certainly, by 1996 neither LCS-96 nor AES showed a statistically significant difference between the union propensities of men and women. In AWIRS95, men were more likely to want to belong but also more likely to *not* want to belong than women, leading to no difference in their net union propensities. By contrast, the 1990–91 SEMSE had shown women's union propensity to be below that of men by a small but significant amount (6 percentage points).

Because SEMSE was not a fully representative sample, we cannot be certain from this evidence alone that there has been a change in the relative union propensity of women. The absence of a propensity differential is consistent with overseas evidence: US union certification studies show gender to have no independent effect on the probability of union membership or pro-union voting (Scoville 1971; Getman et al. 1976; Hammer & Berman 1981; Youngblood et al. 1984). British studies suggest that 'a woman's personal responsibilities have no effect on her decision to unionise' (Booth 1986; see also Payne 1989; Gallie 1989:15–17).

In SEMSE, female employees had lower union instrumentality than male employees, consistent with observations in previously mentioned studies about the poor performance of unions in providing benefits to female members. This matched American evidence that unions had served their female members poorly, and that females were less likely than males to perceive that their union acts instrumentally (Fiorito & Greer 1986). Studies in Britain (Cunnison 1983) and Japan (RIALS 1993) also pointed to the poor perceptions female employees had of union performance.

This did not, however, reflect lower levels of union responsiveness or protection perceived amongst female union members. To the contrary, union responsiveness in SEMSE was scored slightly higher by females than males, but the difference was not statistically significant. Similarly, in LCS-96, women's attitudes to the performance of workplace unions were either similar to men's or more positive: women were, for example, less likely (by 11 percentage points) to agree that unions did a poor job in keeping in contact with their members, and less likely to say that unions should be doing more about wages, job security, or the chance to have a say in work. In AWIRS95, women were happier than men with the way in which unions took notice of members' problems and less dissatisfied than men with the overall service provided by their unions. These patterns are consistent with the proposition that women are more likely to be in member-driven unions.

Does greater satisfaction with unions' responsiveness amongst women merely reflect their lower expectations of unions? While differences in satisfaction with the level of support provided by a union might theoretically reflect different expectations, this should not affect perceptions of whether the performance of unions has improved or deteriorated over a certain period. So we can look at data on changes in union performance to see whether unions representing women are doing a better job of improving their performance, and thereby also to test whether the narrowing gender gap in union density partly reflects improvements in the way in which unions offer services to female members and in their responsiveness to women's concerns.

In SEMSE there were significant differences in perceptions of changes in union responsiveness that offer some support for the hypothesis that unions have been improving their services to female employees. Female employees were slightly more likely than male employees to say that unions were more effective than they were two years earlier in taking notice of employees' problems and complaints (17 per cent compared with 14 per cent), and much less likely to say that unions were now less effective in taking notice of complaints (14 per cent compared with 29 per cent). This relationship held amongst union members in both open and restricted jobs.

Several significant results were also found in the AWIRS90 data, each suggesting that female-dominated workplaces were more likely to show increasing union density. Workplaces where management indicated union density had increased had a higher female-employment share than those where it had not increased. The same pattern arose in workplaces where management said that major organisational change had led to an increase in unionisation, and where the senior union delegate said that organisational change had led to an increase in union membership.

The AWIRS panel data (discussed further in chapter six) also showed the rates of deunionisation between 1989–90 and 1995–96 amongst workplaces with high female employment (greater than 60 per cent) to be significantly lower, at 3 per cent, than the 9 per cent rate amongst workplaces with lower levels of female employment. Similarly, the rates of union collapse (also explained further in chapter six and table 6.2) were slightly lower in workplaces with high levels of female employment.

Finally, LCS-97 asked employees how they compared the performance of their union now with its performance 12 months ago. Women tended to rate their union's performance more positively (29 per cent) than more negatively (21 per cent) compared with a year earlier. Men had the opposite pattern (28 per cent more positive, 37 per cent more negative). This difference in ratings also held when only full-time employees were considered.

This pattern across questions and data sets tentatively suggests that the decline in the gender gap might be due to improving female union propensity possibly associated with improvements in union responsiveness for female members, a greater concentration of women in member-driven unions and, perhaps most importantly, the declining differential in compulsory unionism.

Because gender differences in unionisation reflect differences in the employment patterns of men and women, it cannot be concluded that the increasing share of female employment explains any part of the decline in union density. If female employment had increased but there had been no increase in casual employment and no shift from the public sector or to low-density industries, occupations or size bands, there would have been no structural effect of female employment on union density.

What of the gendered patterns in attitudes to unions? The problem for women has historically been that male-dominated unions have given scant regard to women's interests. The current problem for men may be that the sorts of structures that made their territory-driven unions unresponsive for many years to women's interests are now the major barrier, in a rapidly changing environment, to their providing adequate support to their male members.

The Future Labour Market and Implications for Unions

Many of the changes in union density over the past decade can be explained by structural changes in the labour market: the growth of casual and part-time employment; the growth of low-density industries and occupations; the relative decline of the public sector; and the reduction in average workplace and firm size as large organisations restructure while new and existing small organisations grow.

It is difficult to estimate accurately the cumulative effect of these factors, as they are non-additive. For example, the shift from the public to the private sectors overlaps with the casualisation of the labour force and the decline in average workplace size. Moreover, a small part of the shift can be discounted as not representing a 'true' structural effect because it partly reflects shifts in employment shares from groups that previously had high union propensity to groups that had low union propensity (e.g. from the public sector to the private sector) when the objective conditions (e.g. hazard and unpleasantness) of private-sector work may be no worse than those applying to public sector work. However, a reasonable estimate is that something around half of the decline in union density in the decade to 1992 can be explained by these factors.

Importantly, there is no consistent evidence of an acceleration of structural change during the 1990s. Yet the decline in union density has accelerated during the 1990s, and in particular since 1992. The acceleration of the decline in union density cannot even be partly explained by structural change.

While the nature of structural change appears to fluctuate somewhat from one year to the next, there is little reason to believe that the near future will see a turnaround in these structural forces. Employment growth will continue to be concentrated in industries and occupations with low union density. There is no reason to believe that the increasing casualisation of employment and growth of part-time work will be permanently reversed in the near future.

While there has been substantial structural change in Australia, it is not clear whether this country has experienced more substantial *industrial* change than other industrialised nations. Visser's (1991) comparative shift-share analysis did not show Australia to be amongst the countries most strongly affected by inter-industry change.[9] On the other hand, amongst 10 major OECD nations over the 1980–90 period, the growth in the share of employment taken by two services industry groups (finance, insurance, real estate and business services; wholesale and retail trade, restaurants and hotels) with low density was second highest in Australia (Godbout 1993). By 1990, the share of employment accounted for by these industries was higher in Australia than in any of the other nine major countries examined.

Where Australia has clearly experienced a faster rate of structural change than most other industrialised countries is in the area of part-time employment: between 1983 and 1990, the part-time share in total employment grew by 3.8 percentage points, the second highest growth in the OECD (behind New Zealand) and over five times the OECD average (OECD 1991:46).

All of this hardly means that ongoing decline in union density is inevitable. The discussion in chapter one of developments during the large part of this century suggests that structural influences can be quite small when compared with the influence of union, employer and state strategy. There were long periods in which the changes in union density were far more substantial than could be explained by structural change in the labour market, such as when structural change tended to disadvantage unions but union density increased, or vice versa. It appears that structural change accelerated in the 1980s to a level more potent than at any time at least since World War II.

The problem that the fastest growing sectors of the labour force have been the hardest to unionise is 'a problem as old as the union movement' (Archer 1995). Structural change may make it easier or more difficult for unions to recruit members and for employers to resist unionisation. Ultimately it is the interaction between unions, employees and employers that determines the conditions under which restricted jobs are created or transformed and the conditions under which union propensities are determined.

The fact that, for most of the past two decades, the decline in unionisation has been greater than that which could be explained by structural change suggests that other, non-structural, forces are at work. The next chapter discusses the most important of these.

CHAPTER 5

The Institutional Break in Union Membership

Earlier chapters have shown us that: the decline in union density can be partly explained by structural change in the labour market, but that this change cannot explain the deterioration in union membership in the 1990s; that declining union density cannot be blamed on falling sympathy for unions – indeed, it appears that sympathy for unions has increased since the early 1980s; and that what little evidence there is does not suggest that there has been a decline in employees' perceptions of union performance or union propensity. In this chapter we turn from structural to institutional influences on decline in union membership: changes in the approaches of employers and governments to unions, and in the fundamental determinants of union membership.

An Overview of the Institutional Break

Price and Bain (1989) proposed that, while relationships governing union membership would mostly be stable and cyclical (explicable by business-cycle variations), at particular times there could be fundamental changes or 'paradigm shifts' to those relationships. These institutional breaks emerge from particularly forceful conjunctions of social or economic events and powerful alliances of some of the participants in industrial relations, and alter the institutional arrangements surrounding the employment relationship. A paradigm shift creates 'new patterns in the context of industrial relations', principally changes in 'labour laws and the powers and roles of regulatory agencies, employer policies towards unionisation and collective bargaining, and union structures, political activities and ideologies' (Chaison & Rose 1991). According to Price and Bain, the changes in union fortunes in the US and the UK are attributable to paradigm shifts which have fundamentally altered the determination of union membership. While, as Mason and Bain (1993) argue, their exposition probably places too much reliance on business-cycle explanations of movements in unionisation between paradigm shifts, the notion of 'paradigm shifts' or institutional breaks represents an important advance in the consideration of the determinants of union membership.

It is a central contention of this book that there has been an 'institutional break' in the determination of union membership in Australia. Australia, like New Zealand, first experienced an institutional break in industrial relations with the establishment of the arbitration systems in the 1890s and 1900s. And Australia, like New Zealand, has been going through a new institutional break in the determination of union membership since around the mid-1980s.

In this second institutional break, the decollectivisation of the employment relationship is being actively pursued by, to varying degrees, employers and the state, after nearly a century in which collective employment relationships were accepted, often grudgingly, as the norm. Individual contracts are being promoted by employer associations, individual employers and governments as the most effective means of developing a 'close' or 'meaningful' relationship between employers and employees. Almost all State Governments, and now the Federal Government, have introduced laws facilitating the use of individual contracts as an alternative to collective regulation. So a new institutional environment is being created in which the determination of union membership is being fundamentally altered.

This decollectivisation principally involves challenges to the ability of unions to represent employees, but also involves challenges to the legitimacy of arbitration authorities to regulate the employment relationships governing those employees who are not members of a union. In most systems, the signing of an individual contract (commonly called a 'workplace agreement' or something similar) takes the employee beyond the jurisdiction of a tribunal, except to the extent that tribunal decisions may affect the minimum standards that contracts have to comply with when they are first signed.

In this 'institutional break' the role of demand- and supply-related factors is changing – a point that will be returned to shortly. Critically, compulsory unionism is ceasing to be a significant determinant of union membership, as employers withdraw support for such arrangements and as the state delegitimises them. In the context of the arbitration system, compulsory union membership had become the most common form of union membership in Australia, although technically, the federal tribunal could not require union membership, it could only award preference to union members, and the majority of compulsory arrangements arose from employer–union agreements or practices, not tribunal decisions (Callus et al. 1991). A circumscribed arbitration system persists in Australia (unlike in New Zealand), but most State Governments, and now the Federal Government, have introduced laws to make compulsory unionism and even preference for union members illegal.

Part of the decline in compulsory unionism is certainly attributable to structural change in the labour market (the relative growth of industries and occupations with low levels of compulsory unionism). But this explains only a minority of the decline in compulsory unionism, the great bulk being attributable to changes in government policy and employer strategy.

At the margins, where unions exist but they are weakly organised and represented, union members are being picked off by employers seeking alternative employment relationships. In some cases, employers and unions are in a form of 'hearts and minds' competition – or some might say an 'auction' – in which the employer seeks to wean employees from attachment to unions by offering them seemingly attractive, individualised employment relations. The key result for employers is obtaining an individualised employment relationship, not necessarily being able to get 'closer' to their employees.[1] In many cases where unions are weakly represented and organised (as measured, for example, by the absence of union delegates or the non-involvement of unions in bargaining), members are walking away from unions that are simply seen as doing little or nothing for their members – not least where poor union performance arose from the complacency bred by compulsory unionism.

While the institutional break occurred more rapidly, and has been completed, in New Zealand, it was still under way in Australia in the mid- to late 1990s. With the passage of the *Employment Contracts Act 1991*, taking effect from May 1991, compulsory unionism, previously very common in New Zealand, was made universally illegal. Union membership fell by 29 per cent in one year, and has continued to fall since (Harbridge & Crawford 1997). In Australia the demise of compulsory unionism has been spread over a number of years. This is perhaps partly because employers in Australia were initially more divided and less belligerent towards unions and compulsory unionism than in New Zealand. But the main reason is probably that the transformation in the legislative treatment of compulsory unionism has been more incremental as a result of the different timetables within which State legislatures, and finally the Federal Parliament, have sought to abolish compulsory unionism, due in turn to the different time periods in which the ALP was in power in New Zealand and at the State and

Federal levels in Australia. With the *Workplace Relations Act 1996*, in effect from 1997, only unions under State awards in New South Wales retain a capacity for compulsory unionism in certain limited circumstances.

Much of the rest of this chapter examines the most important single feature of this institutional break – the collapse of compulsory unionism. The size of the collapse is estimated, as is its impact on union density. In this context the failure of compulsory unionism in Australia to typically create strong attachment to unions is also considered, as this helps us understand why the collapse of compulsory unionism has had such an impact on overall union density. The role of governments in engendering the collapse is also considered. Other aspects of this institutional break – in particular, the collapse of union membership within certain workplaces – are canvassed in chapter six.

The Collapse of Compulsory Unionism in Australia

The ABS does not collect data on compulsory unionism. However, a number of social surveys and opinion polls suggested that between 1969 and 1979, 63 to 72 per cent of unionists were under closed shops[2] (Rawson 1978; APAS 1979; Morgan Gallup 1976, 1978; Morgan 1992a). Subsequent studies showed a much lower rate of compulsory unionism. The 1988 Issues in Multicultural Australia (IMA) survey implied that 57 per cent of union members were employed in closed shops (Grimes 1994). Rawson's 1990 survey indicated a figure of 54 per cent (Rawson 1992). Analysis of AWIRS90 data suggests that, amongst workplaces with 20 or more employees in 1989–90, approximately 54 per cent of employees were covered by compulsory unionism (Peetz 1995). The most valid direct comparison of like and like is between Rawson's surveys, showing conscripts at 67 per cent of unionists in 1978 and 54 per cent in 1990 (Rawson 1992).

If compulsory unionism had significantly fallen between 1976 and 1990, in the period from 1990 to 1996 it plummeted. Data from the AES in 1996 indicated that 25 per cent of union members were in compulsorily unionised jobs. A figure of 28 per cent was produced from LCS-96, undertaken at around the same time.

Applying the proportions[3] in such surveys to the union density figures in the members survey (using data from 1976, 1988, 1990 and 1995) suggests that, as a consequence, the proportion of employees in compulsorily unionised jobs fell from 34 per cent in 1976 (Rawson 1978) to 23 per cent in 1988 (Grimes 1994), 21 per cent in 1990 (Rawson 1992) and around a mere 11 per cent in 1995. This is illustrated in figure 5.1, which also shows that the proportion of employees who are non-members has increased as compulsory unionism has declined. Likewise, the proportion of employees who belong to a union and who are not in a compulsorily unionised job has increased as compulsory unionism has declined.

During the late 1970s and 1980s, the incidence of compulsory unionism amongst employees was declining by nearly one percentage point per year. During the 1990s, it has been falling at double that rate. Extrapolating from this trend, compulsory unionism can be expected to be approaching a negligible proportion by the end of the decade. This is especially so because the federal Workplace Relations Act makes union preference and compulsory unionism illegal both for employees covered by the federal system and for those outside the federal system but within the reach of other Commonwealth powers.

Consistent with this trend, since the mid-1980s density has declined by more amongst blue-collar employees (who had relatively high incidence of compulsory unionism) than amongst white-collar employees, by more amongst males (who had higher incidence of compulsory unionism) than females, and by the greatest amount in the industry (mining) with the highest incidence of closed shops according to data from AWIRS90. At the industry level there is a strong correlation between the members survey estimate of the decline in union density

Figure 5.1 Estimated composition of employment by union and job status, 1976–95

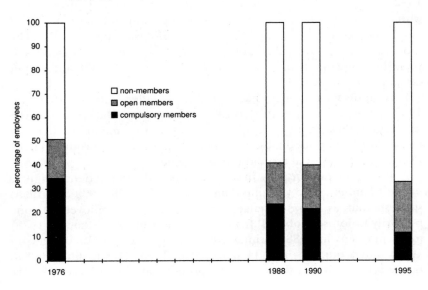

from 1986 to 1994 and the proportion of employees in an industry estimated by Wooden (1992) to be in closed shops in 1990.[4]

Further evidence for the continuing decline in compulsory unionism and the employer role in it, can be found in research commissioned and published by the Business Council of Australia (BCA). In 1988 and 1992, managers in a non-random sample of workplaces that were part of BCA member firms (in turn, amongst the 80 largest firms in Australia) were surveyed by the National Institute of Labour Studies.[5] In 1988, 82 per cent of surveyed workplaces reported that they had closed shop arrangements. Just four years later, the figure had fallen to 74 per cent.

This does not appear merely to reflect compositional change in the sample. In the 1992 survey, 15 per cent of BCA workplaces reportedly experienced a decrease in closed shop coverage of employees between 1988 and 1992, while just 3 per cent reported an increase in closed-shop coverage (Hilmer et al. 1993:198–9). 'Voluntary unionism' was reportedly of high and rising importance on the list of 'preferred changes' reportedly sought by chief executive officers of BCA companies.[6] Whereas, a decade earlier, it was 'the received wisdom by the majority of British and Australian industrial relations academics that sensible pragmatic managers ... saw that the advantages of the closed shop clearly outweighed the disadvantages', by 1989 a survey of Western Australian managers showed 65 per cent agreeing (48 per cent *strongly* agreeing) that compulsory unionism should be discouraged, and just 18 per cent wanting to encourage it (Geare 1990).

An objection could be made along the following lines: compulsory unionism arose where unions were strongest and where employees were most favourably disposed to unions. By this argument, undoubtedly true in some instances, compulsory unionism was merely a reflection of positive attitudes amongst employees towards unions, and the formal removal of it should not have had much of an effect on union membership. However, the loss of compulsory unionism appears to be concentrated in those workplaces where employees were already weakly attached to unions, particularly where the loss of closed shops arose from employer behaviour rather than legislation. This can be seen by comparing the proportion of union 'conscripts', who would rather not be in a union, at two points in time. The 1988 IMA survey indicated that up to 46 per cent of conscripts may have been unwilling (Grimes 1994), and a similar figure was found in Rawson's 1990 survey (Rawson 1992). By 1996, however, LCS (using a different question) indicated that only 33 per cent of conscripts were unwilling, while AWIRS95 suggested a figure of just 21 per cent. This suggests that, since the late 1980s, the loss of compulsory unionism has, if anything, been greater where employees were less attached to union membership. It is reasonable to expect that employers would initially seek to remove compulsory unionism where it was easiest to do so, and this seems to be what has happened. In the next section we can look more precisely at the performance of unions under compulsory unionism to see how well unions 'benefiting' from compulsory unionism performed.

Unions and Employees Under Compulsory Unionism

Our interest here is in comparing the perceived performance of unions benefiting from closed shops with unions whose members are in 'open jobs', at a time before the decline in compulsory unionism had gained its full momentum. We therefore mainly refer to data from SEMSE taken in 1990–91, at around the start of the acceleration in union decline. If, at that time, compulsory unionism on average reflected positive attitudes amongst employees towards unions, then unions benefiting from closed shops should have been perceived as being more effective and responsive than other unions.

We refer to these early data because, by the mid-1990s, unionists under compulsory unionism should have more positive attitudes towards unions than unionists under 'voluntary' unionism because only those workplaces where members had a strong affiliation to unions would still have any compulsory unionism. By the late 1990s, of course, almost all compulsory unionism arrangements would be illegal, and therefore could only survive in the context of near unanimous member and employer support.

Union Responsiveness

As shown in table 5.1, members in compulsorily unionised jobs rated their unions significantly lower in terms of union responsiveness than did their counterparts in open jobs. Indeed, even *non*-members in open jobs gave unions at their workplace a slightly better *net* responsiveness score than members in compulsorily unionised jobs gave their unions. This is so despite their having a much more strongly anti-union ideological orientation than members in compulsorily unionised jobs as measured by responses to other questions (Peetz 1995). To illustrate differences in union responsiveness, while 26 per cent of unionists in open jobs were dissatisfied with the way that 'unions here keep in contact with employees', dissatisfaction was 39 per cent amongst members in compulsorily unionised jobs. Similarly, on measures of perceived union protection, members in compulsorily unionised jobs were more negative than those in open jobs.

More recently, LCS-96 showed a surprisingly similar pattern. Both union members and non-members in open jobs were less likely to agree

Table 5.1 Union responsiveness and compulsory unionism in SEMSE

	Union responsiveness index					
	High responsive-ness (%)	Neutral (%)	Low responsive-ness (%)	Total (%)	Net score*	N
Union members in compulsorily unionised jobs	39	15	46	100	−7	262
Union members in open jobs	53	16	32	100	+21	236
Non-members in open jobs	36	30	35	100	+1	93

Source: SEMSE
Population: Employees in workplaces with 20 or more employees (Sydney area)
* Net score = 'high responsiveness' minus 'low responsiveness'

that 'unions at your workplace do a poor job at keeping in contact with their members' than were compulsorily unionised members (table 5.2). In the AWIRS95 employee survey, members in compulsorily unionised jobs were less likely than members in open jobs to agree that the union took notice of members' problems and complaints, and more likely to disagree that the union gave members a say in how the union operates.[7]

However, in LCS responses to the statement 'unions at your workplace do what their members want them to do' showed no significant differences between union members in open and compulsorily unionised jobs. This is more what we would expect, if unions who have operated under compulsory unionism suffered disproportionate membership losses amongst those employees who considered they were not doing what their members wanted. The pattern described in the previous paragraph probably indicates that the loss of membership amongst poorly performing territory-driven unions was not yet complete.

One hypothesis on union responsiveness might have been that unions that operated under compulsory unionism may have had to be, amongst other things, more responsive than others in order to obtain the employee support necessary to secure compulsory unionism. It does not appear that this was the case at the start of the decade (and still might not have been the case in the middle of the 1990s because of slow adjustment amongst territory-driven unions). Rather, it appears that compulsory unionism was associated with less responsive behaviour

Table 5.2 Union responsiveness and compulsory unionism in LCS

	Unions do poor job at keeping in contact				
	Agree	Neutral	Disagree	Total	Net score*
	(%)	(%)	(%)	(%)	
Union members in compulsorily unionised jobs	64	0	36	100	−28
Union members in open jobs	45	4	52	100	+7
Non-members in open jobs	51	10	39	100	−11

Source: LCS
Population: All employees
* Net score = 'disagree' minus 'agree'

from unions, presumably as they did not need to offer such a high level of responsiveness in order to secure continuing membership.

Voice and Participation

Employee participation in decision making at the workplace appeared to be weaker amongst employees in compulsorily unionised jobs than amongst other employees. For example, in SEMSE only 17 per cent of members in compulsorily unionised jobs said that employee say in decisions had increased over the past two years, compared to 27 per cent of union members in open jobs, 25 per cent of non-members in open jobs, and 33 per cent of non-members in restricted jobs. Agreement with the statement that employees have a lot of say in decisions was just 28 per cent amongst members in compulsorily unionised jobs, compared to 37 per cent amongst union members in open jobs, 36 per cent amongst non-members in open jobs and 37 per cent amongst non-members in restricted jobs.

Thus in SEMSE members in compulsorily unionised jobs were more likely to agree that unions did *not* help their members have a say in their work (33 per cent) than were union members in open jobs (22 per cent). (In LCS, the proportion of union members saying their union should be doing more about 'the chance to have a say in your work' was 29 per cent amongst those under compulsory unionism compared to 21 per cent amongst those in open jobs, but with smaller sample size these lesser differences were not significant.)

It appears that the relatively low participation recorded by employees in compulsorily unionised jobs reflected some weaknesses amongst unions benefiting from compulsory unionism. Such unions appeared to be weak in terms of their responsiveness to members' priorities and their ability to ensure employees had effective participation in the organisation of their work and in decisions that affect them.

Union Power at the Workplace

Employees in compulsorily unionised jobs in SEMSE were more likely than employees in open jobs to agree that unions in their workplace were strong. Managers and delegates were also less inclined to view unions as weak in compulsorily unionised jobs. This is what we would expect, as union strength was one of the important factors enabling unions to establish compulsory unionism in the first place, or was considered a consequence of the existence of compulsion.

However, the power of unions in workplaces with compulsory unionism appeared to be abating, compared to that of unions in workplaces under open jobs. This was evident in data from employees, delegates and managers, which indicated that union strength was declining most (or increasing least) amongst unions benefiting from compulsory unionism (table 5.3). Employees of both kinds indicated that union strength had declined, but by a greater margin in compulsorily unionised jobs. For the other two groups caution must be exercised because of the small sample size, but the pattern of difference remains the same: managers of employees in compulsorily unionised jobs were more likely than not to consider that union influence had decreased over the preceding two years, whereas managers of employees in open jobs were more likely than not to consider that union strength had increased; delegates considered that union strength had increased for both groups, but by a lesser margin in compulsorily unionised jobs.

Changes in Union Satisfaction

SEMSE sought information about whether respondents were more or less satisfied with unions than they had been two years earlier. Falling union satisfaction was much more a phenomenon amongst unions benefiting from compulsory membership than amongst other unions. While only 15 per cent of union members in open jobs said that they were now less satisfied with unions, this was the case for 23 per cent of

Table 5.3 Perceptions of changes in influence of unions at the workplace

	Employees in compulsorily unionised jobs			Employees in open jobs			N
	Rose	About the same	Fell	Rose	About the same	Fell	
	(%)	(%)	(%)	(%)	(%)	(%)	
Perceptions of employees**	10	62	28	14	69	19	690
Perceptions of managers	18	53	29	32	46	22	27
Perceptions of union delegates	49	22	29	52	30	18	23

Source: SEMSE
Population: Employees in workplaces with 20 or more employees (Sydney region)
Weights: To enable comparisons with employee responses, responses for
              managers and union delegates are weighted to refer to the number
              of employees they represent.
** Inter-group differences (between employees in open and compulsorily
   unionised jobs) significant at 1 per cent level.

members in compulsorily unionised jobs. (In both cases, 10 per cent of respondents reported being more satisfied with unions than two years earlier.)

More recent surveys do not combine questions on changing satisfaction with questions on compulsory unionism. However, the material that is available suggests no end to the trend shown early in the decade. In LCS-97 the group with the most negative views about changes in their union's performance was blue-collar male unionists, amongst whom 39 per cent rated their union's performance more negatively than 12 months earlier, compared to 27 per cent who rated it more positively. This group, in LCS-96, had the highest incidence of compulsory unionism (44 per cent of union members). Amongst the rest of the sample of unionists (with a compulsion rate of just 21 per cent), only 28 per cent were more negative about their union, and 29 per cent were more positive.

Workplace Union Organisation

It might be expected that union compulsion, if it arose from unions' ability to enforce unionism at the workplace, would be associated with more intensive union organisation as measured by the member-to-delegate ratio. If anything, the reverse was the case. In AWIRS95, there was no difference between workplaces with and without closed shops in terms of the presence of union delegates, once workplace size was controlled. However, the member-to-delegate ratio was higher for members in compulsorily unionised jobs in SEMSE while in both AWIRS90 and AWIRS95 the member-to-delegate ratio was higher in workplaces that had at least some employees covered by a closed shop, even after controlling for the fact that high member-to-delegate ratios and closed shops were both more common in larger workplaces.

If unions maintaining compulsory unionism were active at the workplace and able to demonstrate the benefits of unionism to conscripts, then closed shops could be a useful part of an effective strategy for securing union membership over the longer term. No doubt, for some unions this was the case, and there is evidence of instances where workers under closed shops have stronger union commitment than workers in the same union in open jobs (Thorpe 1998). This is precisely because, in such instances, closed shops have arisen because of the strength of the members' support for the union, and is reinforced by regular contact with delegates and officials. But overall, the comparisons made here suggest that on average this has not been the case in Australia, and reinforce propositions put forward by Zappala (1992): that in the long run it may not have been in unions' interests to rely on compulsory unionism because of the effect it may have on union performance and employee attachment to unions at the workplace, and because of the dysfunctional characteristics it encourages in territory-driven unions.

The Role of the Collapse of Compulsory Unionism in the Decline in Union Density

Shift-share analysis indicates that approximately one-third of the decline in compulsory unionism from 1982 to 1990 can be attributed to structural change in the labour market – that is, the relatively strong growth of industries that have a low level of compulsory unionism. However, the decline cannot be attributed principally to this, and must instead be explained by changes in employer strategies and the institutional framework, to which I shall turn shortly. The acceleration in the decline of compulsory unionism since 1990 cannot be explained by any acceleration in the rate of structural change in the labour market.

One of the most notable aspects of the trend of union decline is that union density amongst employees who are not in compulsorily unionised jobs has remained fairly stable over time. As figure 5.2 shows, union density amongst this group has remained between 23 and 26 per cent over the period, and was approximately 24 per cent in 1995.

If a fall in the demand for union membership (for example, because unions were actually performing more poorly from the point of view of their members) played a major independent part in union decline, then we might have expected that union density amongst employees who are not in compulsorily unionised jobs would have fallen significantly over time. On the surface, the failure of this to occur would suggest no need for demand-based explanations for union decline at all. The counter argument might have been that employees previously covered by compulsory unionism would be more inclined to union membership than those not covered by compulsory unionism. This would arise from the proposition that unions would have had to have a large amount of support from employees in the first place in order to secure a compulsion arrangement. If this were the case, as compulsory unionism declined, union density amongst people not covered by compulsory unionism should have increased. However, the data in the preceding section provide little reason for believing that employees under compulsory unionism were permanently attached to unions.

Using a survey conducted in 1988, in which overall union density was 46 per cent (4 points above the ABS estimate), Grimes (1994) estimated that the average probability of a closed-shop employee maintaining their union membership if compulsion was removed – I call it the 'retention ratio' – was between 35 and 54 per cent. (This compared with density amongst employees not in closed shops of 24 per cent.)

Figure 5.2   Union density: overall and excluding compulsorily unionised jobs

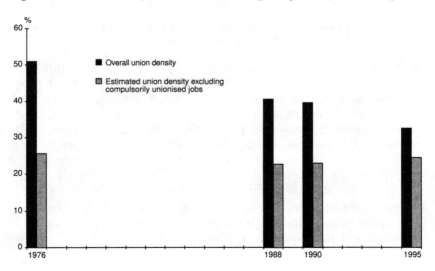

The retention ratio of people moving out of closed shops is used to calculate the impact of the closure of closed shops on union decline between 1990 and 1995. Where, within this range of 35 to 54 per cent, is the best estimate of the retention ratio? If the higher estimate were correct, then 4.8 points of the 6.6 percentage point decline in union density (on the members survey) between 1990 and 1995 can be explained simply by the withdrawal of compulsory unionism. If the lower estimate (35 per cent) applied, then *all* of the decline in that period could be explained by the withdrawal of compulsory unionism. The higher estimate (based on employees' stated preferences for union membership, or their 'union propensity') could well overstate the actual retention ratio, especially amongst employees who change jobs. This is because, amongst employees not in closed shops, the level of union density is below their union propensity (as discussed in the last section of this chapter).

It is not possible to be definitive on the size of the effect. But for illustrative purposes, suppose (a) that the retention ratio was 10 percentage points higher in the 1990s than in the 1980s, on the basis that employers would remove compulsory unionism first where it was easiest; and (b) that the retention ratio was 50 per cent in the 1990s. On those plausible assumptions, the decline in union density attributable to the loss of compulsory unionism would be nearly 1.1 percentage points per annum over each of the five years, almost double the rate of decline attributable to the loss of compulsory unionism over the 1976–90 period (approximately 0.6 percentage points per annum). This would account for around three-quarters of the decline in union density over the 1990–95 period (which proceeded, on the members survey, at a rate of about 1.4 percentage points per annum over this period).

The vulnerability of unions in Anglo-Saxon countries, including Australia and (as we shall see in chapter seven) New Zealand, to declining compulsory unionism reflects the greater reliance on compulsory union membership in these countries. In most of continental Europe, including the most strongly unionised countries, closed shops have not been an important feature of union organisation – partly because the religious bases of many union federations meant that compulsory membership of a union would amount to compulsory membership of a religiously affiliated body (Archer 1995; Kassalow 1969:141–4).

The States and the Acceleration of the Decline in Union Coverage

Part of the decline in compulsory unionism arises from actions of government. Some studies have sought to look at the impact of government, and in particular of the legislative environment, on union membership. Quantitative studies of the impact of government have used cross-sectional or time-series approaches. The former have often compared different legislative regimes within States and/or provinces in North America, and so have a particular focus on 'right-to-work' (RTW) laws in the US south, which preclude compulsory unionism. Time-series approaches may look at one country or be cross-national, and may use various means of proxying for the political complexity of the state. Various studies have argued that the difference between US and Canadian unionisation levels can be partly or largely explained by different legislative environments (Rose & Chaison 1985, 1992; Kumar 1993), different patterns of enforcement of laws against unfair practice (Meltz 1985), the ability of US employers to access the southern 'sunbelt' with laws antagonistic to unions and promoting low wages (Williams 1985) and, more fundamentally, differences in the federal and party political systems themselves (Bruce 1989). Researchers in countries such as Belgium and Israel have pointed to state policies as one of the factors influencing unionisation in their nations (Baupain 1992; Ben-Israel & Fisher 1992). Compulsory arbitration was found to increase union density in US state and federal employment (Hundley 1989) and amongst white-collar employees in the UK (Lumley 1973). Freeman and Pelletier (1990) used an 'index of laws' (depicting the extent to which legislation is favourable or unfavourable to unions) to explain differences in union density between Britain and Ireland, demonstrating the negative impact of the Thatcher Government's laws on union density. Our interest in this section is on what the experiences of the Australian 'States', the second level of government in the federal system, tell us about the role of 'the state' (that is, of government) in affecting union density.

A significant element in the institutional break in Australia has been the introduction of legislation in various State jurisdictions aimed at prohibiting the closed shop and encouraging the decollectivisation of employment relations. The collapse of compulsory unionism has been accelerated by this legislation. The contribution of State Government legislative changes to the decline in union density can be approximated by looking at patterns in union density between the States. Between 1990 and 1995, conservative governments in five of the six States introduced new laws that typically prohibited union compulsion, often encouraged individual bargaining, and made the transition to voluntary unionism, non-unionism and non-award coverage easier.

New South Wales was the first State to introduce such legislation, the *Industrial Relations Act 1991*. Though it sparked a State-wide strike at the time, it would now be considered the mildest of all the reforms introduced at the State level. The Victorian Government was the next and most radical in a succession of Liberal or Coalition State

Governments that came to power between 1991 and 1993, after several State Labor Governments, crippled by financial scandals in those States and the unpopularity of the Federal ALP, lost office. Several Liberal parties, most notably in Victoria, had modelled their policies on New Zealand's *Employment Contracts Act 1991* with some modifications in deference to Australian conditions. The Victorian *Employee Relations Act 1992*, which took effect from March 1993, abolished awards, created employment contracts to replace awards, prohibited compulsory unionism and abolished the Victorian Industrial Commission and with it the capacity of any body to award preference in employment to union members. However, the capacity for radical change was constrained by the existence of the federal system. The passage in late 1992 of a simple amendment to the Commonwealth *Industrial Relations Act 1988* enabled 340,000 employees covered by Victorian awards to move into the federal system by late 1994 and escape most of the effects of State legislation. Other States introduced legislation that retained the award systems but permitted individual contracts to override awards and prohibited compulsory unionism: the Western Australian *Workplace Agreements Act 1993* (taking effect from December 1993); the Tasmanian *Industrial Relations Act 1994*; and the South Australian *Industrial and Employee Relations Act 1994* (taking effect from August 1994).

The immediate impact of these laws can be estimated by examining the two time series on union membership, the members survey and the union census. A simple estimate of the immediate impact of these laws on union density is illustrated in table 5.4. The second column of the table shows the decline in union density in those States that introduced new legislation in each period for which data from the August members survey are available since 1990, starting with New South Wales, in which legislation was introduced in 1991. In three of the four periods, States that enacted new laws during that period experienced a more rapid decline in union density than those that did not.

Under this simple methodology, the contribution that conservative State legislation made to the decline in union density is calculated by comparing the actual decline in national union density with the decline in other States that did not introduce new laws (shown in the fifth column). Over this period, the immediate impact of new State laws contributed 2.2 percentage points[8] (around 0.5 percentage points a year) to the national decline in union density. However, this methodology is very likely to underestimate the actual impact of legislative changes, as in most instances it only takes account of effects in the year in which the legislation is introduced. It also includes, amongst 'other States', some States that had introduced legislation in the previous year, which may still be having an effect in the second year of operation.

Moreover, the estimates for each year are subject to sampling error which, for the smaller States (e.g. South Australia) is quite high.

A better estimate can be made by using the June union census data. This is for two reasons: estimates of the numerator from the union census were not subject to sampling error, a major advantage for the small States in particular (though density estimates are still subject to sampling error because the denominator is calculated from a survey); and the union census was collected annually, enabling more accurate estimates to be made for the earlier part of the period. This enables estimates of the 'second-year' effects to also be made.

The estimated impact of State legislation on union density varies between the States, as would be expected given the impact of sampling error on density estimates in the union census and particularly the members survey, the different details of legislation arising from each State Parliament, the different times of the year when they took effect, and the different levels of State award coverage in each State. But the key point emerges from the aggregation of these data into the 'simple estimates' of the average immediate impact, which are similar in both series. The introduction of anti-union legislation in a State reduced union density within that State by between 2.3 percentage points (members survey) and 2.6 percentage points (union census) in the year in which it was introduced, and across the whole period these first-year

Table 5.4　Immediate impact of State legislation on union density: simple estimates from the members survey

Period (August to August)	States introducing major legislative changes	Decline in density			Apparent immediate impact of legislation	Initial contribution of major legislation to total decline in density
		Total	In States with major legislative changes	In other States		
		(1) (% pts)	(2) (% pts)	(3) (% pts)	(4) (% pts)	(5) (% pts)
1990–92	NSW	0.9	3.1	–0.2	3.3	1.1
1992–93	Vic	2.0	3.6	1.5	2.1	0.6
1993–94	WA, Tas	2.6	6.2	2.1	4.1	0.5
1994–95	SA	2.3	1.7	2.3	–0.6	0.0
average		1.9	3.7	1.4	2.3	0.5

Source:　ABS Cat. No. 6303.0, 6325.0, 6342.0.
Note:　Column 4 = column 2 minus column 3. Column 5 = column 1 minus column 3. Rows may not appear to add due to rounding.

Table 5.5 Short-term impact of State legislation on union density: estimates from union census

Period (June to June)	States introducing major legislative changes	Decline in density			Apparent immediate impact of legislation	Contribution of major legislation to total decline in density
		Total	In States with major legislative changes	In other States		
		(1) (% pts)	(2) (% pts)	(3) (% pts)	(4) (% pts)	(5) (% pts)
SIMPLE ESTIMATES: *immediate impact*						
1991–92	NSW	2.4	3.0	2.1	0.9	0.3
1992–93	Vic	1.8	4.0	1.0	3.0	0.8
1993–94	WA, Tas	4.3	8.4	3.7	4.7	0.6
1994–95	SA	3.2	5.0	3.0	2.0	0.2
average					2.6	0.5
TWO-YEAR ESTIMATES: *First-year impact*						
1991–92	NSW		3.0	2.1	0.9	0.3
1992–93	Vic		4.0	0.1[a]	3.9	1.0
1993–94	WA, Tas		8.4	3.2[b]	5.3	0.6
1994–95	SA		5.0	3.1[c]	1.9	0.2
average					3.0	0.5
Second-year impact						
1992–93	NSW		2.0	0.1[b]	1.9	0.6
1993–94	Vic		5.0	3.2[c]	1.8	0.5
1994–95	WA, Tas		2.4	3.1[d]	−0.7	−0.1
1995–96	SA		1.0	0.7	0.3	0.0
average					0.8	0.3
Combined (two-year) impact						
1991–93	NSW		5.0		2.7	0.9
1992–94	Vic		9.0		5.7	1.4
1993–95	WA, Tas		10.8		4.6	0.6
1994–96	SA		6.0		2.2	0.2
average					3.8	0.8

Source: ABS Cat. No. 6323.0.
Note: For derivation of columns 4 and 5 see table 5.4.
a   excludes NSW
b   excludes Vic
c   excludes WA, Tas
d   excludes SA

effects contributed 0.5 percentage points each year (both sources) to the decline in union density (see the top quarter of table 5.5).

As mentioned, these estimates understate the impact of legislative change. To get a better estimate, we look at the apparent effects over both the first and second years, by comparing the decline in density in States that have introduced legislation to the decline in density in those States that had not introduced legislation in either that year or the preceding year. This methodology raises slightly our estimate of the impact of legislation in the year of introduction (to 3.0 percentage points in the State concerned), but also suggests a second-year impact in the State concerned of another 0.8 percentage points. Taking account of second-year effects raises our estimate of the total impact of State legislation to nearly 0.8 percentage points per annum over the four years from 1991 to 1995. Averaging this over five years, from 1990 to 1995, produces an annual average contribution to the decline in union density from State legislation of 0.6 percentage points.

This figure is of similar magnitude to the 0.5 percentage point difference between the rates of decline in union density that would be attributable to the collapse of compulsory unionism before 1990 (0.55 points per annum) and after 1990 (1.06 points per annum) if the illustrative assumptions set out in an earlier section were accepted. However, we should treat the fact that these numbers turn out to be the same as more coincidence than anything else – not just because of the effects of sampling error and assumptions, but also for conceptual reasons. The 'State effects' include the impact not only of changes to compulsory unionism but also the legislative facilitation of non-union (usually individual) contracts to establish a stronger legal infrastructure for the decollectivisation of employment relations. Equally, the acceleration in the collapse of compulsory unionism probably reflects not only changes in State policies but also a further hardening of positions adopted by employers and employer associations.

So we cannot treat 'State effects' and 'compulsory unionism' as being equivalent, nor can we simply add those two effects together, and we do not know how much of the decline in compulsory unionism since 1991 is due to State legislation, and how much is due to employer strategies independent of legislation. But we can say that the combined effects of changing employer strategies on compulsory unionism and changing state legislation have been substantial and have probably subtracted, on average, something above 1.1 percentage points per annum from union density over this period.

One other notable point is that the first-year impact of the legislation is substantially larger than that in subsequent years (the second-year impact being 30 to 50 per cent of the first-year impact, depending in effect on whether averages are calculated unweighted or with State workforce weights). This might be partly because it is more difficult to measure second-year effects due to the greater 'noise' in the system, but it also suggests that there is a significant 'demonstration' effect from the introduction of legislation; that is, the legislation provides a signal to employers that new, more antipathetic forms of behaviour regarding unions are both possible and desirable. Indeed, it seems plausible that some employers may begin to move against compulsory unionism and to introduce more individualised employment arrangements even before the legislation is passed, after the content of proposed legislation has been announced.

It is important not to conceive of the impact of State government policies as being exogenous to the industrial relations system but rather to understand them as part of the institutional break that has occurred. Many studies of the impact of government on union density are complicated by the problem that 'the law is endogenous', that is, 'the state' is not an independent actor but is influenced by the other actors and events in the system (Hirsch & Addison 1986:55). Events in industrial relations can occasionally determine the party that holds office. And the factors that influence unionisation (including the parties' 'taste' for unionism) can also influence government policy: that is, aggressive employers or indifferent employees may discourage unionism and also encourage laws that give the appearance of discouraging unionism. Hence some US researchers claimed that low unionism was facilitating the passage of 'right-to-work' laws (Lumsden & Petersen 1975; Moore & Newman 1975), while others argued that State/ provincial laws had a separate, negative impact upon union organising (Ellwood & Fine 1987), total union density (e.g. Meltz 1989) and public-sector unionisation (Saltzman 1985; Hundley 1989). The introduction of anti-union legislation in so many Australian States within a period of just four years was not coincidence: it reflected the changes in State and employer ideology that have occurred since the mid-1980s; and it reinforced and accelerated the development of union-antagonistic strategies amongst employers.

Why the Institutional Break?

The collapse of compulsory unionism and the deunionisation of work-places (discussed in the next chapter) are symptoms of a broader trend: the institutional break (or 'paradigm shift') in the determinants of union membership in Australia.

Employer attitudes have been critical in influencing the extent of compulsory unionism (Hanson et al. 1982; M. Wright 1983). Employers may have supported compulsory unionism for a number of reasons: because it made it easier to deal with all employees; because it introduced a 'moderating' influence into union decision making or encouraged 'right-wing' unions; because it reduced friction and resentment by unionists of non-unionists; or because it reduced the need for a physical presence for union officials at the workplace (Cameron 1982; M. Wright 1983; BCA 1989 part:15; Zappala 1992). Some of these motivations may have declined in importance and other, more pressing motivations for employers may have taken precedence. For example, the end of the Cold War removed the need felt by some employers to provide closed shops for 'right-wing' unions to keep communist unions out. But by the end of the 1980s there were strong anti-closed shop feelings amongst employers, as noted earlier in a survey of Western Australian employers (Geare 1990).

The BCA and other employer organisations have made the abolition of compulsory unionism a major priority (Hilmer et al. 1993:113–14, 317–27). Since 1987 the BCA has campaigned actively for major changes in the role of unions and the award system, most recently for the abolition of the award system and its replacement with a system of individual contracts, modelled on the New Zealand Employment Contracts Act (e.g. BCA 1987, 1989, 1993; Frenkel & Peetz 1990a, b; Dabscheck 1990; Hilmer et al. 1993). The BCA has been joined in this campaign by the major employer confederation, the Australian Chamber of Commerce and Industry, which abandoned its accommodatory position in industrial relations policy. The BCA rhetoric is clearly aimed not just at policy makers but also at changing employer ideology, and may not just be reflecting but also creating changes in employer strategy regarding union reach.

There appears to have been a major change in employer ideology in regard to unions and the arbitration system. Clearly, in 1978 and 1980 there was overwhelming employer support for the arbitration system (Spillane 1980; McNair & Layton 1980). In 1982 a major study found that 'few Australian managers show(ed) any sign of seeing the union-free plant as a legitimate strategy ... Unlike the United States approach, Australian corporate thinking (did) not seem to dwell on strategies for doing away with unions' (Niland & Turner 1985:147, 174).

Various large firms in particular have been attempting to diminish or dismantle some of the industrial relations structures that encourage or enable unionism within their workplaces, and have been introducing changes with the effect of reducing award coverage (which, on ABS estimates, fell by nearly 5 percentage points over 1985–90 amongst firms with 100 or more employees).[9] The BCA survey shows that, over the period from 1988 to 1992, managers from 26 per cent of surveyed workplaces reported that the proportion of employees covered by awards or agreements had fallen. Only 7 per cent reported an increase in award and agreement coverage (Hilmer et al. 1993:203). Some of this may have been due to the incidental growth of occupations that did not traditionally have award coverage, but some of the increase may also have been due to changes in the award status of particular occupations.

It may be that reductions in award coverage are concentrated in workplaces and jobs that were union-free anyway, and therefore the resistance to award removal would be low. But there are also cases of firms using changes to award coverage as part of a strategy of deunion-isation. An illustration is provided by one of the BCA's largest member companies. In 1994 CRA Ltd (now Rio Tinto) used the offer of individual contacts containing pay increases to induce a large majority of employees in several highly unionised workplaces to move from award coverage to 'staff' status, and thereby persuaded many of them to resign their union membership. In one workplace this was hampered by an AIRC decision to ensure that employees moving to individual contracts retained award coverage and that employees not accepting individual contracts received comparable pay to those moving to con-tracts. The AIRC decision, the subject of an appeal to the High Court, pointed out that the company had 'deliberately deceived' certain employees (AIRC 1994:41; MacKinnon 1996; McDonald & Timo 1996). The CRA move was the most visible manifestation of a wider trend.

It may well be that the turning point in employer attitudes was sometime in the mid-1980s, when major changes in product markets started to take effect, when some employers engaged in high-profile and generally successful disputes with unions, and when the mobilisation of 'new right' employer attitudes around the H. R. Nicholls Society took effect. But by the mid-1980s, in the context of rapid economic change, a new belligerence in employer strategy was becoming apparent. Employers at the Robe River iron ore mine in Western Australia, the Mudginberri meatworks in Northern Territory, the Dollar Sweets confectionery factory in Melbourne and the State-owned South East Queensland Electricity Board had taken on and defeated unions using common law or trade practices law, which effectively made all industrial action illegal, and they appeared to have considerable support from their fellow senior managers (Guille 1985; McCarthy 1985; Light & Pollack 1986; Creighton 1987; Coghill 1987). Over a decade later, these victories were critical in persuading employers, the National Farmers' Federation and a Coalition Government that they could take on, and wipe out, the waterfront union. They were thwarted by the Govern-ment's 'freedom of association' laws, which, ironically, had been designed to bolster employer resistance to unions.

There is other evidence, from the 1990s, of increasing employer resistance to unions. A survey of 300 firms found that one-quarter of firms who had entered into an enterprise agreement sought 'reduced union involvement' as an objective, and around one-fifth claimed to have achieved it (Arthur Andersen/Holding Redlich 1993). The impact sought and achieved upon unionisation was not recorded. (The following chapter, however, discusses evidence of the impact of employer strategies on union membership changes within workplaces.) It might be the case that Australian employers had become unusually belligerent. Alternatively, it might have been part of an international trend, as it appeared that managers in many parts of the industrialised world were on the offensive by the latter 1980s in the search for greater flexibility (Frenkel 1990).

The impact of changing employer resistance to trade unions has been identified as a reason for the 1970s increase (Bain & Price 1983) and 1980s decline (Price & Bain 1989; Hartley 1992; Millward 1990:39, 1994; Smith & Morton 1994) in union density in the UK. Increasingly active management opposition to unions and unionisation explains a significant part of the 1980s decline in US union density (Freeman & Medoff 1984:233–6; Freeman 1985; Freedman 1985; Dickens & Leonard 1985; Cornfield 1986; Edwards & Podgursky 1986; Goldfield 1987; Maranto & Fiorito 1987:234; Freeman & Kleiner 1990; Farber 1990; Bernstein 1994), especially by comparison with Canada (Rose & Chaison 1993; Thompson 1993). These studies are consistent with the arguments of a number of authors that the growth of unions is likely to be greater where employers are willing to recognise unions and confer bargaining rights upon them over a wide range of issues (Bain 1970; Clegg 1976; Gallie 1989; Visser 1992; Beaumont & Elliot 1992; Waddington & Whitston 1993).

What factors determine the general strategies management has adopted? Two explanations used in the US context might be said to apply here also. Several authors (e.g. Farber 1990; Hirsch & Addison 1986) have suggested that growing US employer opposition to unions is partly a response to increasing pressure on profits, due to increasing import competition and deregulation in unionised industries. Piore (1982, 1991) has pointed to the changes to economic organisation that have taken place in recent decades: as work organisation has allegedly moved from mass production to flexible specialisation, union job control and the adherence to job demarcation and fine classification structures, once beneficial to employers, have become liabilities. Yet most industrialised countries have experienced greater internationalisation of their domestic markets and increasing competition, and few in continental Europe have experienced the employer strategies evident in the US. The change in management philosophy towards human resource management (HRM) models is certainly evident in the US (Kochan et al. 1986), but many European countries have not experienced such an apparently sharp shift to HRM because they had adopted fairly consultative managerial strategies for a considerable time. Management there had not needed to disable unions in order to succeed (Kochan & Dyer 1992; Regini 1992:126).

Economic change may have played an unusually important role in Australia as a result of the form of the terms of trade and currency crises of the mid-1980s. Few other advanced industrialised countries were so dependent upon commodity exports, and none suffered as severe a terms-of-trade fall in 1985–86 as occurred in Australia. This in turn might explain some aspects of Australian employer ideology and strategies in the mid- to late 1980s.

But perhaps a significant part of the explanation for the institutional break concerns employer and government culture and ideology. Just as unions from the English-speaking world seem to have different approaches and priorities to unions from continental Europe, so might be the case with employers. Overwhelmingly the texts and materials that educate and motivate Australian managers are either of American origin or American-inspired. Intellectually, they emanate from a country where 'most ... private nonunion employers view the prospect of being unionised as the corporate equivalent of catching AIDS' (Feuille 1991:86). Few Australian managers read European materials not presented in English. Few would accept the more consensus-based approach to industrial relations that has a stronger tradition in European culture. The shift to economic fundamentalism or 'economic rationalism' in government policies has been prominent in Anglophone countries, not least Australia (Castles 1993).

The point to be made, then, is not just about language: Australia, the UK, Canada and New Zealand are the countries whose cultures most closely resemble that of the US (Johnson & Golembiewski 1992; Hofstede & Bond 1988), and we might expect that in their cultural heritages there are some common traits that predate the latest trends in management theory. Still, this 'Anglo-Saxon' factor should not be exaggerated. It is difficult to evaluate the extent to which any differences in employer ideologies between Australia and Europe result from cultural/educational factors and the extent to which they result from the economic and industrial relations circumstances of the countries concerned, in particular the institutional heritage and the nature of union organisation and behaviour. The fact that Canadian unions have been able to largely resist the trend to deunionisation that has occurred in the US suggests cultural/educational factors common to the English-speaking nations are not the single most important predictor of employer responses.

Several other reasons for employer strategies have also been advanced in overseas studies. These have included: the legislative environment; the strategies of unions themselves, including their adaptation or otherwise to the changing economic environment (Piore 1991); management's own values or ideology (Beaumont & Rennie 1986); the relative profitability of union and non-union labour (Freeman 1990); the likelihood of an employer being a target for a union recruitment campaign (Beaumont & Harris 1993); and the balance of power between employers and unions.

Some of these possible reasons are taken up in later chapters, but the first is particularly apposite. Certainly, in Australia, a critical element in the institutional break has been the introduction of legislative changes across State jurisdictions (and then the federal jurisdiction). As mentioned, this cannot just be seen as the natural outcome of having Liberal and National Party Governments in power. There is nothing new about conservative parties holding office, yet it was only in the 1990s that legislation to decollectivise employment relations and prohibit compulsory unionism and union preference swept through the State and Federal Parliaments. It requires, perhaps, another study to explain the shift in political ideologies within the conservative parties. Associated with the economic changes brought about in the mid-1980s, there was a general shift to the right in the economic policies of most Australian political parties, and this encouraged a shift to the right in political debate generally and a more radical position for the conservative parties on industrial relations. It was apparent that the conservative parties were heavily influenced by their primary constituency, the employers, and by the harder line employers were now taking against unions and collectivism. It was also clear that the conservative parties were influenced by developments in other Anglophone countries, having been inspired by the successes on key industrial relations fronts enjoyed by the Thatcher and Reagan Governments and having visited New Zealand to investigate the experience of the Employment Contracts Act. Without these factors, it is unlikely that the legislative changes that occurred in the 1990s would have transpired.

A Brave New World of Employee Choice?

In this institutional break, the role of 'demand'- and 'supply'-related factors is changing. On the supply side, the factors that influenced the establishment of closed shops need no longer have a role in determining union membership. This in turn might suggest a much greater role for demand-related factors in determining union membership.

However, the removal of the closed shop, and of related mechanisms such as tribunals' capacity to award preference to union members, also removes an impediment to employer resistance to unions. It therefore makes it easier for employers to establish and maintain non-union workplaces. This in turn can reduce the role of demand-side factors in determining union membership. Employees with a low propensity (demand) for union membership may be less likely than in the past to belong to a union against their will, but employees with a high propensity for union membership will find themselves more likely to be non-members, against their will.

In this context, it is important not to fall into the trap of believing that the level of union density outside of closed shops represents the 'true' level of demand for union membership. In LCS-96, 52 per cent of employees agreed that, if they were totally free to choose, they would rather be in a union than not be in one, yet only 34 per cent of employees were union members.

Table 5.6 shows the extent of consonance and dissonance between employees' preferences regarding union membership (union propensity) and their membership status, over four surveys between 1995 and 1997. In three population surveys (AES, LCS-96 and LCS-97), only 13 to 18 per cent of employees who preferred not to be in a union were union members – following Rawson, I call this group 'unwillingly conscripted'. But 35 to 47 per cent of those who preferred to be in a union were non-members – a group I call 'unwillingly excluded'. In one other survey, AWIRS95, the pattern was (slightly) reversed. Although AWIRS95 had a much larger sample, there are several potential sources of bias that suggest the estimates from the other three surveys are to be preferred. First, AWIRS95 only included workplaces with 20 or more employees. Yet while union membership varies greatly by workplace size, union propensity varies only slightly, if at all. For example, in LCS-97 union propensity was 48 per cent in firms with less than 20 employees, compared to 50 per cent in firms with over 20 employees. Consequently, in workplaces with less than 20 employees there is a large number of non-unionists who would rather be in a union. In LCS-97, 41 per cent of non-unionists in firms with fewer than 20 employees would rather be in a union, compared to 30 per cent in firms with 20 or more employees. Second, some non-union employers would not have wanted their employees exposed to a questionnaire that mentioned unions (the author has direct experience of this phenomenon). Third, despite the assurances of confidentiality given by researchers, some employees would be unwilling to express in writing pro-union views when their employer was overtly anti-union. As a result of these three factors, AWIRS95 will substantially understate the proportion of unwillingly excluded employees, and probably overstate the number of unwillingly conscripted members.

Table 5.6 Union density by employee preferences (union propensity)

	AWIRS95 (1995–96) (Workplaces with 20+ employees)		AES (1996) (All employees)		LCS-96 (1996) (All employees)		LCS-97 (1997) (All employees)	
	Union member (%)	Non-member (%)	Union member (%)	Non-member (%)	Union member (%)	Non-member (%)	Union member (%)	Non-member (%)
Would rather be in a union	80	20	65	35	53	47	58	42
Neutral (neither agree or disagree)	44	56	32	68	23	77	13	87
Would rather not be in a union	23	77	18	82	13	87	13	87

Sources: See column headings.
N: AWIRS95: 6995, 3863, 6197. AES: 283, 174, 304. LCS-96: 278, 23, 260.
          LCS-97: 322, 46, 377.

Table 5.7 presents these same data in an alternative manner – by focusing on those employees whose preferences were inconsistent with their membership status, and expressing them as a proportion of all employees. In the four surveys, 5 to 8 per cent of all employees were 'unwilling conscripts', but 7 to 24 per cent were 'unwillingly excluded'. Again, for reasons outlined above, AWIRS95 was the outlier. In the three population surveys, with larger sampling error but considerably less non-sampling bias, there is a consistent pattern of the 'unwillingly excluded' outnumbering the 'unwilling conscripts' by at least two to one.[10]

North American studies have shown that between 27 and 32 per cent of non-union employees would prefer to be unionised but do not have the opportunity (Kochan 1979; Hills 1985; Leigh 1986; Farber 1990; Princeton Survey Research Associates 1994). Less than half of US employees who wished to be in a union were actually in one. In a Japanese survey, the most common reason non-union members did not join a union was that no union was organised for them; two-thirds of non-members considered that they would be better off if a union was present, suggesting that lack of access to unions was a major reason for low Japanese union density (RIALS 1993). The results here show Australian union membership status moving closer to that prevailing in the US and Japan: in 1996 between 21 per cent (AES) and 37 per cent (LCS-96) of Australian non-union members would rather be in a union, and between just one-half and two-thirds of Australian employees who wished to be in a union were actually in one.

The key finding that emerges from these data is that the demise of compulsory unionism does not mean that this institutional break has brought us to a brave new era where employee preferences prevail. As the demise of compulsory unionism ensures that fewer people who do not want to be in a union have to be in one, it conversely is associated with an increase in the number of people who want to be in a union but are not. This is partly a reflection of the particular role that compulsory unionism has in preventing employers from discriminating against union members, and partly because the institutional break in union membership, of which compulsory unionism is a part, is leading to the decollectivisation of employment relations against the wishes of at least some of the employees concerned. Moreover, those employees who would be relatively undecided about whether or not to join are being strongly pushed in the direction of not joining, whereas previously a significant proportion of them would have ended up as members.

The problem of dissonance between employee preferences and their union membership status is partly because unions are simply not able to reach employees in every workplace, but the data below show that it also arises because of the effectiveness of employer strategies and practices to keep unions away from workers. Amongst non-members in LCS-96 who wanted to belong to a union, some 39 per cent (that is, almost 10 per cent of all employees) said that their employer would not want them to join a union; this group alone clearly outnumbers the unwilling conscripts to unions. And regardless of the reasons for dissonance, it is

Table 5.7 Inconsistency between membership preference and union membership status

	AWIRS95 (1995–96)	AES (1996)	LCS-96 (1996)	LCS-97 (1997)
Non-member, would rather be in a union (% of all employees)	7	13	24	21
Member, would rather not be in a union (% of all employees)	8	7	6	5
Total, preference inconsistent with membership (% of all employees)	15	20	30	26
N	17055	761	561	427

clear that any regulation regime will produce a significant group of employees whose preferences do not match their membership status.

In short, the demise of compulsory unionism does not signal the ascendancy of demand-related influences and the supremacy of employee preferences. Rather, it means that the way in which demand- and supply-related factors influence union membership has been transformed – in effect, making it harder for unions to recruit and retain members. Rhetoric surrounding the legislative proscription of compulsory unionism centres on the notion that doing this ensures employees' freedom of choice on union membership. This notion is challenged by close analysis of the data.

Conclusion

The findings of this chapter can be summarised as follows. The decline in union density has arisen principally from a 'paradigm shift' or institutional break in the determinants of union membership, in combination with structural changes in the economy. The term 'institutional break' refers to particularly forceful conjunctions of events and alliances that lead to a fundamental altering of the institutional arrangements surrounding the employment relationship. This institutional break mostly reflects a change in strategies by employers and governments towards unions: the decollectivisation of employment relations is being sought (though not universally) by employers and the state; previous support for compulsory unionism has been withdrawn; and the role of demand- and supply-related factors in the determination of union membership is being transformed. In short, institutional changes, rather than attitudinal changes, are fundamentally behind the decline in Australian union membership.

This is not to say that collective employment relations have met their demise. On the contrary, the largest single mode of the employment relationship is through collective (enterprise) bargaining coverage (Morehead et al. 1997:535), and there are major economies of scale for employers and voice and insurance benefits for employees in maintaining collective relationships in a great many workplaces. The point is, however, that where change is occurring, the direction in which it is occurring is to decollectivise rather than to collectivise, and that a significant minority of employers are attempting to head in this direction.

The collapse of compulsory unionism probably accounts for a large proportion (perhaps from half to three-quarters) of the decline in union membership and explains the acceleration in that decline since 1990. It appears that compulsory unionism and associated territory-driven unionism can lead to atrophy in union organisation, as reflected in data about the perceived responsiveness of unions, their ability to ensure employees have a say in their work, union influence at the workplace, changing satisfaction with unions, and workplace union organisation.

However, the demise of compulsory unionism does not mean that this institutional break has brought us to a new era where employee preferences prevail. While there are fewer people who do not want to be in a union but have to be in one, we are also seeing an increase in the number of people who want to be in a union but are not. The transformation of the way in which demand- and supply-related factors influence union membership is simply making it harder for unions to recruit and retain members.

CHAPTER 6

Within the Workplace

While previous chapters have looked at various types of data concerning individual employees, much of the change in union membership is change that takes place in the workplace. It is the workplace, then, that is the focus of this chapter. What are the characteristics of workplaces that influence union decline and growth? What do they tell us about the influence of union and managerial behaviour and strategy on union membership? What do they tell us about the efficacy of the Australian union movement's amalgamationist strategy?

This chapter examines the issue of within-workplace change from four angles: first, changes in union density within workplaces; second, the extreme situations of deunionisation or union collapse; third, the recruitment of new union members and establishment of unions; and fourth, the effect of union amalgamations on union membership. The Australian Workplace Industrial Relations Surveys are the main sources of information, including the AWIRS95 'main survey' of 2000 workplaces and the separate 'panel survey' of 700 workplaces that were surveyed in 1989–90 and reinterviewed in 1995–96, enabling comparisons over a period of almost six years to be made.

All 'workplace' data in this chapter refer to those with 20 or more employees. Although not representative of all workplaces, they account for the great majority of employees in unionised workplaces, and enable us to understand the forces for change within the workplace.

Changing Union Density Within Workplaces

Precise data on union density within workplaces are not available from the AWIRS panel, because of the way the questions were asked.[1] By looking at average density within groups, however, the inaccuracies arising from this imprecision largely cancel themselves out. Estimated union density in workplaces where data were available fell from 65 per cent in 1989–90 to 54 per cent in 1995–96, with a fall of 9 percentage points in workplaces where data were available for both years.[2] *Average* union density in workplaces fell from 55 per cent to 46 per cent, a drop of 9 points. (The discrepancy between these two sets of figures arises because the former is calculated on the basis of *employees* across all workplaces, whereas the latter is calculated as an average across *workplaces*, regardless of their level of employment.) This fall is less than the 13 percentage point drop recorded in the main surveys between 1989–90 and 1995–96 (Morehead et al. 1997:468). The extra 4 percentage points may partly reflect measurement and sampling error but it also incorporates the contribution over the period of structural change between workplaces on the basis of industry, sector and workplace size. It is also worth noting that the 13 point fall between the AWIRS main surveys is greater than the 10 percentage point drop implied in the ABS members survey over the same period. The imprecision of the AWIRS estimation methodology probably accounts for some of this discrepancy, and this has to be borne in mind when considering estimates of the influence of various factors on changing union density.

In workplaces that had a union presence in 1989–90, estimated density fell from 69 per cent to 57 per cent, a drop of 12 points. (Because density in non-union workplaces cannot fall and may rise, it is arithmetically inevitable that the average density decline in workplaces that were unionised in 1989–90 will be greater than the average decline across all workplaces.) The rest of the data in this section only concern workplaces that were already unionised in 1989–90; those that were union-free and became unionised were subject to somewhat different influences, discussed in the third section.

Several factors influenced whether, and by how much, union density rose or fell within a unionised workplace. These can conveniently be grouped together under three labels: union-related factors; management-related factors; and factors related to the structure of the workplace.

Three union-related factors were crucial. The first was prior union density. The higher union density was to begin with, the more scope there was for it to fall and the less scope there was for it to rise. Accordingly, there was a very strong negative relationship between 1989–90 union density and the change in union density between 1989–90 and 1995–96.

The second factor was the presence of a union delegate. After controlling for the effect of prior union density,[3] workplaces with union delegates experienced a change in union density that was 11 percentage points better than workplaces without delegates. This information is presented in the first column of table 6.1. After controlling for the effects of prior density and 10 other variables, discussed below and in table 6.1, workplaces with union delegates experienced an average decline in union density that was 5 percentage points less than did workplaces without delegates (column two).

The third factor was participation in bargaining at the workplace. The AWIRS team classified a workplace as being a 'bargaining' workplace if managers negotiated with a union delegate in the year prior to the survey and the negotiations dealt with at least one issue from a specified list (staffing levels, wage increases, working conditions, occupational health and safety, discipline and dismissals, changes to work practices, or introduction of new technology).[4] Some 19 per cent of workplaces were in this category. After controls, the decline in average density in 'bargaining' workplaces was 11 percentage points less than in non-bargaining workplaces.

The key issue here was involvement of a union (through the delegate) in bargaining. When bargaining occurs directly between management and employees, itself a sign of union weakness, density also declines. In workplaces where enterprise bargaining leading to a formalised written agreement involved employees collectively negotiating with management *without* union involvement, the decline in union density was 10 percentage points greater than in workplaces where this did not occur.

In the context of the bargaining process, two observations about industrial action are also worth making. First, the impact of the most recent industrial action on the output of the employer was associated with a large differential in the change in density in workplaces where industrial action had taken place. Where action did not affect output, union density declined substantially. This was consistent with other evidence that union membership gains from industrial action are dependent on the action being successful (Peetz 1996). Similarly, the decline in union density was lower, the greater was the proportion of employees in the workplace who participated in the most recent industrial action.

While the degree of union involvement clearly influenced changes in workplace density, so too did management strategy. One of the most significant influences on union collapse and deunionisation is employer strategy to enhance productive efficiency, particularly if employers face difficulties in pursuing collective reform strategies through union behaviour or impediments in the industrial relations system. General managers were asked, in AWIRS95, for their views on the statement 'management here think the award system has worked well in the past for this workplace': 59 per cent of managers agreed and just 18 per cent

Table 6.1 Influences on changing union density 1989–90 to 1995–96

	Effect on union density after controlling for prior density	Effect on union density after controlling for 10 other factors
Union delegate in workplace in 1989–90	11***	5^{*a}
Bargaining at the workplace	11***	11***
Management believes award system has worked well	6**	6**
Management used law firms for advice 1995	–8**	–8***
Change involved new senior management	–7*	–6$^{#}$
Change in main activity 1989–95	–15***	–10**
Public sector, 1989–90	8***	3^{b}
Employees receive over-awards	–12***	–8***
Large organisation (effect of >20,000 employees compared to <500 employees)	7**	8**
Non-core workers employment share (effect of 20 point increase)	–3***	–3***
Employment growth (effect of 20 percentage points)	1*	1$^{#}$
Seasonal demand for product/service	–8***	–3^{c}
Industrial action: had no effect on output	–17***	na
Industrial action: proportion of workers involved (effect of 20 percentage points)	3*	na
Adverse effects from joint consultative council	–10*	na

Source: AWIRS95 panel survey
N: 523
Notes:
na not applicable – variable not included in regression because it would unacceptably lower overall sample size.
\# Significant at 10 per cent level
* Significant at 5 per cent level
** Significant at 1 per cent level
*** Significant at 0.1 per cent level
a 8*** when workplace bargaining is excluded
b 5* when organisation size is excluded
c –4$^{#}$ when organisation size is excluded

disagreed. When managers agreed with this statement, the decline in density recorded in the panel was 6 percentage points less than when they were neutral or disagreed, after other factors were controlled. It appears likely that managers pursue more aggressive anti-union strategies where they see the award system as failing. This may be a proxy indicator that unions at the workplace have not been sufficiently 'flexible', in the eyes of management, to overcome perceived in-efficiencies arising from the operation of awards. This finding confirmed earlier, more tentative evidence along these lines in the AWIRS90 data.[5] Managers probably also pursue more aggressive strategies where con-sultation processes involving unions have broken down — as illustrated by the greater decline in density in workplaces where joint consultative committees are perceived by management to have failed.

Further evidence on the role of managerial strategy can be seen in the fact that density fell by 8 percentage points more in workplaces where employers sought advice from lawyers. During 1995,[6] 28 per cent of workplaces made use of law firms for advice on employment matters. Those that did experienced a drop in union density that was, on average, 10 percentage points greater than the decline experienced in other workplaces. For at least some employers, the use of lawyers is part of a wider strategy of undermining unions.

There is also a suggestion that major changes in managerial strategy associated with the introduction of new management teams can be aimed at reducing union influence and membership. In 9 per cent of workplaces, the organisational change in 1995 with the most significant effect on employees involved a major change in senior management (e.g. a new senior manager, chief executive officer or division head). Workplaces of this type appeared to experience a greater decline in average union density than other workplaces, though the relationship was only slightly significant. Evidence presented later will imply that, often, a change of management has no impact on unionism, but when it does it can be very serious for unionisation.

A central aspect of managerial strategy is the level of employee remuneration, including whether any over-award payments are made to employees. Where over-award payments were paid, the fall in union density was greater.[7] Presumably when employees are paid at a high rate relative to the award, they perceive less of a need for union membership. Employers may use this device to discourage or diminish unionism, or it may simply occur as an innocent byproduct of benevolent managerial practices.

Workplaces in the public sector, and in large organisations (with 20,000 or more employees), showed a lower rate of decline in union density than did workplaces in the private sector or in small and medium-sized organisations. A somewhat unusual pattern of interaction between these two variables arose. When just these variables (and prior density) were entered into an equation, sector was a more powerful influence than organisational size (which was only slightly significant). When the other variables were entered, however, size became more important than sector, which lost its significance altogether.

Differences in union collapse rates between private- and public-sector workplaces, and large and small organisations, may partly reflect patterns in employee attitudes towards unions (in the case of sector) and in the difficulties facing unions in keeping track of members in smaller, private-sector workplaces. Sectoral and size effects may also be proxies for the effects of particular managerial strategies. It is not that public-sector managers have been slower than private-sector managers to embrace change. Indeed, public-sector managers in the panel were 10 percentage points more likely than their counterparts in the private sector and in small organisations to say that the approach or philosophy towards managing employees was significantly different to what it was like five or six years earlier. On average, however, public-sector and non-commercial managers, and workplace managers in large organisations, have apparently been less enthusiastic in embracing new anti-union strategies than their private-sector counterparts. In unionised workplaces, just 4 per cent of private-sector managers, compared to 15 per cent of public-sector managers, disagreed with the proposition that 'management here prefer to deal with employees directly, not through trade unions'. Similarly, just 5 per cent of managers from medium and small organisations, compared to 14 per cent of managers from large organisations, disagreed with this proposition.

Other influences on changes in density also related to the structure of the workplace. The decline was significantly greater in workplaces with a high proportion of 'non-core' employees (part-time employees and related workers and contractors). The decline might have been slightly greater (though the effect was not significant after controls) in workplaces that experienced seasonality in demand, making it more difficult for unions to retain a stable membership base. There was a weakly significant, positive relationship between changes in density and employment growth within workplaces; that is, on average, as employment fell within a workplace, membership fell disproportionately.

Finally, density fell by 10 per cent more in the 10 per cent of workplaces that were engaged in a different activity in 1995–96 to that in which they were engaged at the time of the first survey. In one sense, this is simply another manifestation of structural change in the labour market — one that contributed about 1 percentage point to the overall decline in density over the period. But the fact that this has been occurring within workplaces, and unions have been unable to prevent these changes in corporate strategy leading to major falls in union density, highlights failings in the union response to structural changes. As discussed below, in some cases major changes in corporate strategy are closely integrated with major changes in industrial relations strategy, to the detriment of unions.

One point worth making concerns a variable that was not significant: there was no noticeable effect on changes in union density, within already unionised workplaces, arising from visits by full-time officials over the preceding six years which were perceived by management as being aimed at enrolling members. These visits had allegedly occurred in nearly half of unionised workplaces. These data should be treated warily. It is quite possible that management misreport or do not understand the reasons for visits by full-time officials: according to delegates, when asked about the main reason for the last visit by a full-time official, less than one per cent replied that it was to recruit members. In addition, there are problems of recall when asking a question concerning a six-year period. More interesting, perhaps, are the findings in relation to successful recruitment in unionised workplaces (that is, where management said that, as a result of this attempted recruitment, some employees had become union members). 'Successful recruitment' was, as would be expected, positively related to changes in union density over the panel period. But once the factors listed in table 6.1 were controlled, it had no independent impact on changes in union density. That is, successful recruitment in already unionised workplaces most commonly occurred when it coincided with the factors, discussed above, that promote union growth within unionised workplaces: workplace bargaining, delegate presence, low managerial resistance to unions, and favourable structural characteristics, including a low proportion of non-core employees.

To summarise: in workplaces that were already unionised, density rose or fell according to a series of factors that concerned how unions related to their members and management, how management approached unions, and the structural difficulties for unions in recruiting and keeping in touch with members. On average, union density fell by about 12 percentage points, but falls were smallest (and rises most common) in workplaces with a delegate presence, where unions engaged in bargaining with management and where unions were successful in organising members into effective industrial action when it was necessary to do so. Meanwhile falls were greatest in workplaces where managerial strategies had the intended or unintended effect of making life more difficult for unions or where workplace characteristics made it more difficult for unions to get in touch with and keep track of employees.

Deunionisation and Union Collapse

Regardless of any limitations on the AWIRS95 panel data on union density, the data are sufficiently robust to enable us to identify where a union has changed from having a union presence in 1989–90 to not having a union presence in 1995–96, a process referred to here as *deunionisation*. They are also robust enough for us to consider very large changes in union density within a workplace, of 50 percentage points or more. Where a workplace has either deunionised or suffered a 50 percentage point decline in estimated union density, it has experienced *union collapse*. We first examine deunionisation.

Amongst workplaces that had a union presence in 1989–90, one in thirteen had deunionised by 1995–96. Some 3.3 per cent of employees in workplaces with 20 or more employees were in workplaces that had deunionised over this period, implying that deunionisation accounted for at least 1.2 percentage points of the total decline in union density of approximately 8 percentage points over this period.[8]

There was a relationship with workplace size: larger workplaces (with 100 or more employees) had a deunionisation rate of 3 per cent, while smaller ones (20 to 99 employees) had a rate of 9 per cent.[9] Similarly, workplaces with lower union density to begin with were more likely to deunionise: average 1989–90 union density was 37 per cent in workplaces that later deunionised, compared to 73 per cent in workplaces that did not. Both of these are partly to be expected: if the probability of all employees leaving a union was identical, then workplaces with fewer union members would have a higher probability of deunionisation than large ones simply because it required fewer people to change their union status for deunionisation to occur. However, simple calculations show that these patterns are not simply explicable by chance.[10] Rather, there are clusters of factors which explain why smaller and weakly unionised workplaces have higher deunionisation probabilities. Chief among these is the low incidence of union delegates and active unionism in small workplaces and workplaces with lower union density, already suggested by the importance of union delegates demonstrated in chapter two.

Union Activity

The impact of union delegates and union activism in preventing deunionisation is startling. Amongst workplaces without a delegate in 1989–90, 21 per cent had deunionised by 1995–96. Amongst those with a union delegate in 1989–90, just 2 per cent had deunionised by 1995–96. In workplaces with active unions in 1989–90, the rate of deunionisation, at 1 per cent, was even lower. Where unions were inactive, the rate of deunionisation stood at 10 per cent. Workplaces were classified as actively unionised if, in AWIRS90, the senior delegate from the union with most members at the workplace spent one hour or more per week on union activities and carried out tasks beyond recruiting members, and one other condition was satisfied: either there was a general meeting of members held at least once every six months; or a union committee regularly met with management; or delegates met with management above first-line supervisor level at least once a month (Morehead et al. 1997:326).

The high rates of deunionisation in workplaces without delegates or with inactive unions are of considerable significance. Unionised workplaces without union delegates made up 30 per cent of unionised workplaces (though, because of deunionisation, this is down from the 34 per cent figure of 1989–90) and account for 14 per cent of union members in workplaces with 20 or more members. Moreover, 76 per cent of unionised workplaces have 'inactive' unions, and these account for 53 per cent of union members in workplaces with 20 or more members.

There was also a substantial amount of turnover in the population of actively unionised workplaces. Only 56 per cent of workplaces that had active unions in 1989–90 (8 per cent of all workplaces) still had active unions in 1995–96. However, this loss of active workplaces was almost offset by previously inactive but unionised workplaces becoming actively unionised.

Our second, broader measure of union performance is union collapse: where a workplace either deunionised or suffered a decline of at least 50 percentage points in union density. The advantage of this measure is that it enables us to also detect large declines in union density in previously heavily unionised workplaces, declines which may not be large enough to cause deunionisation but which lead to a fundamental change in the nature of union representation in the workplace.

Between 1989–90 and 1995–96, 14 per cent of previously unionised workplaces experienced either deunionisation or a fall in union density of 50 percentage points or more. Union collapse was, as we would expect, related to union activism, with the rate of union collapse being 17 per cent in workplaces with inactive unions, and just 8 per cent in workplaces with active unions. Similarly, in workplaces with delegates, the union collapse rate was just 8 per cent; in unionised workplaces without delegates, it was 29 per cent. Nonetheless, it is noteworthy that neither union activism nor the presence of union delegates serves to guarantee unions will not suffer a catastrophic decline in density; while they make it much less likely that collapse will occur, they do not preclude it altogether in the same way as they almost seem to preclude total deunionisation.

Closely related to union activism is participation in bargaining. Deunionisation was almost exclusively concentrated in workplaces that had neither active unions nor workplace bargaining. Union collapse was over three times as likely in such workplaces as in other workplaces.

Another significant influence on union collapse and deunionisation was industrial action. Unionised workplaces that had never participated in industrial action were significantly more likely to deunionise and to experience union collapse. But the effect, particularly on union collapse, was concentrated in workplaces with inactive unions; that is, if unions were active anyway it did not matter whether or not there had ever been industrial action (table 6.2). A previous history of industrial disputes probably indicated that employees had direct experience of the need for, and reserved the right for, collective action where management was failing to meet employees' expectations.

Management Strategies and Union Collapse

Delegate presence and union activism are keys to preventing union decline. However, a number of aspects of management strategy also have a major impact on deunionisation and union collapse. Several forms of management strategy only have an effect on union collapse if unions are inactive at the workplace. That is, in many instances some sort of conditional relationship exists between management strategy and union membership. However, there are some aspects of management strategy that have such an impact on the nature of workplace relations that they increase the probability of union collapse even in workplaces with active unions.

Table 6.2 shows the interactions between union activism and various factors (mostly management-related) that are associated with union collapse and deunionisation. (They are presented as cross-tabulations for simplicity of exposition, but the attention is given to relationships that show up as significant in multivariate analysis.)

Problems with the award system led managers to pursue strategies which often brought about union decline. Hence the rate of union collapse was 20 per cent in workplaces in which managers were unhappy with, or indifferent towards, the award system, whereas it was only 10 per cent in workplaces where managers were happy with the award system. However, as shown in table 6.2, these strategies to overcome 'inefficiencies' in the award system only led to significant decline in workplaces with inactive unions. In workplaces with active unions, these strategies had no effect: management either were unable to circumvent unions or were able to bring about change without needing to circumvent unions.

Evidence from other questions suggests the former rather than the latter hypothesis probably provides the correct explanation for the

Table 6.2 Deunionisation and union collapse, union activism and workplace characteristics

		Rate of deunionisation (%)			Rate of union collapse (%)		
		Total	Inactive unions	Active unions	Total	Inactive unions	Active unions
Bargaining workplace	*not bargaining*	10***	13*	1	18***	20**	11
	bargaining	0	0	0	3	1	5
Ever been industrial action at workplace	*yes*	3***	4***	0*	8***	7***	8
	never	18	20	5	28	30	10
Management believes award system has worked well	*no*	9	13	<0.5	20**	25**	8
	yes	6	9	1	10	11	8
Management used law firms for advice 1995	*no*	5**	7**	1	12#	14*	8
	yes	15	26	<0.5	21	30	8
Ownership change 1989–95 affected way work is done	*no*	15	11	1	12**	13***	8
	yes	5	7	0	42	54	<0.5
Change involved new senior management	*no*	6**	8***	<0.5#	12***	14***	6*
	yes	24	30	5	37	39	31
Change in location 1989–95	*same address*	6**	8**	0	12**	14**	6#
	moved address	16	23	1	28	32	18
Organisational status, 1995–96	*non-commercial*	2**	3*	0	3***	5**	1*
	commercial	10	14	1	20	22	14
Sector, 1989–90	*private*	12***	15**	1	21***	22**	15*
	public	1	2	0	4	4	3
More a team philosophy	*not volunteered*	5#	10	1	13#	15*	9
	volunteered	15	24	0	26	42	<0.5
Employee share ownership scheme	*no*	7	10	0	12***	14***	7
	yes	8	12	1	31	37	17
Employees receive overawards	*no*	3***	4***	<0.5	6***	9***	5#
	yes	16	22	2	26	30	15
Female employment share	*below 60%*	10*	15**	1	17#	22#	10
	60% and above	3	3	0	10	11	3
N		620	337	283	620	337	283

Source:　AWIRS95 management and delegate surveys
Population:　Workplaces with more than 20 employees which had union members in 1989–90 and which were still operating in 1995–96.
\#　　　Significant at 10 per cent level
*　　　Significant at 5 per cent level
**　　Significant at 1 per cent level
***　Significant at 0.1 per cent level

absence of a link in active workplaces. There was a link between deunionisation and the use of law firms, again suggesting that for at least some employers, consultations with law firms were about finding means to subvert unions. However, as shown in table 6.2, deunionisation and union collapse were only associated with consultation with law firms in workplaces where unions were inactive. In workplaces with active unions, the rates of deunionisation and union collapse were, on average, unaffected by management's seeking advice from lawyers.

Major changes in the business strategy of management can have a substantial impact on union presence. This is probably because a fundamental recasting of business strategy is often integrally associated with a fundamental recasting of industrial relations strategy. In 9 per cent of workplaces, a change in ownership of the workplace had a major effect (according to management) on the way work was done. As already mentioned, in (a mostly different) 9 per cent of workplaces, new faces in senior management were the change that had the biggest effect on employees. Both these forms of change were strongly associated with union collapse (see table 6.2), suggesting that when these changes in managerial strategy took place they involved aggressive approaches towards unionism more commonly than they involved congenial approaches towards unions. This pattern was clearly evident in workplaces with inactive unions but, in the case of major changes in senior management, it was even evident in workplaces with active unions, suggesting that union activism in itself may not be sufficient to always prevent concerted anti-union strategies from having an effect.

Sometimes management may decide to relocate a workplace to an entirely new site, and in the process seek to bring about a major change to workplace industrial relations, through devices ranging from replacing a large part of the workforce to changing the spatial relationships in site layout that might facilitate collectivist behaviour. Deunionisation and union collapse were both significantly more common in workplaces that had changed address between the two survey dates. Even in workplaces that originally had active unions, the effect is still weakly significant (the lower significance primarily reflecting lower effective sample size rather than a weaker effect as such).

Deunionisation and union collapse were both higher in commercial workplaces, in private-sector workplaces and in workplaces that were part of small organisations (in the last case, the relationship with union collapse was only slightly significant). As noted, this pattern may be partly a proxy for the effect of particular managerial strategies.

Several other aspects of management strategy are more concerned with the relationships between management and employees. When asked to explain their changing philosophy, some 5 per cent of managers volunteered that there was more of a 'team philosophy' than in the past. In workplaces with inactive unions, this was associated with a higher rate of union collapse. More significantly, union collapse was associated with the existence of employee share ownership schemes in workplaces with inactive unions. This might suggest that 'human resource management' (HRM) strategies are associated with union decline, consistent with evidence from an earlier, shorter panel period (1989–90 to 1992–93) (Peetz 1997a). Yet, overall, the evidence for a (conditional) link between HRM strategies and deunionisation or union collapse is considerably weaker in the period covered by the 1989–90 to 1995–96 panel than by the earlier, shorter panel, even though the sample sizes are similar. For example, while workplaces with recently introduced regular social functions and joint consultative committees had higher deunionisation rates than other workplaces in this longer panel, the differences were not significant; in the case of quality circles, they were non-existent. Perhaps the wave of enthusiasm for 'caring, sharing' HRM strategies in the early 1990s has been superseded by a more cynical approach which uses HRM strategies as an element in the management of work intensification.

Evidence for this proposition can be found in the AWIRS95 employee survey. We would expect HRM strategies to be closely linked to 'structured' management. The AWIRS team defined structured management as existing where a workplace had at least four of the following seven elements: training in employee relations for first-line supervisors; a joint consultative committee; a specialist occupational health and safety committee; a written policy on equal employment opportunity or affirmative action; disciplinary procedures; monitoring of employees (through any two of the following: measuring labour productivity, work study, performance appraisal); and a frequently used grievance procedure (Morehead et al. 1997:325). Employees in workplaces with structured management reported higher work intensification than employees in non-structured workplaces: 60 per cent of those in structured workplaces reported increased work effort over the previous year, compared with 53 per cent in non-structured workplaces; employees in workplaces with structured management were also more likely to report higher stress (51 per cent to 44 per cent). Workplaces with regular social functions reported higher work effort (60 per cent to 57 per cent) and higher stress (51 per cent to 48 per cent); staff appraisal schemes were associated with higher stress (51 per cent to 47 per cent); new quality circles were associated with higher work effort (61 per cent to 58 per cent) and stress (53 per cent to 49 per cent); and even 'team building' was associated with higher work effort (60 per cent to 57 per cent). These differences are not large but they are significant. They hint at why HRM strategies may have lost their salience as a means of wooing workers from unions to management: no amount of caring rhetoric can disguise the fundamental nature of work intensification. It is likely that the growth of HRM and 'structured management' – the estimated incidence of structured management rose from 39 per cent to 59 per cent of workplaces between 1989–90 and 1995–96 – in part reflects managerial efforts to obviate the effects of change on employees and to persuade them that the organisation has 'no choice' in what it is doing but it still really does care for them. (The growth of structured management also reflects changing legislative requirements in areas such as affirmative action.)

These days, however, it appears that the only HRM strategy that is powerful enough to affect union collapse is money. Workplaces where over-award payments were made (according to managers) had significantly higher rates of deunionisation and union collapse than did workplaces without over-award payments. Even in workplaces with active unions, there was a weak relationship between over-award payments and union collapse, but its efficacy was much greater in workplaces with inactive unions.

In sum, deunionisation and union collapse were closely related to union activity and management strategy. Indeed, an effective delegate presence and active union role were almost guarantees against deunionisation, and were important in reducing the likelihood of union collapse. Some aspects of managerial opposition to unions were only associated with union collapse in workplaces without an active delegate presence. However, decisive changes in management industrial relations strategy that might arise from major changes in corporate strategy – as reflected in a new management team, new ownership, or a new location – could sometimes have devastating consequences for unions. On the other hand, while money mattered, the adoption of HRM strategies did not appear any more to be a major influence on deunionisation or union collapse, perhaps because HRM strategies are sometimes brought in to ease, but cannot negate, the adverse impacts on employees of the drive for competitiveness.

Union Establishment and Recruitment

We have seen that there is considerable similarity in the factors that influence changes in union density and deunionisation and union collapse. It need not be the case, however, that the same factors influence the creation of union presence in non-union workplaces. When management behaves badly in non-union workplaces, employees might join a union. When management behaves badly in already unionised workplaces, workers may feel that not only management but also the union has let them down – the latter because the union was unable to prevent management from misbehaving. We look first at data from the AWIRS95 main survey – this time on union recruitment – before turning to data from the panel on the establishment of a union presence in non-union workplaces.

Recruitment over the Previous Year

Unions are more successful in recruiting where they already have a presence and are active. This much stands to reason. More interesting for our purposes is the question: in what type of *non*-union workplaces are unions most successful at recruiting? To answer this question we use data on recruitment from the AWIRS95 main survey. Our interest is in the non-union workplace recruitment rate – the number of non-union workplaces with successful recruiting of members in the previous year, divided by the total number of non-union workplaces (including those in which successful recruitment took place).

The overall non-union recruitment rate was 4 per cent – that is unions managed to recruit new members in just 4 per cent of all non-union workplaces, which represented 20 per cent of non-union workplaces they visited for recruitment purposes in the year preceding AWIRS95. The following observations, while all based on statistically significant findings in multivariate analysis, should be treated as tentative rather than definitive, pending confirmation by other data, because of the small number of cases (18 out of 389 non-union workplaces) where non-union recruitment took place.

One of the factors influencing the non-union recruitment rate was employment growth within the workplace. The recruitment rate was 9 per cent in workplaces with employment growth of 10 per cent or more, compared with 2 per cent in workplaces with relatively stable or declining employment. There is a multiple logic to unions concentrating recruitment in growing non-union workplaces. New employees might be more open-minded on whether to join a union. If unions establish a foothold in growing workplaces this is a better base for longer-term membership growth than having a foothold in declining workplaces (which seems to be where a disproportionate amount of unionised employment is located).

The characteristics of employment – particularly the use of shift-work – also influence recruitment potential. Non-union workplaces with shift-work had a recruitment rate of 6 per cent, compared with 1 per cent in workplaces without shiftwork. As working hours move from 'traditional' daytime hours to shifts that suit the employer, dissatisfaction with working arrangements may provide a source for future union recruitment.

Recruitment was also influenced by specific forms of workplace change. In particular, recruitment rates were highest (47 per cent) in workplaces that had, in the previous two years, introduced any of four 'modern management' tools: just-in-time programs, computer-integrated manufacturing, quality circles or total quality management. As many other forms of organisational change did not have strong associations with recruitment, it might not be immediately obvious why 'modern management' tools should be related to successful recruitment. However, a hint is found in the employee survey, which suggests that 'modern management' tools may be associated with increased stress, effort and hazard. Although the effects were small, across the entire sample employees in workplaces with recently introduced 'modern management' tools were significantly more likely to report increased work effort (60 per cent versus 58 per cent for other workplaces), increased stress (51 per cent versus 49 per cent) and work-related injuries in the previous year (19 per cent versus 17 per cent), and were less likely to be satisfied with the safety and comfort of their working conditions (59 per cent versus 63 per cent). Certainly, these factors were, in turn, associated with successful recruitment: only 52 per cent of employees in (previously non-union) workplaces with successful recruitment were satisfied with the safety and comfort of their working conditions, compared with 69 per cent of employees in workplaces that remained non-union. Amongst employees in workplaces with successful recruitment, 30 per cent had experienced a work-related injury, compared with just 11 per cent in workplaces which had remained non-union.

Other evidence from the employee survey provides further suggestions as to the factors influencing successful recruitment, all of which relate to managements' treatment of employees. In previously non-union workplaces that had recent recruitment, only 32 per cent of employees agreed that managers at the workplace could be trusted to tell things the way they are, compared with 48 per cent in workplaces that remained non-union. In workplaces with recent recruitment, just 52 per cent of employees believed management at the workplace did its best to get on with employees, compared with 67 per cent in workplaces that remained non-union. Previously non-union workplaces with recent recruitment were also less likely to have employees who were satisfied overall with their job (54 per cent versus 69 per cent), satisfied that they could use a phone at work for family reasons (68 per cent versus 80 per cent), or satisfied with the way management treated them and their colleagues (38 per cent versus 55 per cent). They were less likely to perceive they had been consulted by higher-level management during workplace changes (42 per cent versus 60 per cent) or that their weekly pay had gone up in the previous 12 months (43 per cent versus 56 per cent) and more likely to believe that they had been made worse off by workplace changes (27 per cent versus 16 per cent). In short, successful union recruitment appeared to be associated with poor management, with badly managed workplace change, and with lack of money.

This pattern is particularly significant, as the 1994 Workplace Bargaining Survey (WBS94) showed that 39 per cent of all employees reported that their satisfaction with management was lower than it had been 12 months earlier, with just 18 per cent reporting higher satisfaction. When growing dissatisfaction with management is manifested in non-union workplaces[11] there is substantial scope for unionisation to take place.

One other, unexpected finding from AWIRS95 is worth noting. Based on both management and employee responses, in raw terms workplaces with recent recruitment had higher proportions of casual and non-core employees than workplaces that remained non-union. This appears to be because workplaces with high levels of casual employment were also more likely to be workplaces with high employment growth and shift workers. When these two factors were controlled (in logistic regression equations), casual employment became non-significant in explaining successful recruitment. This is not to deny that recruitment of casual employees is a difficult task; but it does suggest that one way of increasing membership amongst this group is to focus on those in workplaces that are growing and employ substantial shiftwork.

Union Establishment over a Six-year Period

The other source of data on the establishment of unions in previously non-union workplaces is the AWIRS95 panel. Union establishment is a broader concept than recruitment (a union presence can be established at the initiative of the employees rather than following a visit by a full-time official). A key concept here is the *union establishment rate* – the number of workplaces that were non-union in 1989–90 but in which unions had a presence in 1995–96, as a proportion of the number of non-union workplaces in 1989–90. Clearly, union recruitment is one of the key influences on union establishment: the union establishment rate was 34 per cent where full-time officials had visited workplaces for recruitment purposes in the previous year, compared with 8 per cent in other workplaces. Again, we are constrained by small sample size (out of 78 non-union workplaces, there were 11 in which unions were established) so although significant, the conclusions in some cases are tentative. Nonetheless, on certain matters the trend is the same as in the main survey, suggesting that more confident conclusions may be warranted.

Most prominent amongst these trends is the relationship between 'modern management' tools and union establishment. The union establishment rate was 22 per cent in workplaces which had 'modern management' tools in place, compared with just over 1 per cent in other workplaces. The strength of the relationships involving this variable in both the panel and the main surveys indicates that the adoption of new managerial techniques in response to the forces of increasing competition and globalisation provides fertile ground for unionisation of non-union workplaces.

Other panel data gave tentative support to the trends shown in the main survey's data on union recruitment but with limitations arising from the small sample size. In workplaces with 'rotating shifts', the establishment rate was 23 per cent compared with 10 per cent in other workplaces. In workplaces with employment growth of 10 per cent or over, the establishment rate was 22 per cent compared with 12 per cent in slower growing or declining workplaces. In neither case were the differences significant, but both were consistent with the patterns shown in the recruitment data. Workplaces that, in 1995–96, reported expanding demand had an establishment rate of 23 per cent, significantly greater than the 5 per cent rate among workplaces in which demand was stable or contracting, which reinforces the implication that growing workplaces are the better prospect for unionisation.

The relevance of competition is not so clear. While in the panel there was a negative correlation between the degree of product market competition facing a workplace and the likelihood of union establishment, there was no significant correlation between the recruitment rate and either the number of competitors or the intensity of competition in the main survey.

The other major factor that influenced the union establishment rate was the existence of 'structured management' in the workplace. Workplaces that had structured management in 1989–90 had a union establishment rate of 31 per cent, compared with 7 per cent amongst those with non-structured management. A similar pattern, with lower significance, was also seen in the recruitment rate data in the main survey: workplaces with structured management had a recruitment rate of 7 per cent, while those with non-structured management had a recruitment rate of 2 per cent.

One possible explanation is that structured management is more congenial towards unionisation than non-structured management. The main survey showed that, amongst non-union workplaces, managers in structured workplaces were slightly more likely to agree that 'management here would not mind dealing with trade unions should any employee join one' (43 per cent) than were managers in non-structured workplaces (32 per cent). Similarly, amongst unionised workplaces, managers were more likely to strongly agree that 'management here prefer to deal with employees directly, not through trade unions' when the workplace had non-structured management (60 per cent) than when it had structured management (48 per cent).

However, it is also likely that the emergence of structured management reflects a need to respond to the complexity of issues arising from a combination of workplace change, the growing emphasis on decentralised wage bargaining, growing statutory responsibilities, organisational size, workforce diversity and the need to manage growing uncertainty. To that extent, the higher rates of union establishment and recruitment in 'structured' workplaces probably mean that employees are responding to difficult change in the same way that management is: by seeking to introduce greater formality into the employment relationship and reduce uncertainty.

In sum, the factors influencing the establishment of a union presence in previously non-unionised workplaces are quite different to the factors that influence the rise and decline of unions in already unionised workplaces. The growing pressures on managers arising from competition and globalisation may be making management more antagonistic towards unions; but they are also creating the circumstances that make unionisation attractive to employees. Increasing intensity of work and stress and increasing exposure to occupational hazard are conducive to union joining in workplaces where unions have previously not had a role. The introduction of 'modern management' tools, and difficult working conditions such as those associated with shiftwork, will encourage people to join unions. Where employees in non-union workplaces distrust management, are dissatisfied with management's treatment of them, have been inadequately consulted over change, have been adversely affected by change, or have not experienced pay rises, they are more likely to turn to unions for assistance. Where non-union workplaces are growing, unions are more likely to recruit and establish a presence, partly because it is rational longer-term behaviour on the part of unions to concentrate their efforts in such workplaces. 'Structured' management may arise in response to the same complexities and uncertainties that facilitates unionism and (with some notable exceptions) may itself be more tolerant of the establishment of a union presence.

Union Structure and Amalgamation

The most visible manifestation of the Australian union movement's response to the decline in union density has been the strategy of pursuing union amalgamations. In the latter part of the 1980s the ACTU leadership decided that a radical restructuring of the union movement was critical to its longer-term future, and that fewer, larger unions were needed in order that union members could be effectively serviced, unions could have better-resourced recruitment campaigns and the decline in union membership could be reversed (e.g. Berry & Kitchener 1989; ACTU 1991). Employer groups also complained that efficient work organisation was hampered by there being too many unions. Some even argued that the antiquated structure of the union movement was 'the biggest single industrial relations impediment to more efficient competitive Australian enterprise' (BCA 1989:13). BCA-sponsored research claimed that the average number of unions in BCA-affiliate workplaces had only declined from 4.8 in 1988 to 3.6 in 1992 (Hilmer et al. 1993) and (despite an absence of hard data) that multi-unionism remained a major obstacle to workplace reform. No doubt multiple unionism creates problems for some employers. This in turn may influence some employers' strategies towards unions.

In mid-1986 there were 326 unions in Australia, half of which were registered in the federal system. The original plan of the ACTU (1987) was to reduce, through amalgamation, the number of federally registered unions to 20 within two years. By mid-1996 the total number of Australian unions had fallen to 132, and there were just 47 federally registered unions by the end of 1995. Federally registered unions account for 86 per cent of union membership.

Amongst industrialised countries the strategy of union amalgamation is common (Pankert 1992). As Freeman and Medoff (1984:244) point out, many of the spurts in growth of union membership have been associated with organisational innovations, by new unions led by new unionists along somewhat different lines from traditional unions. Jackson (1982) argued that increased union size would create communication problems between leaders and members, but there is not much prior information on the effect of union structure, reorganisation or amalgamation upon unionisation (Clegg 1970:59–62). Although Gilson and Wagar (1992), in a Canadian study, found that union size had no effect upon the success of union organising, Maranto and Fiorito (1987) found that larger, less centralised unions were more likely to win certification elections. Dworkin and Extejt (1979) found larger ones were also more likely to become decertified, while Barling, Fullagar and Kelloway (1992:134) also found larger unions were associated with lower membership participation. Explanations include the greater diversity of membership, centralised governance, bureaucratic administration, and union officials' attempts to enhance their power while negotiating mergers (Chaison 1986). Members of larger unions were more satisfied than those in smaller unions in Leicht's study (1989). Chaison (1986) found little evidence one way or another from union growth statistics to indicate whether amalgamations assisted union organising or whether they actually retarded it by providing a low-cost 'alternative to the hard, slogging job of organising employees who are not yet in unions' (Brooks & Gamm 1976). Attitudes to single unionism (having only one union within a workplace) have been barely researched, although a British study by Wedderburn and Crompton (1972) found single-union representation within a workplace supported by a majority of employees. Some have argued that union structure can have an important influence on union growth or decline if it leads to resources being wasted over jurisdictional disputes (Western 1993a; LO 1991) or to what Willman (1989) calls 'market-share' unionism rather than 'expansionary' unionism. As Beaumont (1983) found in a British study, inter-union competition is negatively correlated with union success in winning employee support for recognition.

A widespread view within the Australian Council of Trade Unions (ACTU) is that Australia's union structure in the 1980s was, in part at least, responsible for the decline in union membership, as it had led to a poor response to the structural shift in jobs, under-resourced unions, inadequate services to members, insufficient training of officials, damaging conflict within union ranks, and failure to seek new members in poorly organised sectors or to improve services for existing members (e.g. Shaw et al. 1990). Yet others have argued that the ACTU's reponse, its amalgamation strategy, was 'fatally flawed' (Costa & Duffy 1991). Given the importance of this issue for the 'future directions' of the union movement (ACTU 1987), it is perhaps surprising that the consequences of union structure for union membership have not been substantially researched in Australia. Internal reorganisations of some Australian unions were associated with significant growth in membership as organisational efficiency has increased (e.g. Sheridan 1975:303), but there are few recent, published data on consequences of the amalgamation strategy for members' attitudes to or behaviour regarding union membership. Virtually all that were available were some poll data from the early 1980s suggesting that Australians supported (by a small majority) union amalgamations and (by a convincing majority) the encouragement of industry-based unions (McNair 1988:27).

To examine the efficacy of the amalgamation strategy we briefly consider some preliminary evidence from SEMSE and AWIRS90 before examining AWIRS95, the first major source of data on the effects of union amalgamation at the workplace.

Attitudes to Union Rationalisation and Cohesion

SEMSE data, collected before the main phase of amalgamations was underway, suggested that there was considerable employee support for the rationalisation of union organisation at the workplace. Some 55 per cent of union members with an opinion agreed that 'there should be only one union representing employees in this workplace' while just 18 per cent disagreed. Most employees in SEMSE seemed content with the degree of union cohesion they observed, that is, the extent to which unions appeared to be working together rather than fighting with each other. Only 15 per cent of employees with an opinion agreed that 'unions at this workplace spend a lot of time fighting each other', while 53 per cent disagreed.

Where unions were seen as spending a lot of time fighting each other, however, the effects upon unionisation were quite serious. Employees who said unions fought with each other had lower union satisfaction, scored unions lower on responsiveness and protection, and had lower instrumentality and propensity. More importantly, low union cohesion was probably associated with a lower union joining rate and higher union exit rate and definitely associated with lower union density (see logistic regression equations reported in Peetz 1998). In short, union in-fighting led to lower unionisation.

Union Size and Attitudes

Data preceding the main period of union amalgamations also enable us to make some assessment of the presumption that larger unions are more effective at recruiting and retaining members. Data on union growth by union size (Rawson & Wrightson 1980, 1985) do not indicate a strong relationship between union size and growth. Over the 1970s and early 1980s the growing and declining unions seemed to be fairly evenly spread between the larger and smaller unions. Wooden and Balchin (1992) found an uneven relationship between union size and workplace union density although, using the same data set, Harris (1993) found union density to be highest in workplaces where the largest union had over 75,000 members.[12]

Data from SEMSE did not suggest a powerful *employee* preference for larger unions. General union propensity was no higher amongst employees in unions that had over 75,000 members than it was in unions with under 40,000 members, or those in between. Perceptions of union voice did not differ by union size, although satisfaction with union delegates and the way in which unions kept in contact with their members was higher in large unions.[13] However, union apathy was a more significant problem in smaller unions, and union apathy commonly led to union exit (Peetz 1997c).

Union size also appeared to affect employer strategy. Management in SEMSE workplaces appeared more critical of smaller unions than of larger ones. Managers in workplaces with small unions appeared to have lower trust of unions, be less likely to say that they tried to cooperate with management, be more likely to say unions were doing a worse job than previously, and be less likely to encourage union membership.

So there might be several mechanisms by which increased union size may encourage employees to unionise in Australia. First, reducing the number of unions at the workplace would probably increase the attraction of unions to employees and employers. Second, larger unions would presumably also be in a stronger financial position to withstand employer offensives along the lines of some of the battles of the 1980s. If unions are able to do more for their members, they may benefit from increased union propensity and reduced exit. (Larger unions also appear better positioned to overcome union apathy.) There are other issues that may also affect the impact of the amalgamation strategy on union membership, such as the effect on union cohesion and competition for membership, or 'market-share' unionism. These issues shall be returned to below.

The Perceived Effects of Amalgamation: General Patterns

Managers and delegates were asked different questions about union amalgamations in AWIRS95. Understanding the effects of amalgamation first of all requires an understanding of the different perceptions of managers and delegates and the different meanings of the questions they were asked.

In the AWIRS95 main survey, managers from 10 per cent of unionised workplaces reported that there had been a reduction in the number of unions in the previous *two* years. This reduction was attributed by slightly over a third to the effects of union amalgamation, so that overall, amalgamation had led to reductions in multi-unionism in 5 per cent of *multi-union* workplaces. Because most of the union amalgamation process had been completed before 1994 (and because in some workplaces the number of unions would have increased without amalgamations) these figures substantially understate the impact of amalgamation in reducing multi-unionism: the panel showed that 25 per cent of multi-union workplaces had experienced reductions in multi-unionism due to amalgamation over the six years from 1989–90 to 1995–96.[14]

Amongst senior delegates, 58 per cent reported that their union had been part of an amalgamation *since 1988*; 17 per cent indicated that this had led to some employees who previously were covered by different unions coming together in the same union. Given the pervasiveness of the ACTU's amalgamation strategy, it is likely that the former figure significantly understates the actual extent of amalgamation (particularly amongst delegates of large unions that have absorbed smaller unions not represented in their own workplaces), and it is better thought of as an indicator of delegate awareness of amalgamation than of the true incidence of amalgamation. Those senior delegates who had also been a member of their union at the workplace before the amalgamation took place (84 per cent of those in amalgamated unions) were asked a series of questions about the impact of amalgamation on a number of aspects of unionism.

The general pattern was that amalgamation was usually perceived to have had no impact on delegates' contact with full-time union officials, the training opportunities provided by their union, delegates' own say in union decisions affecting their workplace, their unions' ability to recruit and retain members at the workplace, the services provided to delegates or members at the workplace, or their unions' ability to assist them in dealing with issues that arise at the workplace. Where delegates did have a view, it tended to be more positive than negative. Hence 12 per cent of delegates thought that amalgamation had made it easier to recruit and retain employees, whereas 6 per cent thought it had made it more difficult. A larger proportion, 20 per cent, thought that as a result of amalgamation the union seemed more able to help them deal with issues, while just 6 per cent thought they were now less able to help delegates deal with issues. Twenty-five per cent thought that training opportunities offered by the union had increased since amalgamation, with just 8 per cent perceiving a decline. On other important issues the margins were much closer: 13 per cent thought that there was more contact with union officials, and 10 per cent less contact; 13 per cent thought that they now had a greater say in union decisions affecting them as a result of amalgamation, while 11 per cent perceived a lesser say.

Still, on that basis we would expect that amalgamations would be associated with small positive effects on union membership. Yet a first inspection of the data suggests that this is not the case. Delegates and managers were asked about their perceptions of changes in union membership in the preceding 12 months. In workplaces where the main union had been through an amalgamation, 24 per cent of delegates claimed that membership of their union had increased in the past year, while 25 per cent claimed it had declined. By contrast, where they believed they had not been through an amalgamation, 27 per cent claimed an increase in membership but just 10 per cent conceded a decline. A similar pattern was evident in managers' perceptions of union membership change: amalgamation had little effect on managers' willingness to claim a membership increase, but they were significantly more likely to say that membership had declined in workplaces where they reported a change in the number of unions due to union amalgamation (24 per cent compared with 13 per cent) or where the senior delegates' union had been through an amalgamation (21 per cent compared with 12 per cent).

There are, however, doubts about the accuracy of data based on perceived changes in union membership. For example, delegates more often say that membership has increased than decreased, but overall union density declined in this period. In addition, changes in membership can reflect not just changes in union density but also changes in the total number of employees in a workplace. For example, when we exclude those delegates who indicated that the change in their union's membership only reflected changes in the size or structure of employment in the workplace, the proportion of 'amalgamated' delegates reporting a decline in union membership falls to 12 per cent (and to 5 per cent among 'non-amalgamated' delegates). And amalgamations may have taken place at any time over the seven years preceding the survey, whereas these data merely purport to represent changes over the preceding year. Accordingly, we turn to the panel data for more reliable information over the longer period that is relevant to amalgamations.

Amalgamations, Changing Union Density and Union Collapse

The panel shows that the rate of union collapse was not significantly different between workplaces where the senior delegates reported their unions had been amalgamated (5 per cent) and those where amalgamations were not reported by the delegates (6 per cent). However, the overall estimated decline in union density across workplaces where the senior delegates' unions had been amalgamated was 11 per cent, compared with just a 4 per cent decline across workplaces where the delegate did not report an amalgamation.

Yet quite a different picture is obtained by looking at data from managers on whether the number of unions had been reduced through amalgamations. Where managers reported a reduction in unions through amalgamation, the rate of union collapse was just 4 per cent, compared to 8 per cent in workplaces elsewhere (a non-significant difference on weighted data, though significant on unweighted data). The average estimated decline in density across workplaces where multi-unionism has been reduced by amalgamation (8 per cent) was virtually identical to the decline elsewhere (9 per cent).

How do we reconcile these different patterns in data from delegates and managers? It appears likely that the issue is not just whether amalgamations lead to more or less efficient unions but also whether amalgamation leads to more or less efficient workplace arrangements. In workplaces where delegates reported that, as a result of amalgamations, some employees who used to belong to different unions had become members of the same union, the rate of union collapse was only 1 per cent. In workplaces where delegates reported amalgamations had taken place, but delegates reported no reductions in the number of unions, the rate of union collapse was 7 per cent. While this difference was not significant (though it is weakly significant in unweighted data), it reveals a pattern that enables us to reconcile the seeming inconsistency between the evidence from the AWIRS95 managers' and delegates' questionnaires.

The implication is that amalgamation is likely to benefit union membership principally where it leads to a reduction in multi-unionism in the workplace. Given the earlier evidence of employees' and managers' preferences for fewer unions in the workplace, this proposition is plausible. It is also possible that amalgamation has been of more benefit to minority unions (where delegates did not participate in AWIRS95) than to the unions that have typically had dominance of workplaces. Employee attitudes also help us understand the effects of amalgamation.

Again, in the AWIRS employee survey (not part of the panel) there was an over-riding tendency for amalgamation not to have much effect one way or the other: there were no differences in the rates of within-workplace union exit amongst employees on any of the measures of amalgamation. And again, in the employee survey, there is dissonance between the apparent effects of the amalgamation of the main delegate's own union, and the effects of amalgamations that reduce the number of unions in the workplace. When senior delegates reported that their own union had been amalgamated, employees in those workplaces had lower union propensity (44 per cent) than in workplaces where the delegate's union had not been amalgamated (50 per cent). However, union propensity was higher in workplaces where the senior delegate's union had been in an amalgamation that reduced the number of unions at the workplace (46 per cent) than where it had not (44 per cent). And in workplaces where managers identified a reduction in multi-unionism from amalgamations, union propensity was significantly higher (48 per cent) than in multi-union workplaces where no reduction in multi-unionism from amalgamation had occurred (42 per cent). The implication is still that amalgamation, if anything, is more likely to be associated with more positive employee attitudes when it leads to reductions in multi-unionism.

When questioned about union performance, the benefits from reduced multi-unionism were less ambiguous. Employees from workplaces where multi-unionism had been reduced were more likely to agree that 'unions here give members a say in how the union operates' (30 per cent versus 26 per cent), 'unions here do a good job representing members when dealing with management' (42 per cent versus 37 per cent) and 'overall, I am satisfied with the service unions here provide to members' (43 per cent versus 39 per cent).

Did the impact of amalgamation on employee attitudes depend on anything more than just the impact it had on the number of unions at the workplace? To answer this, we compared delegates' views on the effects of amalgamations with employees' attitudes to unions. The data suggested that some of amalgamation's effects on employee attitudes were determined by the way it influenced the effectiveness of unions as organisations. The two factors of note here were whether amalgamation led to an increase in union training opportunities, and whether it led to an increase in the contact delegates had with full-time officials. Where training opportunities had increased, employees were more likely to say they were satisfied with union services than when training opportunities had decreased (45 per cent versus 37 per cent), they were more likely to say that unions took notice of members' problems and complaints (50 per cent versus 41 per cent), and they were more likely to say unions were doing a good job of improving pay and conditions (41 per cent versus 36 per cent). When contact with full-time officials had increased, employees were more likely than when it had decreased to say that they were satisfied with union services (43 per cent versus 33 per cent) and slightly more likely to say that unions took notice of members' problems and complaints (46 per cent versus 40 per cent).

In sum, the effects of amalgamation on workplace unionism appear ambiguous and conditional. Overall, it probably has not had a great deal of impact one way or the other. Where amalgamation has led to a reduction in multi-unionism at the workplace – a reduction which is consistent with both managers' search for efficiency and employees' desire for single unionism and union cohesion – amalgamation has probably been of net benefit to unions. Where amalgamations have led to no change in multi-unionism, the effects are less positive. From the limited evidence available, there is little to suggest that smaller unions would be better for union membership. Where amalgamated unions have been able to take advantage of economies of scale, and provide better training and workplace support for and contact with their members and delegates, union membership has held up. But if amalgamation does not lead to the organisational improvements that enable unions to improve their training and support for the workplace, the tendency is probably for more negative effects.

The benefits of amalgamation may be fewer for the larger unions at the workplace (which are not necessarily the larger unions overall), and given earlier data about the weakness of smaller unions, it is possible that the main beneficiaries of amalgamation have been employees in relatively small unions and unions that previously had a relatively minor role at the workplace. However, more data are required before this proposition can be verified.

Conclusion

The workplace-level data presented in this chapter indicate that managerial strategies indeed matter for the future of union membership. The creation of a union presence often arises in response to poor management of workers and poor management of workplace change. Once unions have established themselves, management strategy towards unions has a crucial impact on union membership. Where an organisation undergoes major strategic changes, that might involve new management, new owners, new principal activities or new locations, there may be intended or unintended consequences for union membership – typically adverse, sometimes catastrophic. Clearly management sometimes deliberately seeks to undermine unions and may, for example, involve lawyers in the employment relationship as part of the process of weakening unions. On other occasions unions may suffer collateral damage, being unable to adjust adequately to the strategic changes brought about by management.

Is the implication for unions that they face a bleak future at the workplace, largely beyond their control? There are several reasons why the answer is 'no'. First, unions are not passive actors in this process. Their own strategies on such matters as workplace efficiency and competitiveness also influence management strategy towards unions themselves. At the heart of union success or failure is their strategies towards their members – the extent to which unions have managed to organise themselves at the workplace, the extent to which they are active at the workplace, and the extent to which they engage in bargaining with management and thereby represent the interests of their members. Indeed, it appears that an effective delegate presence increasingly resembles a prerequisite for securing the continuing membership of a union in a workplace. Active, representative unionism may be an inoculation against deunionisation and a strong barrier to union collapse. Unions with members who did not have workplace-based union delegates to represent them, and those that were otherwise inactive at the workplace level, are in a poor position to prevent employee exit (as discussed in chapter two) or to resist management attempts to deunionise. Some aspects of managerial opposition to unions only appeared to facilitate union collapse in workplaces without an active delegate presence. Still, major changes in management industrial relations strategy that might arise from major changes in corporate strategy could have devastating consequences for unions even where unions were active.

Second, while the adoption by management of HRM strategies has often been seen as damaging for unions, and may in the past have created particular problems for them, these strategies appear to be losing their efficacy as union-busting devices. The same market pressures for organisational change that are encouraging management to introduce HRM strategies, in an attempt to ameliorate the impact of change on employees, are also highlighting the need for employees to obtain or retain union membership.

Third, these same pressures for competitiveness in the context of globalisation make unionisation an attractive proposition for some employees in non-union workplaces. Where modern management tools increase pressure on employees, where poorly managed non-union workplaces expose workers to growing occupational hazard under the pressure of competitiveness, where the use of shift-work increases and where worker dissatisfaction with management grows, the potential to unionise non-union workplaces grows.

However, the benefits for unions need to be kept in context. Amongst workplaces in our sample (that is, those with 20 or more employees), the decline in union density (including deunionisation) within previously unionised workplaces contributed 10 percentage points to the decline in union density over the period. The establishment of unions in non-union workplaces produced an offset of less than 1 per cent against this trend.

Another point to bear in mind here is that the 'modern management' tools or fashions, such as just-in-time, total quality management, quality circles and computer-integrated manufacturing, which facilitate the unionisation of non-union workplaces, have little effect on membership in workplaces that are already unionised. This is partly because, to some extent, unions 'share the rap' with management for the good and the bad effects they generate.

What of the workplace implications of the union movement's structural responses to the unfavourable environment for unionism? Willman (1989) referred to a distinction between 'market-share' unionism – competition in areas of existing, often high-density, membership – and 'expansionary' unionism – in which unions seek to attract new members in growing industries with previously low density. This distinction is particularly apposite for Australia, where demarcation and jurisdictional disputes between unions have been perceived to be common and costly (K. Wright 1983). The way that union structure has evolved under the arbitration system (and from its earlier occupation-based heritage) can be seen as having promoted market-share unionism at the expense of resources that could have been devoted to expansionary unionism. If unions pursue market-share unionism then they would not be able to offset the effect of structural shifts in the economy as they will not be able to make sufficient inroads into new areas of rapid employment growth.

The union movement is seeking to reorganise and restructure itself through a program of amalgamations. In some respects, this strategy seems consistent with the preferences of employees: dissatisfaction with multi-unionism at workplace level led to lower general union propensity; smaller unions also appeared to possess lower union responsiveness and induce greater apathy. The trend towards amalgamation should also serve to reduce employer resistance to unions where multiple unionism causes problems.

But does this mean that union amalgamation will promote union-isation? There is little evidence to support the proposition that, within the Australian framework, a policy of promoting small unions would be an effective way of dealing with union decline. And it may be that, through the union amalgamation strategy, larger unions will be better resourced and in a better position to support and represent their members. But the answers to several other questions will determine the overall impact of amalgamations:

- Have amalgamations significantly reduced the number of unions operating in each workplace? The evidence provided in this chapter suggests that this is a critical issue, and that, so far, progress in this area has not been as great as may have been hoped for by employers (and employees).
- Have amalgamations significantly reduced the resources devoted to market-share unionism, freeing them up for expansionary unionism? In other words, are amalgamations promoting union cohesion or union in-fighting? Anecdotal evidence (there is no systematic evidence) suggests that several unions that have been formed through amalgamations have undergone major internal faction fights, to the detriment of officials' ability to service their members.
- Have amalgamations enabled unions to take advantage of the economies of scale that should be created to substantially improve the training opportunities available to members and delegates, and is contact between the union organisation and delegates being strengthened or weakened? The evidence so far is that gains in some areas have been made but they have been patchy.
- Are amalgamations reducing or increasing the complexity of union coverage and therefore the difficulty that unions have in identifying their members' interests? The overall pattern of amalgamations in Australia to date has presumably been to add to this complexity by increasing the number of industries that most unions cover. What may be important is what amalgamations have *not* done to reduce the

complexity of occupational and multifaceted coverage and the associated focus on demarcation, territorialism and incumbency.
• Will new union structures be adapted to the objectives and strategies of unions, or will they merely reproduce the old structures? The adaptation of union structures to the decentralisation of wage fixing was an issue that many New Zealand unions faced with great difficulty in the early 1990s (Peetz et al. 1993). As Griffin and de Rozairo (1993) foreshadowed, the growth of single-employer bargaining is more demanding and expensive for Australian unions than more centralised use of the arbitration system, leading to a likely deterioration of union finances in the 1990s when combined with declining union membership. Notwithstanding the ACTU's capacity to coordinate union strategies, there are, as Pocock (1997) points out, serious doubts about the receptiveness of union structures to pressures for change and about their adaptability in the face of new constituencies with new ideas and interests and new methods of working.

We do not have complete answers to all of these questions; some are beyond the scope of this book, and are raised, not with the hope of answering them, but to make the point that it is still too early to draw firm conclusions about the relationship between trends in union structure and union membership. What can be said is that single unionism and union cohesion promote unionisation; that multiple unionism, union in-fighting and (possibly) the proliferation of small unions, other things being equal, retard it; and that so far the expectations of neither the strongest advocates nor the severest critics of the strategy of amalgamation have been met. In the meantime, however, amalgamations have taken up considerable resources of unions. The opportunity cost of those resources, and the opportunity that might have been lost in some unions for more fundamental restructurings, would have to be considered in any assessment of the overall impact of amalgamations.

Whatever the impact of amalgamation, it is clear that, at the moment, it is not the main game determining the welfare of unions at the workplace. Managerial and union strategies at the workplace level, in dealing with each other and with employees, have been the principal determinants of union rise and fall in the workplace.

CHAPTER 7

The Accord and the Post-Accord Industrial Relations Order

The Accord played the central role in union policy in the 1980s and 1990s. Consequently it has played a central role in popular explanations of union decline in that period. This chapter critically examines the impact of the Accord on union membership and the further changes that might be expected in the light of the Liberal–National Party Government's enactment of the *Workplace Relations Act 1996*. It identifies the propositions underpinning the argument that the Accord was a significant cause in the decline in union membership, considers ways of testing these propositions, and discusses the relationship between the Workplace Relations Act and union membership.

The Two Halves of the Accord and Their Impact on Union Membership

There are several ways in which the possible impact of the Accord could be tested. In order to do this, we first need to identify the plausible mechanisms by which the Accord could affect union membership. There are in effect three main mechanisms by which the Accord could influence the decline in union membership.

The first is a potential 'real wage' effect. The decline in real wages associated with the Accord could have led to employee dissatisfaction with unions and declining union propensity. Members may then have left unions since they no longer saw unions doing what they were meant to be doing – raising real wages.

The second possible mechanism is an 'alienation effect', and it concerns the processes more than the outcomes of the Accord. The centralisation of decision making within the union movement may have alienated rank and file union members who no longer had an input at

145

the workplace level into the decision making processes that affected them. They may have seen that they did not need to make a contribution to or struggle for gains in wages and conditions, and therefore they no longer needed to belong to a union to gain the benefits of union membership. Like the 'real wage' effect, the 'alienation effect' operates through influencing union propensity.

The third possible mechanism is an 'institutional effect', and concerns the impact of the Accord on union reach rather than union propensity. The Accord could have influenced the political and legal environment or the attitudes of employers to unions at the workplace, thereby increasing or reducing the difficulty of union organising and the incentives for employer resistance.

The first two mechanisms imply that some periods of the Accord would be more clearly associated with 'explanations' of union decline than other parts. So, for the purposes of testing the propensity-related mechanisms, it is necessary to divide the Accord into two periods. The first period, which coincided with Accords I to V, covers the time from 1983 to 1990. The second period, which coincided with Accords VI and VII, covers the rest of the time to 1996. Within the 13-year history of the Accord, the first period lasted for something over seven years and the second period for something under six, and it is therefore convenient, albeit not literally accurate, to refer to them as the first and second 'halves' of the Accord respectively.

The first half was the period of varying degrees of centralisation in wage fixation, which coincided with a gradual decline in real wages (figure 7.1).[1] The second half of the Accord was the period of enterprise bargaining, commencing in 1990 with Accord VI and with a key stage being its implementation through the October 1991 Australian Industrial Relations Commission decision to introduce the enterprise bargaining principle (Hancock & Rawson 1993). This was the period when decisions about wage increases were substantially being made by individual unions and on an enterprise-by-enterprise basis, involving union members directly and reversing whatever alienation they had previously felt from centralised wage determination. And, as can again be seen from figure 7.1, it was a period when real wages increased.

The first half of the Accord is far more relevant than is the second half to both the real wage and alienation mechanisms linking the Accord and union membership. These two mechanisms can be tested as we would expect several consequences to follow from them. If either mechanism held we would expect: that the decline in union membership should be greater under the first half of the Accord than under the second half of the Accord; and that it would not be possible to explain the decline in union membership without reference to the Accord. If

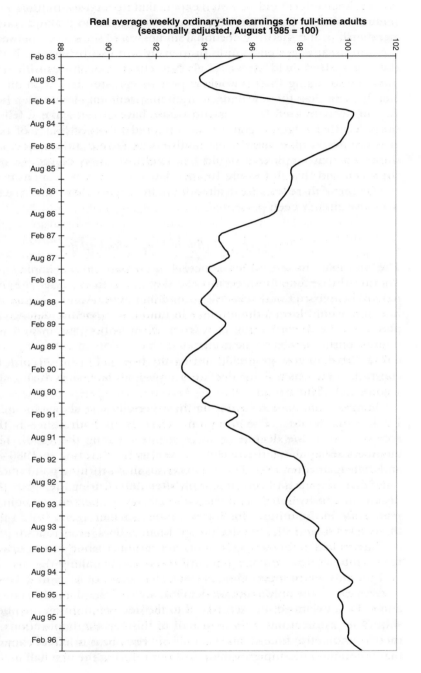

Figure 7.1 Real earnings during the Accord

the real wage effect held we would expect that time-series studies would generally show a positive relationship between real wages and union membership; and that cross-sectional studies would show a link between declining real wages and union propensity and exit behaviour. If the alienation effect held we would also expect that countries with centralised wage-fixing systems would experience greater decline in union membership than those with decentralised system; that union membership in decentralised New Zealand would have grown while it fell in Australia; that wage bargaining (as opposed to other forms of bargaining) would have made a substantive difference to union membership; and that employees would have negative views of the Accord approach and that this would be correlated with union propensity or exit. Three of these tests are dealt with briefly because they concern data that have already been presented.

The Timing of the Decline in Union Membership

The first issue to test, which concerns both possible mechanisms, is whether the decline in union membership was greater under the first half of the Accord than under the second half of the Accord. Figure 1.1 in chapter one showed the changes in union membership during the period of the Accord using data from the members survey and the union census. It clearly demonstrated that union membership was either stable, or rose gradually, during the first half of the Accord. By contrast, there was a sharp decline in union membership during the second half of the Accord.

Changes in union density during these periods were shown in figure 1.2 in chapter one. The common theme from both series is the acceleration of the decline in union density during the 1990s. The members series shows the decline in density accelerating in 1986–88 and then again after 1992. The union census shows turning points more clearly: density starts to decline sharply after 1991. During the 1980s, the decline in density in the members series averaged 1 percentage point a year, while in the union census it was much smaller again. But in the three years since 1992, the decline in the members series totals 6 percentage points (2 percentage points per annum) while in the union census it totals 9 percentage points (three points per annum).

One study worth mentioning at this point is that of Kenyon & Lewis (1992, 1996) – the only major academic analysis of the alienation effect, and one that claimed the Accord led to the decline in union membership. The problem was, they appeared to misread the implications of their econometric time-series study. Their equations in effect showed that union membership growth was no lower during the first half of the

Accord than would have been expected, based on modelling of trends during the preceding 33 years, except by comparison with the unusual period of the 1972–75 Whitlam Government, during which a number of exceptional policy changes were implemented. Their 1996 study reveals a very sharp decline in union membership growth in the second half of the Accord, also contrary to the hypothesised alienation effect. A more detailed critique of the methodology used by Kenyon and Lewis can be found in Peetz (1997b).

The failure of union membership to decline by more in the first half of the Accord, associated with centralised wage fixing and real wage declines, casts considerable prima facie doubt on both the 'real wage' and 'alienation' mechanisms. This is not to deny that workplace union organisation tended to atrophy during the centralised period of the Accord. The point is that this atrophying had been going on for the best part of the century as a result of the way in which the award system directed union attention to a different focus. Workplace wage bargaining may have been retarded under the Accord, but unions that were capable of bargaining over wages bargained over other matters and, as we shall see later, it is bargaining *per se* that matters most. If centralisation was the key issue, then we would expect this to be reflected in other evidence.

International Trends

A second test of the effect of the Accord on union membership, which concerns the alienation theory, is to ask whether countries with centralised wage bargaining and centralised union organisation experienced greater decline in union membership than countries with decentralised bargaining and wage determination. The rationale for this test is that, if the 'alienation effect' applies in Australia, it should apply in other countries also. If it does not apply cross-nationally, then there must be something else happening to explain trends in Australia.

The literature on this subject has been discussed in chapter one. It showed that, if anything, centralisation should have enhanced rather than eroded union membership. The trend throughout the studies examined was that centralisation in union movements or wage fixation or 'corporatism' in one form or another is typically associated with higher union density and lower declines in union density than is decentralisation.

Alternative Explanations

If union density fell as a result of effects of the Accord on union propensity, then there would be a substantial component of the decline in union membership that could not be otherwise explained. However, the evidence presented in previous chapters, particularly chapters four and five, shows that alternative explanations can be found to explain the decline in union membership. For example, depending on the assumptions made about the retention rate, over the period 1976–90 the fall in compulsory unionism could have explained approximately 0.6 percentage points per annum of the fall in union density. Over the period 1990–95, the decline in union density attributable to the loss of compulsory unionism and State Government legislation appears to be at least 1.1 percentage points per annum over each of the five years – out of a total fall in union density of just 1.4 points per annum. The increase in casual employment would have led to a drop in union density at a rate of 0.3 percentage points per annum, averaged over this five-year period – mostly in addition to the decline arising from the withdrawal of compulsory unionism. (There is some overlap as the probability of being in a compulsorily unionised job is lower for casual employees (7 per cent in LCS) than for permanent employees (12 per cent)). The shift from public- to private-sector employment would be associated with an annual drop in union density of 0.2 percentage points per annum over each of the last five years, which is entirely in addition to the effect arising from the decline in compulsory unionism, as compulsory unionism is less common in the public sector than in the private sector. The institutional break in union membership, associated with the collapse of compulsory unionism and the attempted decollectivisation of employment relations by employers and governments, in combination with structural change in the labour market, provides ample quantitative explanation of the decline in union density and membership. It is therefore not necessary to resort to the Accord to explain the decline in union membership.

Accord Processes, Values and Outcomes

One proposition that might underpin the alienation mechanism is that the fundamental notions underlying the Accord, requiring cooperation with the Labor Government and the acceptance of certain restraints in wage bargaining in return for the achievement of wider economic or social gains, are inconsistent with employee preferences: the 'support given to the Accord by union leadership has no doubt been perceived as actually being against the interests of insiders', that is, of union members (Kenyon & Lewis 1992:341). It is possible to test whether employee preferences were at odds with the Accord and whether this dissatisfaction led to falling union propensity or union exit.

Respondents to SEMSE were asked a number of questions relating directly or indirectly to the Accord. The responses demonstrate little evidence of employees seeking to break away from corporatist accommodation under the Accord. Of those respondents who had heard of the Accord, 89 per cent thought that the Accord was a good idea; just 10 per cent thought that it was a bad idea that should be abandoned (1 per cent offered no opinion). Another survey in 1985 had found that 82 per cent of union members who had heard of the Accord thought that it was a 'good idea'; a further 10 per cent considered that it 'might be a good idea but they need to start all over again', while only 5 per cent considered it was a 'bad idea which should be abandoned'.[2] In SEMSE, there was no significant relationship between union propensity and attitudes towards the Accord; less than one in seven respondents said they would prefer that unions cooperated less closely with the (Labor) Government; just one in seven wanted AIRC guidelines to be less influential in setting wages; and three-fifths agreed that if it were not for the arbitration system, people in weak unions would fall behind and people in strong unions would get bigger wage increases. Union propensity, density, joining and exit did not significantly vary between occupational groups according to the influence that wage guidelines had (according to managers) on their wages.

This did not mean that employees were generally happy with the Accord outcomes. While 55 per cent of unionists could be classed as saying that they thought that the Accord was working well, this consisted of just 9 per cent who thought that it was a good idea that was working *very* well and 47 per cent who thought that it was working *somewhat* well. A further 34 per cent considered that it was a good idea but that it was *not* working well. However, amongst people who thought that the Accord was a good idea, there was no significant relationship between their views on how well the Accord was working and their union propensity, membership, exit or joining.

It appeared, then, that the fundamental notions underlying the Accord were consistent with employee preferences and did not lead to any decline in union membership.

Wages and the Accord

It is possible to test the real wage mechanism by investigating whether union membership unambiguously declines when real wages fall, through an examination of both the existing literature and survey data from SEMSE on the link between wages and union membership.

The impact of real wages on union membership or density has usually been examined in the context of business-cycle studies modelling the impact of macroeconomic variables through time-series econometric analysis. However, one of the main features of these studies is that there is no consensus at all on the impact of real wages upon unionisation. Bain and Elsheikh (1976) argued that unions are 'credited' with achieving real wage increases when they occur and hence real wage growth encourages demand for unionism. Carruth and Disney (1988), however, found that real wage growth was strongly and *negatively* related to union density in Britain, and some micro-level studies have found a negative relationship between wages and union support (Hills 1985) or union satisfaction (Leicht 1989). The Australian business-cycle evidence is also contradictory: Sharpe (1971) and Borland and Ouliaris (1989) found a negative relationship between real wages and union membership, while Kenyon and Lewis (1992) and Bodman (1996) found a positive relationship.

If there is any impact (in either direction) on union membership arising from the impact of the Accord on real wages, account also needs to be taken of the effect that wage restraint under the Accord had in enhancing employment growth (Russell & Tease 1988; Lewis & Kirby 1987; Flatau et al. 1991; Chapman et al. 1991; Chapman & Gruen 1990) which would, if anything, promote the growth of union membership (Bain & Elsheikh 1976; Carruth & Disney 1988; Booth 1983; Sharpe 1971; Borland & Ouliaris 1989; Western 1993a).

If the time-series studies do not consistently indicate that declining real wages lead to declining union membership, what can we tell from micro-level evidence in Australia? SEMSE data show that, in terms of whether or not they felt that they had benefited from union membership (that is, 'union instrumentality'), there were no significant differences between those workers who believed that the value of their real pay packets had gone down, and those whose real pay had appeared stable. This was partly because the blame for real wage cuts fell even more heavily on the employer than on their union (the impact that declining pay packets had on satisfaction with management was twice as strong as the impact on satisfaction with union leaders and officials). And it was partly because those employees who had perceived falling real pay happened to be more likely to be covered by 'stronger' unions, as perceived by the employees. (Where unions were weak or absent, management had greater control over those workers' pay and, at the time, was exercising its discretion to pay these workers the 'market' wage, whereas workers in 'strong' unions were more heavily constrained by the prevailing wage guidelines.) Presumably the strength of these unions would have been demonstrated by union-achieved gains in areas other than pay – indeed, there would be something strange about a union that was well organised but which dealt only with pay issues at the workplace level. For those employees, the perceptions of real wage falls were not serious enough to offset the other gains achieved by the unions.

More importantly, the impact of declining pay upon the rate of 'union exit' was dependent upon whether unions were seen to be providing benefit to their members or being responsive to them (table 7.1). If union instrumentality or union responsiveness were high, the union exit rate did not vary substantially in response to perceived changes in pay. But the combination of declining pay with low union instrumentality or responsiveness was severe in its impact upon unions. Hence, amongst employees who felt that the value of their pay packet had fallen, the rate of union exit was only 2 per cent where they were satisfied with how unions kept in contact with their members, but 17 per cent where they were dissatisfied. If unions were, in the minds of employees, performing their other jobs properly – if they were continuing to keep in contact with their members and ensuring their members receive a fair go – then changes in real pay had no impact upon union membership. But if unions were allowing their members' pay to fall *and* were not offering them proper protection or other benefits and remained remote from them, then many members decided that they had had enough, especially if management appeared to be doing a reasonable job otherwise.

Table 7.1 Same-workplace union exit rates by change in pay and union instrumentality and responsiveness

| | Same-workplace exit rate when: | | |
	Pay packet has risen or stayed about the same (%)	Pay packet has fallen (%)	N
Union instrumentality			
– benefited from union membership	4	3	142
– made no difference or worse off	5	22	162
Union responsiveness			
– satisfied with how unions keep in contact	0	2	96
– neutral/dissatisfied with how unions keep in contact	5	17	184

Source: SEMSE
Population: Employees in open jobs
The same-workplace exit rate is the number of employees who have left a union at their current workplace, divided by the total from adding this group to the number of current members at the workplace.

On average, union exit rates were higher amongst employees who were dissatisfied with what unions at their workplace were doing about wages – but again, if employees rated their union above-median on the protection scale, or were satisfied with the way the union kept in contact, dissatisfaction had no impact on union membership.

In sum, the link between real wages and union membership under the Accord is more complicated than would first appear. There is not consistent evidence of an aggregate relationship over time between real wages and union membership. Nor is there much reason to believe that any negative effects, if they existed, for union membership from real wage declines would offset the beneficial effects for membership of job creation during wage restraint. At the micro level, the evidence suggests that the impact of declining real wages on union membership will depend on whether unions are performing their other traditional functions of providing protection, securing non-wage gains for workers and, critically, keeping in touch with their members. It is where unions are already weakly organised, inactive or invisible at the workplace that real wage falls can lead to membership losses.

Workplace Wage Bargaining and Union Membership

Another test of the 'alienation' effect is to examine whether unions at workplaces that engage in wage bargaining fared better in terms of union propensity, exit or collapse than those that only engaged in bargaining over other (non-wage) issues and those that do not engage in workplace bargaining. As discussed in chapter six, amongst workplaces that were classified at the time of AWIRS90 as having engaged in workplace bargaining, the rate of deunionisation over the six years to 1995–96 was less than 1 per cent. But amongst those that had not engaged in workplace bargaining, deunionisation stood at 11 per cent.

In examining the relationship between the Accord and union membership, the most important question is whether bargaining over wages has taken place at workplace level. Consequently, in this discussion bargainers are divided into 'wage bargainers' – those bargainers in which negotiations over wage increases had taken place – and 'other bargainers' – in which negotiations over other issues,[3] but not wage increases, had taken place. Amongst SEMSE employees, 29 per cent worked in organisations that were classified as wage bargainers, 35 per cent worked in other bargainers, and 36 per cent worked in non-bargainers.

Notably, deunionisation was not influenced by the subject matter of bargaining. The rates of deunionisation amongst non-wage bargainers and wage bargainers were identical (less than 1 per cent).

Likewise, there was no significant difference between the rate of union collapse amongst wage bargainers (9 per cent) and other bargainers (6 per cent).

In SEMSE, union propensity was stronger amongst employees in bargainers (44 per cent) than in non-bargainers (35 per cent). So too was union instrumentality: employees in bargainers were notably more likely to say that they had benefited from belonging to a union (51 per cent) than non-bargainers (38 per cent). However, they also showed slightly more pro-union sympathy, so some of the differences between bargainers and non-bargainers probably reflect differences between the orientations of the workers.

Whether bargaining over wages took place at workplace level was not particularly important in explaining union propensity and attitudes. There were no significant differences in the union propensity of employees in wage bargainers and those in other bargainers. There were also no significant differences in union density of wage bargainers and other bargainers for employees in open jobs in SEMSE or for workplaces in AWIRS90. Employees in wage bargainers were much more satisfied with their delegates than were employees in other bargainers. But there were no differences between wage bargainers and other bargainers in terms of employees' perceptions of union voice, union responsiveness, union instrumentality, employees' willingness to rely upon unions, their perceptions of changes in the purchasing power of their pay packets, or their satisfaction with what unions have done about wages. Union joining, exit and density were not affected by the subject matter of bargaining.

In the Workplace Bargaining Survey 1992 (WBS92) respondents were asked about the way in which most employees received wage increases at their workplace. Amongst workplaces where wage increases were obtained 'mainly through increases to award rates only', which would generally be through procedures external to the workplace, the rate of deunionisation (over the three years to 1992–93) was only 3 per cent. But in workplaces where wage increases were determined through internal procedures – adjustments for inflation matching the market rate for particular occupations, productivity increases or, most commonly, performance appraisal or annual review – the rate of deunionisation was as high as 11 per cent. Many of these forms of workplace-based wage determination may be solely the prerogative of management, or the subject of individual 'bargaining' between management and the employee.

The problem for unions then occurs not so much if wage determination is centralised beyond the workplace. It occurs if management is determining wages at the workplace directly with employees, and unions are not involved. In workplaces where negotiations with unions had taken place within the previous year and wage increases were (according to AWIRS90 data) normally negotiated with unions, the rate of deunionisation (to 1992–93) was 1 per cent. Where wage increases were not normally negotiated with unions, deunionisation was 6 per cent. Where wage increases were determined internally at the workplace rather than externally, but they were not normally negotiated with unions, the rate of deunionisation (to 1992–93) was 12 per cent. There is also anecdotal evidence from unions that the active involvement of unions in single-employer bargaining has enabled some unions to significantly increase their membership base (Adams 1994).

In sum, management incorporation of employees through workplace agreements could lead to reduced unionisation if unions failed to perform active bargaining functions. Workplace-based wage determination had the potential to severely undermine union membership unless unions became directly involved in wage bargaining. The impact of workplace-based wage determination on union membership depended on whether, and in what way, unions became directly involved in wage bargaining. The existence of bargaining over any subjects appeared to be positively associated with general union propensity and instrumentality, although not with open density. However, there were no significant differences between workplaces that engage in wage bargaining and those that engage in bargaining over other (non-wage) issues, in terms of union instrumentality, propensity or in rates of deunionisation. If bargaining assisted unionism, then, it was not the subject matter of bargaining that was critically important in determining the effect on unionism. The caveat to this comment is that, if management deals directly with employees over wages, then unions run a risk of losing membership if they do not become involved in workplace wage negotiations.

Hence, the centralisation of wage determination away from the workplace under the first half of the Accord probably had little or no effect on union membership in workplaces where bargaining was able to take place on other matters. However, had the ACTU and the ALP Government not responded to the growing employer pressures for single-employer bargaining over wages, chances are that many employers would have shifted the focus of wage bargaining to the enterprise or workplace level anyway, often without union involvement. Had this happened, it would probably have been the worst of possible outcomes for unions.

The New Zealand Experience and the Accord

Another test of the 'alienation effect' is to consider whether the growth in Australian union membership during the period to 1991 was significantly lower than the growth that occurred in New Zealand under a Labor government during the same period. This comparison can also illuminate the third possible mechanism – the 'institutional' effect – mentioned early in this chapter.

The aim of this approach is to make use of the possibility of comparing Australia with a country with similar political and industrial history and institutions, but which chose a non-Accord path, and to see whether the decline in Australian union membership is substantially greater in Australia than in the comparison country. There is only one country with which such a close-pair comparison can validly be made: New Zealand. For most of the post-war period, New Zealand and Australia experienced comparable political and industrial histories. Both had long periods of conservative rule from 1949 (in New Zealand's case, interrupted for three years by Labour in the late 1950s); both had labour governments elected in 1972, defeated in 1975 and re-elected in 1983 (Australia) or 1984 (New Zealand). Both had moderately strong levels of unionisation. Both countries had award-based systems of industrial regulation and arbitration tribunals. Both systems enabled compulsory unionism. The main point of departure occurred in the early 1980s.

In 1983 the Australian labour movement signalled its intention to adopt a corporatist strategy to policy making, through the agreement between the Parliamentary Australian Labor Party (ALP) and the ACTU in February 1983 to the prices and incomes Accord. At the federal election the following month the ALP won office (Carney 1988). It subsequently retained office in elections in 1984, 1987, 1990 and 1993. Throughout this period the Accord was the central feature of wages and industrial relations policy, and an important element in economic and social policy. From 1983 until 1986 wages were directly linked to prices through a form of wage indexation determined in a series of national wage cases. From 1987 onwards a series of developments in wage fixation, occurring within the framework of the Accord and under the titles 'second tier', 'award restructuring' and 'enterprise bargaining principle',[4] led to a gradual decentralisation of wage fixing, although the parameters under which bargaining occurred remained set by agreements under the Accord.

In New Zealand, a very different path was taken (Bray & Walsh 1994). Nothing comparable to the Accord was negotiated before the New Zealand Labour Party came into office in 1984, or during its term in office. Wage bargaining was formally decentralised, though characterised by a form of 'pattern bargaining' (whereby wage increases in leading firms or industries are replicated in other firms or industries). The Labour Party was re-elected in 1987 but defeated in a 'landslide' in

the 1990 election. The incoming National Party Government introduced the *Employment Contracts Act 1991* which abolished the award
system and replaced it with an industrial relations system based on the
law of contract. Individual employers and employees could seek to
negotiate individual or collective contracts, either directly with each
other or through the appointment of a bargaining agent. Employers
and employees were able to appoint any individual or organisation to
negotiate a contract on their behalf. Unions had any special or exclusive
representation rights removed. Union membership was made com-
pletely voluntary and union compulsion or preference outlawed. The
automatic right of union access to workplaces was removed, except
where the union was already the authorised bargaining agent of
employees.

Comparing Australia and New Zealand serves two purposes. The first
is that a comparison between Australia and New Zealand up until 1991
enables a direct comparison between the operation of the Accord and
the experiences of a Government and union movement that pursued
decentralisation in wage fixing under an award system without providing a strategic framework for institutional reform or the encouragement of workplace-level reform. It is analogous to what might have
happened in Australia had a Labor Government not followed an
Accord strategy. The second purpose is that the experience in New
Zealand under a National Party Government that abolished the award
system and pursued radical decentralisation, including through abolition of the institutional framework and construction of a new one, is
analogous to what might have happened in Australia had a Labor
Government subsequently been defeated and replaced by a conservative
Government, particularly one elected after 1990. It also serves as a
starting point for analysis of what would be expected to happen to the
Australian union movement under a Liberal–National Party Coalition
Government.

Figure 7.2 compares changes in union membership in Australia and
New Zealand, with the key period being from 1983 to 1991. For almost
all of this time there were labour governments in both countries but
Australia had an Accord while New Zealand did not. The data are
expressed as an index and use, as much as possible, similar data sources
in the two countries. Prior to 1987, most public-sector unions in New
Zealand were not included in the official statistics because they were not
registered under the Industrial Relations Act. From 1991, with the
implementation of the Employment Contracts Act, official statistics on
union membership were no longer even collected. However, a team at
the Victoria University of Wellington, led by Raymond Harbridge, has
collected union membership data since then. The index joins the

private and total membership series in 1985. As the New Zealand data are from censuses of unions, the Australian data are taken from the directly comparable union census.

The graph clearly shows that, during the critical first half of the Accord, union membership was stable in Australia but actually fell in New Zealand. Between 1983 and 1991, the number of members fell by a total of 17 per cent in Accord-free New Zealand, while rising by 13 per cent in Australia.

What does the comparison of the two countries tell us about the 'institutional effect' of the Accord? The events leading up to the sharp divergence in trends in union membership that occurred after 1991 can be seen as critical junctures in the two countries, that is, watersheds in political and industrial life that opened up certain directions of change and foreclosed others in ways that are likely to shape politics and unionism for years to come. The term 'critical junctures' has been taken from Collier and Collier's (1991) framework for critical junctures and historical legacies. A number of historical analysts have focused upon critical junctures under one name or another as a means of explaining subsequent developments. For example, Collier and Collier draw their terminology from the work of Lipset and Rokkan (1967) and others whose work points to the importance of particular crises or 'cleavages' within the labour movement, or between labour, capital and/or the state, as having a profound effect in shaping subsequent developments

Figure 7.2 Union membership, Australia and New Zealand, 1980–96

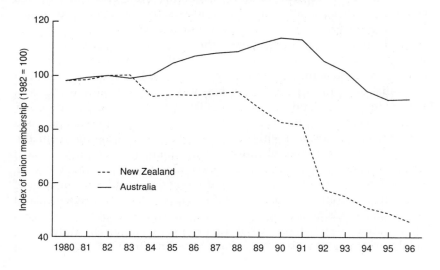

in national and industrial politics (see also Frenkel 1993). Price and Bain's (1989) idea of paradigm shifts applies this tradition to unionisation: the changes in union fortunes in the US and UK are attributable to paradigm shifts which have fundamentally altered the determination of union membership. The changes in the determination of union density in New Zealand after 1991 clearly also represented a paradigm shift or institutional break, perhaps an even sharper one than those observed in the US and UK, and certainly more dramatic than occurred in Australia over the course of a decade or more.

There were several key moments of critical juncture for labour in Australia and New Zealand in the post-1974 period. But probably the most crucial point of departure between labour strategy in the two countries was the decision by Australian labour over the period 1979–83 to adopt the Accord and the choice of New Zealand labour to eschew such a strategy. What followed after this critical juncture was ultimately a result of the choices made. In Australia, the choice made was to pursue an essentially corporatist approach to policy making, which moderated heavily pro-market sentiments in microeconomic policy. In New Zealand, the choice made was to pursue an ostensibly market-based approach to industrial relations and, indeed, to virtually all economic areas. The strategic decisions to adopt or reject corporatist policies in the labour parties and union movements can be understood in terms of the differences in the constitutional frameworks in the two countries, the roles of tribunals, the economic and political developments of the early 1970s, and the leadership of the two countries.

The period from 1985 to 1989 can be seen as a second key moment in the period of critical juncture, occurring after crises of external economic imbalance affected both countries, but particularly Australia. It was one in which the Australian union movement made efforts to adapt its structures and strategies to the economic circumstances of the time, while adaptation within the New Zealand union movement was much slower. Structural reform proceeded on the basis of consensus in Australia. Reform of product markets was more radical and less consensual in New Zealand, but reform of labour markets was hampered by the absence of an effective institutional framework for change. As a consequence of reform within unions and of the impetus from the Government and powerful industrial tribunals, the Australian award system was gradually restructured to more closely approximate the wage and benefit systems that management seemed to require in the face of changing economic circumstances. Over this period, the New Zealand award system was becoming increasingly obsolete except in those areas where unions were persuaded of the need for change. The differences in labour strategies across the Tasman arose in part from differences in institutional processes but also from differences in the ideology and vision of the leadership of the two labour movements.

In both Australia and New Zealand there were substantial moves to decentralisation from 1990, but they were more radical and, as we have seen, devastating for the union movement in New Zealand. Indeed, the third key moment of critical juncture occurred in the early 1990s, when both countries experienced a move to greater use of single-employer bargaining. In both, there were market pressures and pressures from employers for wage fixing to take this direction. In both countries, most parties agreed on the need for some form of decentralisation in wage bargaining. The differences in parties' motivations and organisation reveal much about the reasons for success or failure in their strategies.

In Australia, the strategic decisions to make the move were taken by labour in the context of the Accord, while legislative and institutional change provided the means of production of the outcome. The sixth and seventh phases (or 'marks') of the Accord were negotiated, providing for increased encouragement of or reliance upon single-employer bargaining. In New Zealand, the key strategic decisions were now out of the hands of labour. Instead the forces of capital held sway and the newly elected National Party Government recast the industrial relations environment with the Employment Contracts Act.

The main effect of the Accord that is of relevance here was probably to ease the rapidity of the institutional break in the determination of union membership and to change (at least temporarily, perhaps with lasting effect) some of detailed institutionalised arrangements eventually put in place.

The Accord as a political and economic strategy helped the Australian Labor Government stay in office for several more terms than its New Zealand counterpart (Australian Labor won five elections from 1983; New Zealand, two). This was for several reasons: Labor's 'cooperative' industrial relations strategy was consistently (for five elections) preferred by voters over the Coalition's (Age Poll 1988; Newspoll 1989, 1991, 1992; Goot 1990; Jones et al. 1993; Savery & Soutar 1993); the Accord helped create employment and inflation outcomes that voters preferred (the New Zealand labour market stagnated); the Accord created schisms in employer ranks between those generally supportive of this approach and those fundamentally opposed (New Zealand employers were united in opposition to Labour) (Frenkel 1988); it ensured close political cooperation between the unions and the ALP, preventing the ALP being 'run over by a bus strike', as the South Australian Labor Government was in 1979 (Badcock 1982), or by a dispute in the oil industry in the lead up to the 1983 election (Kelly 1985:398); and it placed boundaries around the behaviour of the

Federal Labor Government that prevented it, for example, from introducing the Goods and Services Tax (GST) that was enacted by its New Zealand counterpart.

This last point is particularly relevant. Perhaps the most significant question about the Accord is not whether its impact on wage determination processes led to any decline in union membership (as discussed, the evidence is against this proposition) but whether it enabled the union movement to be 'bought off' into accepting a program of radical structural change in the economy that was against unions' interests. Both before and particularly after the terms of trade crisis of 1985 and 1986, there were major policy-induced structural changes to the economy, promoted under the banner of 'microeconomic reform', starting with the floating of the dollar and the deregulation of much of the financial system, subsequently encompassing telecommunications, rail, sea and air transport, electricity generation and supply, tariff policy, government business enterprises, privatisation, education, competition policy and numerous other issues. In each case microeconomic reforms have been aimed at increasing the influence of market forces on the allocation of resources. In many cases the reforms have been to the detriment of the employment of union members. In many cases the reforms have weakened the bargaining power of unions in the industries concerned. And in many cases, the benefits of microeconomic reform had been greatly exaggerated by comparison with the benefits achieved (Quiggin 1996).

This line of argument, in effect that the Accord was a betrayal of unions' interests, has been advanced by a number of people – in the case of industry policy by Ewer et al. (1992). It is an argument that has been given impetus by a self-congratulatory speech by former Treasurer John Dawkins to the BCA in which he claimed that the Labor Government had used the ACTU and the business community to help implement its reform policies (Dawkins 1994). The limits to this analysis are: first, that it ignores those benefits that accrued to union members through the Accord, for example in the form of increased employment (discussed earlier), and improvements in the 'social wage' (Saunders & Whiteford 1987; Bradbury et al. 1990; Harding & Landt 1992; Harding & Mitchell 1992); second, it ignores the broader economic forces that led to many of the policy changes; third, that it assumes these changes would not have occurred in the absence of a Labor government; and fourth, it assumes that a Labor Government without the Accord would have been more responsive to the true interests of unions than a Labor Government with an Accord. The third assumption has been shown to be incorrect by the behaviour of the Liberal–National Party Coalition both in opposition and in government. A quick comparison with New

Zealand shows the fourth of these assumptions to be false: if there was only one country that had a more rapid and severe program of micro-economic reform than Australia, then that country would surely be Labour-governed New Zealand during the period 1984–91. The absence of an Accord in New Zealand meant that the Labour Government there paid virtually no heed to the expressed concerns of the union move-ment in devising and implementing its program of microeconomic reform. And if Treasurer Dawkins was so pro-business in his approach to economic policy, would he have been any less so in the absence of the Accord?

The GST was the most notable example of how the ACTU, through the formal or informal mechanisms of the Accord, prevented or (more commonly) ameliorated policies that would otherwise have been introduced by the Federal Labor Government, ranging from such things as the reversal of a decision to introduce a patient 'co-payment' for medical services to the implementation of labour adjustment assistance to enable the retraining and redeployment of workers displaced by microeconomic reform on the railways. Whether the ACTU could have used its influence under the Accord more effectively, especially in relation to industry policy, is a moot point – certainly arguable, but beyond the scope of this book. The key point here is that the Accord made public policy more, not less, sympathetic to working class and union interests than would otherwise have been the case.

In turn, with the assistance given by the Accord in enabling its re-election four times, the Federal Labor Government (in contrast to the stated policies of the Coalition parties) did not introduce policies sought by employers aimed at either decollectivising employment relations, promoting individual contracts or abolishing compulsory unionism. Indeed, when CRA sought to deunionise its workforce through the medium of individual contracts, the Federal Government intervened in the AIRC cases in support of the unions' position. While the Labor Government did introduce laws allowing for non-union agreements ('enterprise flexibility agreements' or EFAs), these were only collective, not individual, in nature, and they were consequently not consonant with the decollectivisation strategy of employers. Cer-tainly EFAs, offered (ineffectively) as a consolation to employers who were otherwise relatively disadvantaged by the *Industrial Relations Reform Act 1993*, were the source of a deep rift between many unions and the ALP Government. However, they had little practical effect, covering less than 2 per cent of employees under federal agree-ments (DIR 1996). The main 'damage' they caused to unions arose from the symbolism involved in acceptance of the notion of non-union bargaining.

In the 1996 election the Labor Government was defeated. The Coalition by then had made significant changes to its industrial relations policies, setting aside the liability that a radically decollectivist policy, by comparison with the Accord, had represented at the 1993 election. Consequently, as discussed later in this chapter, the Workplace Relations Act retained the award system and, by comparison with the 1993 policy (and with the New Zealand Act), gave considerably less active impetus to decollectivisation. There is no evidence that the Coalition would have been any less likely to introduce decollectivist policies if it had not been for the symbolic role of EFAs.

The difficulties experienced by New Zealand unions during the Accord period suggests that the 'alienation' theory tells us little about the relationship between the Accord and union membership. In effect, the union movement through the Accord ameliorated, and bought time to adjust to, the paradigm shift in union membership. The Accord also enabled the union movement to shift its strategy from centralised wage fixing to enterprise bargaining. Real wage declines under centralised wage fixing were leading to some losses in union membership in those areas where unions were already weakly organised, but not where unions were strong; that is, they were quickening a process that would have happened anyway.

The move to enterprise bargaining, however, did not reverse the decline in union membership. Indeed, the decline accelerated after the introduction of enterprise bargaining. But this was not *because* of the introduction of enterprise bargaining under the evolving Accord. It was because there was an acceleration in the institutional break or paradigm shift and in the withdrawal of compulsory unionism, through changes to the legislative environments operating at the State level and probably through some hardening of employer positions. The trouble with the devolving of wage determination to the enterprise or workplace level was that, in unionised workplaces where unions were *not* well organised and represented, enterprise-level wage determination by the employer, perhaps after 'negotiations' with employees, could highlight to members the irrelevance or impotence of unions in relation to their own wages. With over one-third of unionised workplaces lacking a single union delegate, Australian unions were vulnerable to being severely eroded at the edges no matter which formal wage determination system was in place.

Australian Unions under a Federal Coalition Government and the Workplace Relations Act

The end of the Accord was brought about by the election of a Liberal–National Party Coalition Government in March 1996. Within months this Government had introduced into the Parliament new industrial relations legislation. Although it faced an initially hostile Senate, its passage was secured after an agreement was reached between the Australian Democrats and the Coalition Government. In summary, the main features relevant to union membership were that it:

- increased the scope for individual contracts, by enabling 'Australian Workplace Agreements' (AWAs) to be made directly between employers and individual employees;
- prohibited compulsory unionism and abolished the capacity of the AIRC to grant preference in employment to union members;
- encouraged the establishment of new unions, including enterprise unions, and the break-up of existing unions;
- increased sanctions for industrial action, including by creating major penalties for unions engaged in 'secondary boycotts' (that is, industrial action directed at one employer that is aimed at persuading another employer to accede to certain demands) and prohibited employers from paying employees engaged in work bans, overtime bans or any other form of industrial action; and
- made union access to workplaces more difficult by requiring union officials to have permits to enter workplaces and give notice to employers of their intended visit, and restraining them (unless suspected award breaches are involved) to only speaking to employees during meal breaks.

This section discusses the potential impact of the Workplace Relations Act on union membership, by reference to the provisions affecting compulsory unionism and union preference; the fragmentation of unions; sanctions; and the way it will interact with the reform strategies of management and unions. The last in particular is done by reference to the New Zealand experience and what such a comparison will tell us about the likely consequences in Australia.

The Prohibition on Compulsory Unionism and Union Preference

The Workplace Relations Act put the seal on a permanent and irrevocable departure from earlier patterns of compulsory unionism. The prohibition of compulsory unionism and preference clauses affects some unions more than others, but on average the unions that are already weakest and most poorly organised would be hardest hit – just as they had already been hardest hit by the decline in compulsory unionism that had occurred over the preceding decade. With the loss of compulsory unionism until 1996 having been concentrated in workplaces where unions were already weak or inactive, removing it from genuine union strongholds would not have such a strong effect on union membership.

While the near-national prohibition on compulsory unionism will make union recruitment more difficult and employer resistance easier, it would be counter-productive in the long term for unions to seek to rebuild compulsory unionism on the basis on which it previously existed. As was shown in chapter five, it appears that compulsory unionism in Australia led in the past to atrophy in union organisation in at least some areas. Certainly, there would seem to be little short-term point in attempting to maintain compulsory unionism arrangements, unless there is consent amongst employees and employers, when the substantial resources of the Office of the Employment Advocate were devoted to uncovering, thwarting and penalising such actions.

Union Fragmentation

Several provisions in the Workplace Relations Act were aimed at fragmenting union organisation, in part through creating competition between unions for members and in part through facilitating the breaking up of recently amalgamated unions. The 'conveniently belong' restriction[5] was abolished, to make it easier for enterprise unions and other new unions to be registered. A union only needed a minimum of 50 (rather than 100) members to be registered. Enterprise unions could be established on application to the AIRC, and they could not be opposed on the basis of the 'conveniently belong' rule; and could only be opposed on the basis that the existing union would more effectively represent the employees concerned. Former constituent unions of, or branches in, recently amalgamated unions could, by ballot, break away through 'disamalgamation'. One new union was registered in the first year of the Act.

The freedom of employees to select the union of their choice did not go so far as to threaten the convenience of employers. The AIRC retained the capacity to determine union coverage where there was a demarcation dispute and the behaviour of a union was, or threatened to be, restricting the performance of work or harming the business of an employer.

The Workplace Relations Act could be seen as encouraging unions to engage in 'market-share' unionism, where they are competing against each other for members, rather than 'expansionary' unionism, where they are competing against the efforts of employers to prevent them gaining the affiliations of employees. By maintaining a role for the AIRC in determining contested union coverage and the break-up of unions, the legislation gave unions the opportunity to expend substantial financial and human resources in jurisdictional fights before the AIRC and divert attention from organising workplaces and recruiting members.

Some amalgamations appear to have led to worse in-fighting within the union movement than would have occurred if the unions had remained separate, and some disamalgamations might therefore be less traumatic for the unions concerned than maintaining the existing structures. But when unions respond to the new laws by focusing on 'market-share' unionism, especially if their main theatre of activity is within the AIRC, they seriously undermine their ability to devote resources to rebuilding union membership – resources that were already stretched to the limit by enterprise bargaining and a shrinking financial base.

Sanctions

A range of sanctions provisions was included in the workplace relations legislation that, if activated, could create severe resource crises for unions, threatening their capacity to provide even the most basic of services and therefore threatening their ability to maintain their membership. The AIRC was given greater powers to direct that industrial action stop or not occur, with directions enforceable by court injunctions, and non-compliance with injunctions leading to fines or imprisonment for contempt or union deregistration. Industrial action was prohibited while an agreement was in force with penalties of up to $10,000 and the possibility of court injunctions. Employers were prohibited from making, and employees prohibited from accepting, payment (even in part) for periods while employees were engaged in work bans, overtime bans, work to rule or any other form of industrial action – again, with penalties of up to $10,000 and court injunctions. Most importantly, secondary boycott provisions that were inserted into the Trade Practices Act (which otherwise deals with corporate misbehaviour) by the Fraser Liberal–National Party Government, and removed by the Keating Labor Government (with alternative provisions inserted into the Industrial Relations Act) were reinstated into the Trade Practices Act, with remedies including injunctions, damages and fines of up to $750,000. Provisions allowing a three-day conciliation period before a court remedy could be sought were deleted. The wording of the secondary boycott provisions acted to encompass many primary boycotts (that is, disputes directly between the employer and employees). Additional sections were inserted into the Trade Practices Act effectively prohibiting industrial action with the purpose and likely effect of substantially hindering a third person engaging in international trade, a provision clearly directed at the waterfront union and its supporters. Reflecting the fiction that the secondary boycott provisions deal with competition policy, most were included in State and Territory laws implementing the national Competition Code.

In relation to some industries (such as the waterfront), bold and elaborate strategies were being devised to break the union 'hold', in a manner somewhat reminiscent of the way in which the British Conservative Government had planned for years – starting in Opposition – its strategy of breaking the British union movement by defeating the miners' union in a prolonged strike (Beynon & McMylor 1985). The legislation opened up new possibilities for employers and anti-union lobby groups (such as the National Farmers' Federation) and closed off many traditional union tactics. The battle for the waterfront attained a symbolic significance that went far beyond the economic consequences of waterfront 'reform'.

Decollectivisation, the Undermining of Unions and the Interaction with Employer Strategies

The Workplace Relations Act, like the Employment Contracts Act in New Zealand, provided mechanisms for employers to bypass unions and deal directly with employees, thereby decollectivising employment relations. The main mechanism was 'Australian Workplace Agreements' – individual contracts that overrode awards but were subject to an amended, and weakened, 'no disadvantage' test.[6] 'Non-union' certified agreements could be used to the same effect where an employer secured the support of a majority of employees but was unable to persuade a (unionised) minority to accept individual contracts. The formal usage of these mechanisms has been low by comparison with formal collective mechanisms, but they also serve an important demonstration effect for employers in regard to how they should structure their formal and informal employment relations. The impact of these provisions on union membership depends in part on the strategies adopted by management and unions in this new environment.

A starting point for analysing this issue is to recognise that employers may adapt different workplace reform approaches which may give greater or less attention to productivity or labour costs. Two polar categories have been identified by authors such as Curtain and Mathews (1992). The 'productivity enhancement' approach is said to focus upon improving functional flexibility of labour – the ability of labour to be deployed flexibly and to the most efficient use, emphasising skills acquisition, multiskilling, flexibility in work assignments, quality and devolution of authority. The 'cost minimisation' approach is said to focus more upon achieving numerical flexibility in labour costs or employee numbers. Although Curtain and Mathews portray these as two competing strategies, or possibly polar extremes on a continuum, this ignores the possibility that management may adopt both strategies. It is more useful to think of them in terms of two axes that produce a diagram with four quadrants, as shown in figure 7.3. The labels given to the four types of management strategy build upon typologies constructed by Boxall and Haynes (1992) and HTM (1992). Organisations with a high level of change that focus upon productivity enhancement are referred to as 'reformers'. Those with a high level of change that focus upon cost minimisation are called 'revisionists'. Those that do not have a high level of change are referred to as 'traditionalists'. Conceptually, cost-minimisation and productivity-enhancement strategies may be directly opposed, as the former implies a strategy focused on 'control' while the latter implies a strategy focused on 'commitment'. These two strategies, pursued properly, seem mutually exclusive (Walton 1985). Nonetheless, a number of firms attempt to pursue, imperfectly, both strategies: hence the category, 'mixed strategists'.

Cluster analysis undertaken by HTM (1992), and other research (reported in Peetz et al. 1993), showed how such management strategies are each associated with particular patterns of change in union membership. These effects, though, are not predetermined. The impact of management strategies on unionism is contingent upon the nature

Figure 7.3 A typology of management strategies

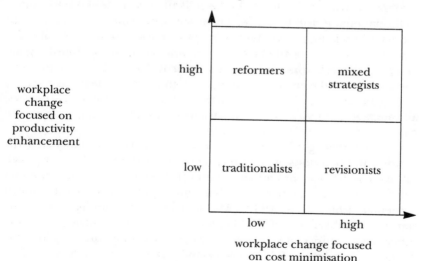

of the institutional framework and on union strategy at the micro and macro levels. Most of the rest of this section looks at the two axes of figure 7.3 in relation to union membership in the context of the Workplace Relations Act partly by drawing on the experience of the Employment Contracts Act.

Cost Minimisation, Union Strategy and Union Membership

The first issue is whether, and how, cost minimisation strategies influence union membership, and how these are affected by the Workplace Relations Act. The New Zealand experience indicated that cost minimisation strategies were associated with aggressive approaches to reducing labour costs, particularly penalty rates, attempted exclusion of unions, reduced union rights, falling union membership, the assertion of management's right to manage and sometimes the use of bargaining tactics that went beyond the law (HTM 1992; Harbridge & Moulder 1992; Peetz et al. 1993). Union reach was consequently reduced, as was the employee incentive to unionise, by making access to unions so difficult as to render them ineffective or by persuading employees it was not in their long-term interests to try to involve the union in bargaining. In some cases, harsh bargaining practices by employers increased the employee incentive to unionise (Boxall & Haynes 1992), but these effects were, in aggregate calculations, swamped by the other factors mentioned above. As shown in chapter five, this has also been the pattern in Australian States where public policy has facilitated employer belligerence.

Many Australian employers in the mid-1990s were looking for industrial relations reform to deliver major scope for cost minimisation and reductions in labour costs. They were partly frustrated by the Coalition's fear, informed by the 1993 election experience, of the political impact of industrial relations policies that overtly led to lower wages and conditions. Unlike in New Zealand, then, the award system was retained (albeit in 'simplified' form) and the AIRC kept many of its powers, although it was more severely restricted from arbitrating than in the past.

The minimising of employers' incentive to resist unions had depended upon unions' ability to maintain the 'union wage' through union coordination of bargaining and the extension of collective bargaining coverage through, in Australia and New Zealand, awards (Freeman 1990; Visser 1991). The weakening of unions' bargaining status and subversion of multi-employer bargaining gave special significance to informal employer coordination of bargaining in New Zealand. Employers felt considerable pressure to reduce certain

conditions of employment (especially penalty rates) once other employers had done so in a highly decentralised wage system without an
underlying award framework (Harbridge & Moulder 1992). The shift in
power to employers, the dismantling of multi-employer bargaining and,
therefore, of union coordination of bargaining, produced a strong
market incentive for employers to remove union wages and conditions
and therefore to resist unions.

As a consequence of the 'no disadvantage' test, however, Australian
'revisionists' are constrained as to how far they can legally go in aggres-
sively pursuing cost minimisation strategies when properly scrutinised.
The provisions of the federal system do not mean that no Australian
employers pursue cost minimisation approaches. But a cap is placed on
the employer incentive to deunionise as a means of avoiding the union
wage, albeit a cap that is somewhat perforated by the apparent extent of
illegal, under-award pay and conditions. Still, there are early indications
of a version of the coordinated or 'pattern' bargaining by employers
that was previously seen in New Zealand, especially regarding penalty
rates and other issues relating to working hours.

Productivity Enhancement, Union Strategy and Union Membership

The other axis of employer strategy concerns 'productivity enhancement'. The important point to make here is that the mere fact that firms
sit in the top left-hand quadrant of figure 7.3 – the 'reformers' quadrant
representing the pursuit of productivity enhancement strategies – does
not in itself guarantee security for union membership. Here the New
Zealand experience is particularly pertinent, because while the Workplace Relations Act and the Employment Contracts Act differ in matters
of detail, the fundamental similarity is that both provide a mechanism
for individual contracting while restraining union influence and representation rights.

The key question is whether firms pursue reform strategies based on
collective or individual bargaining with employees. 'Reformers' can be
divided into two categories. 'Individualistic reformers' pursue a produc-
tivity-enhancing strategy without a continuing role for unions. Management is essentially able to reduce the employee incentive to unionise by
offering them a better wages or conditions deal than they previously
had, rendering the union superfluous. 'Collectivist reformers' adopt a
productivity-enhancement approach focusing on high quality and high
wages and generally engage in cooperative relations with unions. Unlike
individualistic reformers, they are not likely to experience reductions in
what had previously been high union membership.

Within a new environment in New Zealand, union strategy was a
key variable affecting employer strategy. Individualistic reformers were

typically organisations in which the previous union relationship was acrimonious and unions were viewed by management as a barrier to better industrial relations. Unions that had been heavily reliant upon compulsory unionism, and had been able to demand fees from a captive membership, without needing to perform or adapt their needs to their members' requirements, suffered large drops in membership (Boxall & Haynes 1992; Peetz et al. 1993:274–9). The abolition of compulsory unionism provided the opportunity for employers following 'individualistic reform' strategies to seduce their employees away from these unions with little resistance.

The New Zealand pattern, then, reinforced the validity of some Australian observations (Peetz 1996, 1997a) regarding the interaction of trust in management and union satisfaction. Employers were able to reduce unionisation or deunionise totally by pursuing strategies that enhance employee trust, *provided* employees were being poorly supported by their unions.

In the new environment of the Workplace Relations Act, Australian unions faced exactly the same challenge as their counterparts faced in New Zealand: to find a way of responding to management's reform agenda that maintains the support of their membership. However, to repeat a point made in chapter two and elsewhere (Peetz 1996), employees might be willing to work cooperatively to improve workplace efficiency but they are not seeking acquiescence from their unions in their interactions with management.

Conclusion

The priorities and processes – although not necessarily the outcomes – of the Accord were essentially congruent with employee preferences. The Accord (like the award system in general) minimised the cost incentive upon employers to deunionise and, by facilitating changes in the wage system that promoted greater productivity and flexibility, the Accord may have reduced the incentive upon employers to deunionise in search of greater flexibility and productivity. While reductions in real wages were not popular, there did not appear to be major losses in union membership arising solely from them, principally because the blame was not solely directed at unions but (principally) at management. However, if real wages were falling and unions were not adequately performing on other matters as well, then unions were in danger of losing members. Likewise, if employers tried to determine wages at the enterprise or workplace level and unions did not get involved, the position of unions was seriously weakened. In the context of rising employer pressure for single-employer wage bargaining, the shift to enterprise bargaining in wage fixing, while it exposed the workplace weakness of unions, might have been better for unions at that time than the alternative of continuing with a highly centralised national wage system.

The main impact of the Accord on the decline in union membership was probably to ease the rapidity of the paradigm shift in union membership and to change some of the detailed institutionalised arrangements eventually put in place. This is most obvious by reference to the comparison with developments in New Zealand over the same period, where, in net terms, union membership fell by greater amounts under both Labour and National Governments.

Clearly, union organisation at the workplace level was in something of a state of atrophy under the Accord – but this had been the case for most of the century as a result of the award system's focus away from the workplace and on the machinations of the tribunal system. Cross-national comparisons show that centralisation of wage fixing is not the problem in itself, but that it needs to be matched by strong union organisation at the workplace (Hancké 1993), the missing ingredient in Australia. For much of this century, the weakness of workplace organisation did not matter so much for unions because membership was commonly reproduced through institutional means. When unions were organised at the workplace, and engaged in bargaining, they reinforced their membership at the workplace – regardless of whether bargaining was over wages or other matters. Workplace wage bargaining may have been retarded under the Accord, but unions that were capable of bargaining over wages still bargained over other matters. The decline and then collapse of compulsory unionism through the 1980s and 1990s, the economic transformation of the mid-1980s, the employer and state offensive against unions and the shift to 'enterprise bargaining' changed the paradigm – suddenly the workplace mattered, and it mattered a lot. It exposed the workplace vulnerability of unions that arose not just from the Accord (Green 1996) but from the system of industrial relations that unions had helped build over 90 years. The award system was simultaneously the strength and the weakness of the union movement.

The environment created by the federal Liberal–National Party Government and the Workplace Relations Act creates a number of problems and dangers for unions. The impact will be shaped by unions' capacity to deal with the removal of most of the remaining compulsory unionism arrangements, avoid destabilising fragmentation in the face of the provisions for disamalgamation and enterprise unions, avoid the full force of the sanctions provisions against industrial action, and devise and adopt strategies for responding adequately to management's workplace reform strategies. It will be the most testing period unions have faced in over half a century.

CHAPTER 8

The Future for Australian Unions

Declining union density has potentially wide implications for society and for the study of industrial relations. Continuing reductions in union density might be expected to lead, unless other forces intervene, to widening inequality and reduced 'voice' for employees in their working lives. As Barbash (1985) has pointed out, it is unclear whether the benign aspects of human resource management would continue in the absence of organised labour's countervailing power. Moreover, the traditional academic discipline of industrial relations is founded, ultimately, upon the study of the interactions between employers and collectively organised employees: the decline in union density in Britain has been claimed to be leading to the 'end of institutional industrial relations' (Purcell 1993), fundamentally affecting the way labour markets are studied. This book has therefore presented a framework for analysing the reasons for union membership and non-membership, and has examined the reasons for union decline.

In the preceding chapters, union membership in Australia has been examined within a 'change-response' framework. This model was used because it focused on the way in which union membership is determined by changes in the environment or in the strategies of major participants in the industrial relations system, and by the way in which other participants respond to those changes. This approach to analysis was aimed at helping to bridge the gap between those theories that focus upon individual attitudes or behaviour, ignoring considerations relating to union and employer behaviour and the wider environment, and those theories that seek to identify macro-determinants of union membership without due consideration of individual behaviour and attitudes. This model is described in chapter one, and there is no need to repeat it here. Rather, this chapter summarises the reasons for union decline in Australia, the reasons why Australian unions have had such a bad experience compared to many of their counterparts overseas, the factors favouring union renewal, the barriers to that renewal, and the strategies unions might adopt in order to bring that renewal about.

Why the Decline in Union Membership?

Three main factors can be identified as causing the decline in Australian union density: structural change in the labour market, the institutional break in the determinants of union membership, and the failure of many unions at the workplace to prevent employer strategies from leading to a decline in union reach and membership.

First, there has been a substantial amount of structural change in the labour market. The casualisation of the workforce, the decline of the public sector, the growth of industries and occupations in which union density is low and the relative growth of small firms has led to an exogenous decline in union reach. Something in the order of half of the decline in union density over the decade to 1992 can be accounted for by reference to structural change. However, it does not explain a high proportion of the decline since then.

Second, and more importantly, there has been an institutional break or 'paradigm shift' in the determinants of union membership. This institutional break reflects a change in strategies by employers and governments towards unions. The most important aspect of this has been the collapse of compulsory unionism, independent of structural change in the labour market, as employers have withdrawn recognition of such arrangements and governments have delegitimised and prohibited them. In addition, the decollectivisation of the employment relationship is being actively pursued by, to varying degrees, employers and the state, after nearly a century in which collective employment relationships were accepted, often grudgingly, as the norm. Individual contracts are being promoted by employer associations, individual employers and governments as the most effective means of developing a 'close' or 'meaningful' relationship between employers and employees. Some workplaces are being deunionised by employers engaged in the pursuit of these objectives. These employer and government strategies appear, in turn, to have either originated in or been exacerbated by the economic changes and perhaps ideological changes amongst employers that took place from the mid-1980s. The impact of this institutional break has accelerated since 1992 with the enactment of legislation in almost all State jurisdictions and now in the federal jurisdiction aimed at prohibiting union preference in employment and compulsory unionism, and encouraging the use of individual contracts in place of awards and collective agreements as the basis for setting the terms and conditions of employment and framing the nature of the employment relationship.

What we have seen, then, is a major decline in union reach, through forces representing a combination of structural and strategic changes. There is little evidence of any decline in the propensity of employees to belong to unions. Sympathy towards unions has, if anything, increased since the early 1980s. Data showing trends in employees' more specific attitudes to the instrumentality of union membership and the performance of unions are harder to come by, but the limited evidence we have does not suggest a deterioration in the perceived performance of unions at the workplace.

The main change that is happening in relation to union propensity concerns the match between employee preferences and their union membership status: employees who do not want to belong to a union are now much less likely to have to be in one, but employees who would rather be in a union are more and more likely to have their wishes unfulfilled. The institutional break in the determinants of union membership, most obviously demonstrated by the collapse of compulsory unionism, is not leading to some brave new world in which employee preferences alone determine union membership. There are still many people who are unable to match their membership preference with their membership status. The main change is that the number of 'unwilling conscripts' is less, but the number 'unwillingly excluded' is greater. It is simply becoming a lot harder for unions to organise workers.

But while there is little evidence of a decline in union propensity, it is important to note that (particularly in terms of sympathy towards unions) Australian unions were starting from a low base a decade ago. The weak level of union sympathy at a time when employment was growing rapidly in the 1980s made new recruitment into unions more difficult. And the decline in union reach has been underpinned by a weakness in union propensity in those workplaces where it has occurred. In the context of a changing economic environment, new management strategies have led to changes in how work is managed and performed. Sometimes the exclusion of unions has been an intended consequence, but other times (perhaps more often) the impact upon unions is merely the by-product of particular employee-focused strategies.

However, the effect of employer strategy on union membership is not unconditional. It is, in fact, dependent upon union behaviour. So the third factor behind the decline in union membership has been the inability of some unions to provide the infrastructure, or adopt the strategies, or act with sufficient vigour or cohesion, to prevent employer strategies from leading to a decline in union reach and membership. In other words, that part of the decline in density that is explained by employer-induced reductions in union reach can itself only be explained by reference to inadequate union performance, most visible at workplace level, in response to management agendas for change. Union membership has declined because unions were not represented by delegates in workplaces where workplace reform was under way, or union delegates were not satisfactorily representing employees, or unions were inactive in terms of bargaining or were not involved in workplace wage determination. In many of those instances direct dealings (not necessarily 'bargaining') between individuals and management have supplanted collective dealings through unions. In some cases, union membership has declined where unions have been weak or ineffective in resisting changes that have been to the disadvantage of employees.

While the union response to changes in the microeconomic environment and management strategy has been important, so too has been the (slow) union response to change in the structure of the labour market. It appears that the focus of much activity to promote union growth was on 'market-share' unionism rather than 'expansionary' unionism. This was most evident in the extensive and expensive battles fought out in the AIRC for coverage of some groups of employees, which represented a substantial opportunity cost that retarded the attraction of union membership for potential new members in growing industries and occupations.

The high level of unemployment (compared with that in the 1970s) that persisted through the 1980s and 1990s, following the 1982 recession, slowed union growth considerably compared with the growth that would have occurred if 1970s conditions had prevailed. On the other hand, the rapid employment growth and reduction in unemployment through much of the 1980s would have made union membership grow faster than would have been the case if the depressed labour market conditions of 1982 had persisted through the decade.

Several factors have partly offset the downward pressures on union membership mentioned above. While deunionisation occurred in some previously unionised workplaces, some other non-union workplaces became unionised. The faster rate of workplace change evident late in the period probably accelerated this process. It was not nearly enough, however, to offset the losses from deunionisation from quite different causes.

The main impact of the Accord on the decline in union membership was probably to ease the rapidity of the institutional break and to change, at least temporarily, perhaps with lasting effect, some of the detailed institutionalised arrangements eventually put in place. The

Accord as a political and economic strategy helped the Australian Labor Government stay in office for several more terms than its New Zealand counterpart by: promoting favourable economic outcomes and an approach to industrial relations that was congruent with voter preferences; dividing employer groups thereby minimising conservative opposition to Labor; precluding politically damaging behaviour by unions; and likewise placing boundaries around the behaviour of the Federal Labor Government. In turn the Federal Labor Government continued to promote and mostly defend collectivised employment relations, although its enabling of collective non-union 'enterprise flexibility agreements' weakened the legitimacy of unions and bolstered the legitimacy of the Coalition alternative. Still, by the time the Labor Government was defeated, the Coalition had softened its industrial relations policies so that its new legislation retained the award system and, by comparison with the 1993 policy (and with the New Zealand law), gave considerably less active impetus to decollectivisation, particularly through cost-minimisation strategies.

The Accord minimised the cost incentive upon employers to deunionise and, by facilitating changes in the wage system that promoted greater productivity and flexibility, it might have reduced the incentive upon employers to deunionise in search of greater flexibility and productivity below what they otherwise would have been. The priorities and processes of the Accord were essentially congruent with employee preferences. While reductions in real wages were not popular, there did not appear to be major losses in union membership arising solely from them, principally because the blame was more likely to be directed at management than at unions. However, if real wages were falling and unions were not adequately performing on other matters as well, then unions were in danger of losing members. At least over its first half, the Accord also maintained the limited focus unions had on workplace activism, a limited focus that was the legacy of nine decades of arbitration. This longer-term legacy was responsible for the underlying vulnerability of unions in the 1980s and 1990s. Where unions had the infrastructure at the workplace or enterprise level to engage in bargaining, the Accord may have retarded their capacity for wage bargaining but it did not prevent them from bargaining over other matters, and in the end it was the capacity for bargaining, not just wage bargaining, that determined unions' longevity at the workplace.

The Accord enabled the union movement to shift its strategy from centralised wage fixing to enterprise bargaining. The move to enterprise bargaining did not solve the problems of union membership; in fact, the decline in membership accelerated. The decline and then collapse of compulsory unionism through the 1980s and 1990s, the economic transformation of the mid-1980s, the employer and government offensive against unions and the shift to enterprise bargaining were central elements in the institutional break in the determination of union membership. For most of the century, unions' performance at the workplace mattered, but it mattered less in determining membership than did their ability to secure appropriate institutional outcomes – including agreements with employers, or award provisions, that secured union membership. But from the 1980s, and especially the 1990s, the situation reversed. The institutional arrangements swung against unions, and union performance at the workplace mattered a great deal. Whereas the ACTU had expected that the shift to enterprise bargaining would boost union membership, it instead exposed the workplace vulnerability of unions, a vulnerability which, given increasing pressure from employers (especially larger ones) for decentralised wage determination, they would probably have been shortly exposed to anyway regardless of the ACTU's preferred wages strategy.

Workplace wage bargaining was, in itself, no more effective at providing incentives for union membership than was centralised award-based pay determination. Still, workplace wage bargaining enabled unions to get involved in issues that, in the 1990s, would otherwise be the prerogative of management alone or the subject of individual 'bargaining' between management and employees. The centralised Accord had little overall effect in reducing union density and performed some functions that were important in holding union density at higher levels than it otherwise would have been. This is most obvious by reference to the comparison with developments in New Zealand over the same period, where, in net terms, union membership fell, by greater amounts than in Australia, under both Labour and National Governments. In effect, the union movement through the Accord bought a small amount of time to adjust to the institutional break in union membership.

Why has the Decline Been So Severe in Australia Compared with Other Countries?

Since this analysis suggests the Accord has acted, if anything, to slightly restrain the decline in union membership, the question that must be asked is: why have Australian unions fared so poorly compared with some of their counterparts overseas? Countries with corporatist arrangements of one sort or another comprise most of the countries that have managed to retain or increase high levels of union membership. Australia is amongst a very small group of countries with centralised or temporarily 'corporatist' bargaining arrangements that have experienced a significant decline in union membership.

There are seven factors that appear to explain the poor relative position of the Australian union movement. The first concerns the workplace organisation of unions. The corporatist countries that have maintained high levels of density have also been countries that have strong workplace or local unions. Strong macro-corporatism has virtually been a necessary condition for the maintenance of strong union density, but it has not been a sufficient condition. Workplace union organisation adequate to support micro-corporatist arrangements may be required as well. In this respect, when searching for international comparisons, Australia may have more in common with the Netherlands than with Sweden. In Sweden, macro-corporatist institutions have been underpinned by powerful workplace organisation as unions 'are incorporated into firm-level decision-making through a legally and institutionally protected position in works councils and other workers' participation institutions' (Hancké 1993:599). The Netherlands, by comparison, is a 'strongly corporatist' country in which 'the unions do not have strong local structures, and this has caused serious recruitment problems' (ibid). Union density in Sweden grew through the 1970s and most of the 1980s; union density in the Netherlands fell slightly in the 1970s and, between 1980 and 1988, fell by 10 percentage points, only slightly greater than the 8 point fall in Australia from 1982 to 1990.

The Australian 'problem' concerns not just workplace structures but also workplace practices of unions. As Hammarström (1992:121) points out, shop stewards in Anglo-Saxon countries have a 'traditionally reactive (role) and they have not in general developed a constructive dialogue with management on investments, training and other areas of business development'. This characteristic helps explain the increased employer resistance that unions in Australia, New Zealand, the US and UK appear to have encountered to varying degrees in the 1980s or 1990s.

The relative shallowness of Australian workplace union organisation partly reflects unions' heavy reliance, by international standards, on compulsory unionism. In most of continental Europe, including the most strongly unionised countries, closed shops have not been an important feature of union organisation. Compulsory unionism in Australia has quite different determinants to union propensity. It also appears to have a (negative) impact upon union responsiveness and performance that has made Australian unions vulnerable to the withdrawal of closed shop agreements. The assault by employers and governments on unions was able to be so effective because Australian unions had become so reliant on compulsory unionism.

The second factor explaining the relatively poor position of Australian unions, which may be partly responsible for and partly a result of the first, is the legal/institutional environment in Australia. Unlike most Western European countries, there has been no legal provision in Australia for firm-level industrial democracy through works councils or other such bodies. The existence of such arrangements does not guarantee strong local unions, but it does provide an institutional framework within which unions can intervene in the 'politics of production' (Hancké 1993). Its absence in Australia would seem to have been an impediment to active workplace unionism (Archer 1995). The award system, by contrast, has historically been associated with a wide definition of the extent of managerial prerogative and a narrow definition of the scope of tribunals' jurisdiction and, by implication, of the matters unions can legitimately raise and bargain with management. This mobilisation of bias (Bachrach & Baratz 1970:43) limited the ability of unions to pursue matters on any micro-corporatist agendas. In recent decades the breadth of managerial prerogative has been eroded by decisions of the tribunals and the High Court, a development important in providing a necessary but not sufficient condition for the development of micro-corporatism in Australia. But the gradual spread of consultative mechanisms under the 'second-tier', 'structural efficiency' and 'enterprise bargaining principles' of the Australian Industrial Relations Commission in the late 1980s and 1990s have fallen well short of the consultation rights guaranteed in much of Europe.

The narrow demarcations of the award system as it existed in the early 1980s acted as an impediment to productivity growth and flexibility. Unions' adherence to award provisions governing work rules encouraged their replication through over-award rules and provided an incentive for employers to seek non-union labour that would not feel obliged to operate under award conditions. Reform of the award system in the late 1980s through award restructuring in Australia was an important element in preventing union labour from attracting too great a competitive disadvantage. Such systemic reform takes time, however, and inevitably in some areas unions were too obstructionist. Consequently the process of change was too slow for those managements to abide. The employer assault on, and destruction of, the award system in New Zealand demonstrated the consequences of allowing the award system to ossify at a time when employers were placing an increasing premium on flexibility.

The third factor, related to these two factors, is the structure of Australian unions. Australian unions, like their declining counterparts in Britain and New Zealand, have an occupational, craft or multifaceted structure which has been disguised but not generally resolved by union amalgamations. The structure of unions has promoted market-share unionism and the wasting of union resources in competition for membership in front of tribunals, thereby enfeebling one of the key advantages Western (1993a) cites for centralised union movements, their capacity to prevent wasteful jurisdictional disputes. The inefficiencies of workplace multi-unionism have promoted employer resistance, retarded employee interest and inhibited the reaping of the gains of economies of scale in workplace union organisation. Amalgamation has had a limited impact in reducing multi-unionism and in reducing market-share unionism, and has sometimes led to increased in-fighting within, rather than between, unions. In some cases amalgamation has enhanced membership by creating opportunities for union training and workplace contact that were not previously there, but (probably) less commonly it has distanced unions further from their members. Most commonly, it has had no effect on workplace unionism, but with considerable opportunity cost in terms of the resources devoted to the process.

The combination of weak workplace union linkages, compulsion in membership, underdeveloped industrial democratic traditions and a focus on demarcation and territorialism may have created a fourth factor: an unusually sclerotic union movement in which significant parts have difficulty in adapting to change. With weak workplace linkages comes a shortage of democratic input (and low conviction by members that their unions are democratic institutions) and inadequate exposure to the changing interests of their members. With compulsion came a limited need to respond to these changing interests. With an absence of industrial democratic traditions comes a combativeness in union-management dealings that finds an equivalent in combativeness in intra-union relations: 'attacks and criticisms are much more common in union halls and offices than are thoughtful planning, problem solving and mutual support' (Pocock 1997:12). With a focus on demarcation and territorialism comes a focus on incumbency, and a belief that 'once in a position, an incumbent has a right to stay' (Elton 1997:113).

The fifth factor is that union sympathy appears to be weaker in Australia than in several other countries. Certainly, differences in union sympathy between countries do not in themselves explain differences in union density, and they are not being put forward here as the most significant factor. Nonetheless, a low level of union sympathy would appear to make Australian unions especially vulnerable to the removal of compulsory unionism and meant that when employment grew rapidly Australian unions were not able to pick up new members in the way they should have been able to.

The sixth factor in relation to Australian unions' difficulties concerns employer culture and ideology. Just as unions from the English-speaking world seem to have different approaches and priorities to unions from continental Europe, so might be the case with employers. Few Australian managers read European materials not presented in English, and there is a strong cultural link between Australia and the US that extends into many areas of social and economic life. It is difficult to evaluate the extent to which any differences in employer ideologies between Australia and Europe result from cultural/educational factors and the extent to which they result from the economic and industrial relations circumstances of the countries concerned, in particular the institutional heritage and the nature of union organisation and behaviour. Certainly, it is not the sole explanation: Canadian unions, in the context of a similar cultural environment but different legislative framework, have been able to largely resist the trend to deunionisation that has occurred in the US.

The final factor concerns the rate of economic change. It is possible Australia has experienced more substantial industrial change than many other industrialised nations. Where Australia has clearly experienced a faster rate of structural change than other countries is in the area of part-time employment. But while this could account for something under 1 percentage point of the difference between union density changes in Australia and an OECD average, it is not enough to explain most of Australian unions' relative performance.

Economic change may have played an unusually important role in Australia, however, in the form of the terms of trade and currency crises of the mid-1980s. Few other advanced industrialised countries were so dependent upon commodity exports, and none suffered as severe a fall in the terms of trade in 1985–86 as occurred in Australia. This in turn might explain some aspects of Australian employer ideology and strategies in the mid- to late 1980s. It certainly played a decisive role in terms of union strategy towards wage fixing and productivity. And it played a key role in directing the Labor Government towards an extensive program of microeconomic reform. In turn, these economic changes brought about pressure for substantial change at the workplace.

These pressures were exacerbated by the manner in which the arbitration system had developed in tandem with the system of industry protection through tariffs in the early part of the century (Plowman 1992). When industry protection was turned on its head in the 1980s, the pressure for change to the award system was considerable. While the Australian award system was clearly more adaptable than its New Zealand counterpart, for many employers, bureaucrats and commentators the tying of deregulation of product markets to the deregulation (and implicitly deunionisation) of labour markets became almost a mantra.

It is, however, difficult to make a persuasive argument that economic change was so unique in Australia that it could explain most of the difference between the decline in Australian union density and the stability in density in other corporatist countries. While economic factors may have contributed to the Australian union movement's poor relative performance, the more important factors would appear to be Australia's union structure and strategy and institutional framework, and Anglophone employer culture.

Is there a Future for Unions in Australia?

The analysis in this book of the reasons for union decline, as bleak a picture as it portrays, does not suggest that union decline is inevitable or that Australian unions are destined to occupy an increasingly marginal role in Australian society. As discussed in the first chapter, unions have gone through periods of decline in the past and risen again. Union density fell severely during the 1930s, and yet unions recovered from that to reach a new high in membership. The decline in Australian union density has been so significant that it may be thought that Australian unions are heading down the American road, which led the US union movement to achieving union density of only 15 per cent by the early 1990s. But this is not necessarily the case. There are many factors that favour a turnaround in the decline in union density and membership in Australia. Equally, there are also many obstacles to union revival. What factors will determine whether unions grow or continue their precipitous decline in the future?

The most important point to make here is that, while the origins of union decline may be largely external to the union movement (that is, reflecting changes in the economy or in the strategies of employers and governments rather than changes in the union movement itself), how they translate into effects on union membership depends on the response of unions to those changes.

The way in which unions relate to their members is the single most important determinant of union propensity. The way in which unions relate to employers and the way in which they search out and recruit new members are the most important determinants of union reach. Whatever change occurs in the system, unions are in a position to respond. When structural change occurs in the labour market, the res-ponse in terms of union recruitment strategies determines the ultimate importance of the structural effect. When employers adopt particular strategies in response to changes in the macroeconomy, in employer ideology, or any other factor, it is the way in which unions respond to employer behaviour that determines whether union membership falls, remains stable or rises. Unions have shown over their history their capacity for response and for making large and sudden gains in membership. Whether they still have that capacity, to overcome the very difficult problems posed by the adverse environment of today, is what is in question.

The union movement has already started to respond to declining union density. This response has taken several forms: a restructuring of unions through amalgamations; changes in the wages system to promote an increasing focus upon workplace wage bargaining; and the devotion of additional resources to union recruitment, including a program 'Organising Works' and the hiring of specialist recruitment officers targeted at particular groups such as migrants and young people.

Certainly, it is helpful to unions that there is a high degree of interest in union membership in Australia – higher than the figures on actual membership would suggest. The number of employees who would rather be in one is roughly equal to, and might be greater than, the number who would rather not be in one.

Moreover, over the past decade and a half, sympathy towards unions has been increasing. It is easier now for unions to overcome the ideological barriers people had to joining unions than it was at the start of the 1980s. However, union sympathy remains at a low level by international standards and this serves as an impediment to recruitment of new members.

Less negative ideological dispositions against unions would facilitate union recruitment, though its importance should not be overstated. Making sustained improvements in this area is a slow task. The weak sympathy for Australian unions is probably attributable to the fairly high levels of industrial conflict that Australia has historically had and the low legitimacy that strike action has had in Australia as a result of the arbitration system. It has gradually improved under the Accord in the context of low industrial disputation levels. Over time, union sympathy will continue to improve if levels of industrial conflict remain relatively low and, in particular, if unions partaking in industrial action are seen to be engaged in legitimate activity.

The relevance of arbitration has been greatly reduced as a means of resolving matters in dispute, since the rise of enterprise bargaining as a form of wage determination and the passage of the *Industrial Relations Reform Act 1993* and (most significantly) the *Workplace Relations Act 1996*. This should help improve the legitimacy of industrial action, at least when it is undertaken in the negotiation of an enterprise agreement (when it is legal and 'protected'). The extent to which this benefits union sympathy depends in part on the extent to which industrial action is focused in the 'bargaining periods' legitimated by statute, and the extent to which the populace is persuaded that industrial action is an inevitable consequence of a wage system that focuses on enterprise bargaining and largely removes access to arbitration when negotiating agreements.

Beyond this, there is the broader question of the general ideologies that exist within society. At issue for unions is not only their ability to develop favourable images of themselves but also to promote ideas of social solidarity that underpin collectivism – concern for fairness in the distribution of income and power in society, a concern that is under-mined by the growth of right-wing ideology – and to link unions to these notions of fairness and freedom (Archer 1995).

Institutional factors are also very relevant. While many employers prefer to maintain existing collectively based relations with their em-ployees, a larger number than in the past are unwilling to accept the turn-of-the-century settlement in industrial relations and are unwilling to continue to recognise unions or deal collectively with employees. As long as the award system continues in place, it provides some defence of the 'union wage' and therefore acts to depress the incentive for employers to avoid unions in order to achieve labour cost advantages. Allowing the gap between union-negotiated wages achieved through enterprise bargaining and award safety net wages often received by non-members to grow too large would increase the incentive to use non-union labour, unless the productivity advantage of union firms was of similar magnitude. In this context, adequate adjustment of the award safety net to reflect movements in community living standards is essential for unions. This is an advantage that Australian unions have over their counterparts in Britain, New Zealand and the US – par-ticularly the latter, where the union–non-union wage differential is reckoned to be so large as to be a major reason for high employer resistance and low union density.

Of course, if the union–non-union wage gap is matched by a pro-ductivity differential favouring union labour, no financial incentive to use non-union labour exists. So for unions there are two ways of avoid-ing the problem: ensuring that union labour has higher productivity than non-union labour, because of superior work organisation, tech-nology or application; or ensuring that union-achieved wage gains are, as much as possible, generalised across the relevant workforces. This proposition may seem to go against the grain for many unions – if, as was found in chapter two, union instrumentality is such a major influence on union membership, does it not follow that union strategies for reversing membership decline should focus on making wage gains exclusive to union members? To conclude this would be to overestimate the importance of wage increases as the primary motivation for union membership, as discussed in chapters two and seven. Even if it were possible for unions to appropriate wage increases for members only, it is unlikely that overall union membership would rise. The employer incentive to fight unionisation is strongest where the 'union wage' is not generalised and the union–non-union wage differential is the highest. Whether the impact of a higher union wage differential in attracting and retaining members in open jobs would offset the loss of membership arising from greater employer resistance to union membership is ultimately an empirical question, but overseas evidence suggests that the answer is probably no.

This is not to ignore the importance of wage campaigns in helping to mobilise and recruit workers into unions. For example, the Transport Workers Union (TWU) was reportedly one of the better performing unions in terms of membership growth during its 1995–96 wage campaign. But the importance of the union–non-union wage differential was reflected in the TWU's efforts (successful in NSW but a failure in the federal jurisdiction) to secure an 11–15 per cent award-based wage increase for that half of the road transport industry's workforce that had not received a wage increase through enterprise bargaining.

Nor is this to say that the award system has been an unqualified plus for the union movement. Part of the reason for unions' poor workplace organisation has been the attention that has been given by unions to operating through the award system at the expense of the workplace and the way the award system defined various workplace issues as being beyond the legitimate scope of union activity. The joint evolution of the award system and union coverage facilitated the growth of multi-unionism within workplaces. But the dangers that would be posed to the union movement through the total loss of the award system, of opening up avenues for large scale cost-minimisation strategies and incentives for deunionisation, could outweigh any benefits that may be gained through increasing the incentive for unions to build up their workplace organisation. The decline in union density over the past two decades is, one would think, sufficient motivation for developing workplace organisation without requiring any additional motivation from the neutering or abolition of the award system. There is a balance to be found in an award system that maintains the safety net at adequate levels while promoting employer efficiency and enabling union involvement in the workplace. The award system also holds a high degree of legitimacy in the electorate. To the extent that unions are able to link their own identity to the defence of that system, they may also enhance their own credibility and membership.

Another aspect of workplace regulation also worth mentioning here is the union movement's approach to industrial democracy. The Australian union movement, unlike its European counterparts, has resisted suggestions that there should be legislative or other provisions encouraging or requiring the establishment of representative industrial democracy mechanisms such as works councils within workplaces. This has been because Australian unions have feared that these would be used as alternatives to unions by employers seeking to avoid unions.

These fears have, by and large, been misplaced. Employers seeking to bypass unions do not generally use alternative collective mechanisms for dealing with their employees; they seek instead to individualise employment relations. The most common manifestation of voluntary collective employee representation is a union; so where collective mechanisms are encouraged (and representative forms of industrial democracy are inherently collective in their orientation) unions are the natural bodies to dominate those mechanisms. This is demonstrated by the practice in Germany, where representation on works councils is most commonly taken by union members or delegates. Works councils appear to have strengthened the position of unions in many countries, except those (for example, in Holland and France) where unions were weak and divided at the workplace level or unable or unwilling to take advantage of the mechanism (Archer 1995).

There are several reasons for believing that industrial democracy mechanisms such as works councils could influence union renewal. They could be expected to assist in the development of workplace union organisation by expanding or formalising the sphere of activity of many union delegates, even facilitating the development of delegates in otherwise poorly organised workplaces. They may assist in the development and implementation of collectively orientated models of workplace reform. And they have the potential to boost the legitimacy of unions (Archer 1995) by building on democratic values, emphasising the voice role of unions, and attracting workers who give high priority to seeking greater involvement in decision making at work. It is noteworthy that the *Unions 2001* report (Evatt Foundation 1995) recommended the commissioning of a detailed study into the advantages and disadvantages of different types of works councils with a view to establishing the most appropriate model for Australia (Archer 1995:133). No action on this front had been taken at the time of writing.

A number of unions, and the ACTU itself, have taken to providing non-traditional services to members as a means of encouraging membership growth. Given the role of instrumentality in determining union membership, it might be thought that these non-industrial services may indeed achieve this goal. The evidence, however, is not very favourable for most such services. There are few people who have joined a union because of the provision of private non-'industrial' benefits to members. The one exception that persistently revealed itself was indemnity insurance offered by nurses' unions, and this is really an example of a union providing the archetypical union service – protection and insurance for its members. Notably, the main such service provided by overseas unions that is known to have a strong positive effect on union membership is the Ghent system of unions providing unemployment insurance for their members in four European countries (Western 1993a, Visser 1991). Israeli unions have benefited from involvement in the provision of health insurance (Ben-Israel & Fisher 1992:95). Other individualistic services, it has been argued, have had little impact on British unionism (Crouch 1982; Kelly 1990). There is already an active market for many of the non-insurance 'discount' services that unions are increasingly offering. And individualistic non-industrial services mostly do nothing to promote the collective identity on which union action is based.

The provision of non-traditional services is unlikely to do any direct harm to union membership. It could produce some gains in retention, though these would probably be quite small except in those specialised cases where the service is a 'hit', as a result of being genuinely tied to the protective notions underlying unionism. The question is, how much will it divert unions away from other activities with a greater impact on union joining and retention? If non-traditional, non-insurance services are not self-financing when all factors are taken into account, they will have an opportunity cost in terms of attracting and retaining members.

Structural change in the labour market will continue to act against unions' interests. Casualisation of the labour force is continuing to grow as part of management strategies responding to the gap between the cost of casual and permanent labour and the greater discretion and power exercisable by management over the use of casual labour. Casualisation in turn makes recruitment and retention of union members very difficult. The public sector is in decline as governments wind back public services, privatise others and move to purchaser-provider models. Industries and occupations with low union density will continue to outgrow the more traditionally unionised ones.

But not all change is detrimental to unionism. The rate of workplace change in the 1990s is faster than in the 1980s (Short et al. 1993). While it may be leading to some improvement in skill levels of employees and broadening of jobs, it is also leading to increased demands on employees, work intensification and increased stress. Modern management tools such as just-in-time, total quality management, quality control and computer-integrated manufacturing are placing increasing pressures on employees. Workplace change creates opportunities for unions to organise. The emergence of knowledge-based industries comprising a 'third wave' of change (Costa 1997) may represent a fundamental challenge to union structures and objectives over the very long run, but the adoption in the mainstream of the economy of new production techniques derived in part from those industries brings about uncertainty and dislocation that facilitates the unionisation of previously union-free workplaces.

In unionised workplaces, models for workplace reform take on importance. The changes in employer approaches to unions have come about in the context of an accelerating pace of workplace reform in the face of rapid economic change. A significant number of employers have decided that working through traditional union-based mechanisms would be inadequate for meeting their organisational needs. For unions, a key issue will be their ability to promote collective means of dealing with workplace reform issues, as alternatives to the atomised model of workplace reform exemplified by the approach of CRA/Rio Tinto, which developed a strategy over more than a decade of decollectivising its employment relations. There are many instances of unions and employers working with a sufficient degree of 'good faith' – albeit not necessarily in total agreement with each other – to enable the employers' agenda for workplace reform and efficiency to be addressed while the interests of employees are satisfied and employment relations remain on a collective basis.

At issue is not just the extent to which the concerns of employers in workplace change are addressed. It is also a question of unions' ability to adequately reflect the interests of their members in workplace change issues. By and large, the initial inclination of the majority of employees is to cooperate with the employer in developing efficient forms of work organisation, as this also promotes job and wage security. They expect the same broad intent from their unions, and may leave their unions if they do not perceive unions approaching workplace reform issues in good faith with employers. But, particularly in the context of increasing insecurity, stress, hours of work and work intensification, workers are not wanting unions to be acquiescent to the management agenda when that agenda conflicts with the interests of employees. Unions can recruit members by organising dissatisfied workers against unreasonable management agendas, and retain members by knowing when to cooperate and when to confront management.

In this context, the more union recruitment is focused on areas where the prospects of success are high (for example, where workplace change is under way), and where the long-term potential for growth is strong (growing enterprises, new industries), the better position unions will be in to offset the deleterious impact upon union reach of structural change in the labour market. Recruitment of new members from non-union workplaces will be important in improving union reach to employees who were previously unable to access union membership. However, it does nothing to address the problems of union exit and the weakening of union presence in previously unionised workplaces which are, in some ways, more severe problems for unions because they require more innovative and controversial organisational responses.

Unions, at the time of writing, faced an antagonistic Federal Government and antagonistic State Governments in five out of six states, with the only Labor State Government unpopular and hanging on to government by a slender parliamentary majority. More so than in the past, conservative governments have been united in their industrial relations policies and willing to collectively enact anti-union legislation. Across the country as a whole, the legal environment is more difficult for unions than at almost any time this century.

In addition, the support that governments have given to unions to facilitate their modernisation has evaporated. The Federal Government has abolished the Australian Trade Union Training Authority. A scaled-down version of it is now run by the union movement itself. Grants and other forms of financial assistance, be they to promote workplace reform or union amalgamations, have been terminated.

While the overall impact on union membership is likely to be negative, some positive effects may also arise. Employees may turn to unions in the context of employer excesses in a new, pro-employer legal environment. Many employers seek to reassert their dominance in the employment relationship through removing union security and decollectivising employment relations. As part of this reassertion of managerial power, and particularly in the context of legislation that shifts the balance of power in favour of employers, some can be expected to take advantage of the new environment and exploit their workforces beyond the level that has been socially acceptable in the past. Patterns of increasing work intensification are just one indicator of the potential for this to occur. Some employers will take the opportunity to reduce wages and conditions of their workers. While this will be facilitated by the reductions in safety nets in many jurisdictions for employees becoming covered by individual contracts, the problem of enforcing compliance with the award system means that many employers can be expected to reduce conditions below the level that the award would legally require them to provide. Such exploitation will provide opportunities for unions to recruit new members – provided that unions themselves are not allowing their own members' conditions to be reduced in this way – and this may offset a (small) part of the membership losses arising from this greater hostility of employers towards unions.

If activated, the sanctions provisions of industrial legislation could create severe resource crises for unions, threatening their capacity to provide even the most basic of services and therefore threatening their ability to maintain their members. A key issue will be the extent to which unions think and proceed strategically, rather than philosophically. Many provisions of the Workplace Relations Act are intended to have the effect of encouraging unions to engage in 'market-share' unionism, where they are competing against each other for members, rather than 'expansionary' unionism, where they are competing with employers for the affiliations of employees. The extent to which unions are lured down the market-share path will determine their ability to devote resources to rebuilding union membership. The unions that survive best will be those that adopt strategic approaches, enabling them to anticipate crises, plan ahead, develop collective commitment to goals, and effectively manage available resources – not just in responding to legislation, but in determining the overall course to be taken by the union over a five- or ten-year period (e.g. Pocock 1997:13).

Ultimately a strategic response by unions to declining union membership in the context of this institutional break could be expected to also require a political strategy by unions, that is, a strategy regarding the legislative and executive arms of the state. The Accord was the political strategy of the union movement (and of the Labor Party) over the period 1983–96. It is beyond the scope of this book to consider to what extent any future political strategy in response to the fall in union membership could resemble the Accord, because that raises a number of policy questions in the areas of wages policy, industry policy, job creation and the social wage that are deserving of lengthier consideration than can be given them here. But it is clear that, without a federal Labor Government in power, there would be no legislative changes to ameliorate the most severe effects on the union movement of the Workplace Relations Act and associated legislation. This is perhaps even more important for unions in the 1990s than previously, because the Workplace Relations Act uses constitutional heads of power (in particular, the corporations power) that have not been extensively used in industrial relations legislation previously to ensure its impact is more pervasive than any previous legislation, while the Competition Code extends the reach of the sanctions provisions in the Trade Practices Act further than in the past.

There would be no point in attempting to reinstitute the capacity for compulsory unionism that existed in the past. But there remains an issue concerning the seeming shortage of balance in the treatment of freedom of association, in particular arising from the prohibition on the AIRC's awarding union preference where issues of discrimination against union members potentially arise. The description of the new provisions as providing for 'freedom of association' is ironic: though they may be strategically used by unions, they cannot guarantee the right of workers to freely choose their union membership status. In the context of the broader changes taking place, they make it easier for employees to freely disassociate from unions, but more difficult to associate with a union.

The critical issue for unions, however, is likely to be their ability to recreate themselves in forms that are democratic, efficient and effective, at both the workplace and organisational level. Certainly, there are many workplaces where unions are holding their own and resisting the trend to decline. These are, typically, workplaces where unions have a delegate presence, are active in affairs affecting their members and are effective in representing and shaping the interests of their members.

Around half of unionised workplaces with five or more employees, and three-tenths of those with 20 or more employees, have no union delegates. In even larger proportions of workplaces with a union presence the union would be considered to be 'inactive'. Unions are most vulnerable to membership losses in these workplaces, and face a major task in rebuilding their presence in them. Even mining – the industry which was thought to be a bulwark of unions and where union membership fell dramatically in the face of individual contracts – the apparent strength of unions at the workplace level was largely illusory, except in coal mining where fewer inroads have been made into the well-organised core of union membership.

Much revolves around the extent to which workplace union organisation develops, builds up a delegate presence and equips delegates with the skills and resources necessary to perform their tasks. Workplace wage bargaining is helpful in as much as it might do three things: encourage the development of workplace union organisation; enable unions to avoid handing over responsibility for wage determination to employers; and remove union-based obstacles to the achievement of employers' agendas for change, thereby reducing the incentive for employers to resist or avoid unions. Yet workplace bargaining also holds dangers for unions: if the workplace- or firm-based union organisation is inadequate to the task of properly representing the interests of employees in negotiating with management, member desertion may follow. Workplace wage bargaining places the greatest pressure on that part of the union movement which (for a number of unions at least) appears most vulnerable: its workplace-level organisation.

Workplace wage bargaining is neither a simple solution nor, given the pressures that led to it, the cause of the 'problem'.

The real issue for unions is whether they have the capacity to undertake the resource and structural changes necessary to establish genuinely effective and representative workplace organisation. Many workplaces already have active, cohesive, responsive, reliable unions present. It is in the workplaces whose unions do not have those characteristics that unions will remain vulnerable to erosion or eviction. The ACTU set a target of creating 10,000 additional union delegates within three years from 1995 – one of the more important elements to the ACTU's strategy to arrest the decline in union membership.

In this context, a major set of factors influencing the retention of union membership comprises how well unions keep in contact with their members, how accurately they identify their members' needs and preferences, and how responsive they are to their members' wishes. A central issue here is communication between the workplace and the union office. The efficacy of any approach will be influenced by the context provided by union organisation: for unions with strong workplace delegate infrastructure, high quality, regular contact between the office and the delegates are important factors; for unions that are less effective in this area, more direct means of communication between the union and its members may be more effective.

Associated with this there are broader issues concerning union structures. The Australian union movement during the 1980s and 1990s has generally been more effectively coordinated than at any other time this century. It would be as fallacious to blame this for the decline in union membership as it would be to blame the increase in union sympathy for it. Rather, overseas experience shows that central coordination gives the Australian union movement several advantages in redressing union decline. It provides the opportunity to avoid squandering resources in costly jurisdictional disputes. It provides the opportunity to analyse problems, define policies and, most importantly, to spread reforms throughout the union movement. Central coordination therefore enables the innate inertia within long-established unions to be, in part, overcome and facilitates the adaptability of unions to new environments. It enables a pooling of resources to develop new models of recruitment. It provides the opportunity for consistent approaches on wages policy, enterprise bargaining and organising to be taken. In this respect, the Australian union movement has an advantage over its counterparts in the US (as well as in Britain and New Zealand). The mechanism is there; the question is whether it is able to be used effectively.

While an amalgamationist strategy might enable advantage to be taken of economies of scale in the provision of union services, the efficacy of such a strategy will depend upon a number of other factors: whether amalgamation will significantly reduce the number of unions operating in each workplace; whether it will reduce or increase the complexity of union coverage and therefore the difficulty that unions have in identifying their members' interests; whether it will promote union cohesion or union in-fighting; and whether it will lead to internal reconstruction of union organisation that will be better adapted to meeting unions' objectives and strategies and dealing with the decentralisation of bargaining. On several of these matters the performance of amalgamations to date has not been strong. A key issue for the future is whether further changes are made to union structure to overcome continuing vulnerabilities arising from multi-unionism and inter-union conflict at workplaces and the increasing complexity of union organisation and coverage. Such changes would involve something other than additional amalgamations: a recasting of the boundaries between unions, be it through exchange of members of different categories between unions (a rare phenomenon to date) or the formation of strategic industry-based federations of unions (Fisher 1998) to overcome *de facto* the within-industry cleavages that encourage 'market-share' unionism and discourage union growth. Instead, despite the potential gains from having a centrally coordinated union movement, and the amalgamation of previously competing unions, extensive competition between unions continues to be fought out at workplaces and in front of the AIRC, with considerable expense and opportunity cost.

Also at issue is whether each union's internal organisation is genuinely suitable to its objectives and strategies, and not merely a conglomeration of pre-existing structures and factions. So far it appears that the internal restructuring necessary to achieve this has often not been undertaken. It seems the potential gains from some amalgamations have not yet been achieved because of faction fighting within the newly created organisations. Such factionalism is a diversion of resources from the provision of services to members and from expansionary recruitment strategies and can worsen the alienation of existing or potential members. Whether it results from or pre-dates amalgamation, factionalism also means that merit and capability is downgraded as the basis for selecting officials and the remaining union resources are accordingly used considerably less efficiently than they otherwise would be.

Of wider relevance is resistance to change within unions. Pocock (1997) describes US unionism, and by extension Australian unionism, as having a three-layered triangular structure: at the top, a layer of new leaders committed to organising, strategic unionism, activist education and inclusiveness; at the bottom, a mix of lively activists; but in the middle, a population of long-serving officials who are the major force for inertia in the system. A centrally coordinated union movement can effect change within the top of the triangle, and can in very limited ways facilitate the development of activism at the bottom of the triangle; but the central layer, armed with the rhetoric of solidarity, the advantage of incumbency, and the culture of defensive attack, can be impervious to all but the most radical environmental changes.

This is seen in perceptions of unions by their members. Unions are often seen as achieving gains and providing protection for their members, but they are criticised for the way in which they keep in contact with their members and are not seen as giving members an adequate say in how the union operates. Workplace union delegates report no net improvement on either of these issues, and the limited evidence from the members themselves does not contradict this view. The failure of unions to keep in contact with members is directly leading to membership loss. The traditional model of the male blue collar union seemingly finds it most difficult to adapt to change and to retain the support of its constituency. In many (but not all) cases, the availability of and reliance on compulsory membership produced a particular union culture that ensured members received certain bene-fits and protections and officials obtained territory and security of tenure. This culture was able to prosper in an earlier environment but it now confronts a new world created in the wake of an institutional break in the determinants of union membership. As Pocock sees it:

> It is not too dramatic to say that the institutions of unions are the sites of a major cultural contest ... To crudely characterise it, on one side are those imbued with historically nurtured habits of solidarity and union organisation that have served them well, consolidating their hold ... Over time, some of these habits have become so solidified that they work against change ... On the other, perhaps, are a set of unions and unionists that are younger and more inclined to look forward than back. This contest has several aspects: while there are exceptions to these generalisations, it sets blue against white, public against private, it is gendered, and it poses contrasting visions of the 'proper unionist'. (Pocock 1997:3; see also Elton 1997)

The outcome of this cultural contest will be crucial in determining the future of Australian unions. Many of the surges in union membership growth have been associated with organisational innovations, by new unions led by new unionists along different lines from traditional unions (Freeman & Medoff 1984:244). Such organisational innovations seem essential if Australian unions are to be reinvigorated. Without them, many Australian unions will continue to show the characteristics of being territory-driven rather than member-driven, and will wither further in face of continuing employer and government opposition and in the context of likely member indifference to their fate.

This book highlights the importance of change, and of responses to change, in determining the direction of union membership. If the strategy of the union movement does not satisfactorily respond to the forces underlying the decline in union density, that decline will continue. Structural changes in the economy are predicted to continue to exert downward pressure on union density. Unions face ongoing challenges from casualisation of labour and the decline of the public sector. Institutional changes and the associated strategies of employers and governments are pushing unions to the edge of the employment relationship. Legislation already in place regarding compulsory unionism and individual contracting will further erode union reach. Employers will continue to seek more forms of flexibility and avenues for growth in profitability and, in the absence of an effective response, union presence will be restricted to a decreasing number of workplaces. Organisation at the workplace is necessary, but it is not sufficient to bring about the turnaround in fortunes that unions so clearly seek. If the Australian union movement is to respond and bring about a renewal of union membership, it must engage in a process of self-examination with which it may not be entirely comfortable. Whether it does so is largely in its own hands.

Appendix
Research Methodologies and Data Sources

ABS surveys are described and discussed in the relevant ABS publications. This appendix focuses on other data sources.

The Australian Workplace Industrial Relations Surveys (AWIRS)

There are several major recent survey databases that have been produced under the sponsorship of the Commonwealth Department of Industrial Relations (DIR) (now the Department of Workplace Relations and Small Business). By far the most important of these are the 1990 and 1995 Australian Workplace Industrial Relations Surveys (AWIRS90 and AWIRS95 respectively). AWIRS90 was conducted from October 1989 to May 1990, and is reported upon in *Industrial Relations at Work* (Callus et al. 1991). It consisted of two surveys. The first was a personal interview survey of 2004 workplaces, involving the administration of between one and four questionnaires in each workplace, plus (in approximately 85 per cent of them) a self-completed questionnaire containing factual data on employment and other matters. The second was a telephone survey, using a shorter questionnaire, of 349 small workplaces with 5 to 19 employees. The sample frames for both surveys were designed by the ABS from DIR specifications and drawn from its register of establishments. The population from which the sample for the main, personal interview survey was drawn comprised all workplaces with 20 or more employees in all industries except two: agriculture, forestry, fishing and hunting, and defence. The response rates were: for the main survey, 86 per cent, and for the small workplace survey, 89 per cent.

AWIRS95 was conducted during 1995–96. The main survey collected data from 2001 workplaces (a response rate of 80 per cent) with 20 or more employees. Unlike AWIRS90, it also contained data from 19,155 employees (a response rate of 64 per cent) in those workplaces. A longitudinal or panel survey of 698 workplaces (a response rate of 90 per cent) that had participated in AWIRS90 was also conducted. As with AWIRS90, the main survey included a survey of union delegates in workplaces with a union presence. Further details on AWIRS95 are contained in Morehead et al. (1997).

198

The Workplace Bargaining Surveys (WBS)

The Workplace Bargaining Research Project (WBRP) consisted of a number of stages and methodologies, undertaken by researchers from DIR and seven universities in Australia and overseas. The first element of the project comprised a review of literature and recent developments in workplace bargaining in eight countries (reported in Peetz et al. 1993). The second phase involved the undertaking of two major surveys. The 1992 Workplace Bargaining Survey (WBS92) was undertaken in December 1992 by AGB McNair on behalf of DIR. Its sample was drawn from a subsample of the workplaces with 20 or more employees that participated in AWIRS90. The WBS92 was a telephone survey with a total of 700 respondents and a response rate of 83 per cent. Thus it represented a panel of AWIRS90, enabling changes between 1989–90 and 1992–93 to be examined. Results of WBS92 were reported in two publications (Short et al. 1993; Short et al. 1994).

A second Workplace Bargaining Survey, WBS94, was undertaken in late 1994. It was undertaken by the ABS on behalf of DIR and was drawn from an independent sample. It involved face-to-face interviews with 1060 workplace managers and self-administered questionnaires completed by 11,000 employees in the majority of those workplaces. Results were reported in DIR (1995).

The Labor Council Surveys (LCS)

The Labor Council Survey (LCS-96) was undertaken on behalf of the Labor Council of New South Wales by Newspoll. It involved telephone interviews with 709 employed people, including 561 employees. Only results for employees are analysed here. Amongst the employees were 195 union members. The weights used are those recommended by Newspoll.

In 1997 a second, shorter survey was also undertaken by Newspoll on behalf of the Labor Council (LCS-97). It contained a small number of items from LCS-96 and a small number of additional questions.

The 1996 Australian Election Survey (AES)

The Australian Election Survey (AES), was undertaken on behalf of researchers at the Research School of Social Sciences (RSSS), Australian National University, shortly after the 1996 federal election. It was a complex self-completion survey with 782 employees, including 300 union members, amongst its 1797 respondents.

The Survey of Employees in Metropolitan Sydney Establishments (SEMSE)

I conducted the Survey of Employees in Metropolitan Sydney Establishments (SEMSE) in 1990–91. In total, 942 employees in 35 workplaces with 20 or more employees were surveyed, using a self-completed questionnaire, between August 1990 and April 1991. Between them, the 624 union members in the sample belonged to 34 unions. The SEMSE sample was a sub-sample of the AWIRS90 sample. The questionnaire was translated into six languages that were common in the localities being surveyed: Vietnamese, Chinese, Italian, Spanish, Turkish and Arabic. Translation was financed by the Ethnic Affairs Commission of New South Wales and undertaken by their contract translators.

Sampling was restricted to workplaces in the greater Sydney metropolitan area as defined by the ABS, ranging from the Gosford/Wyong area in the north, to the Blacktown/Penrith area in the west and the Macarthur region to the south, some 100 kilometres from the northernmost workplace. The Sydney metropolitan area accounted for 73 per cent of New South Wales workplaces and 26 per cent of all workplaces in the main AWIRS90 survey. Moreover, AWIRS findings for New South Wales were 'with few exceptions . . . generally in line with the national figures' (Cully & Fraser 1993:3). SEMSE covered most industry groups, but excluded agriculture and defence (excluded from AWIRS90), mining and electricity, gas and water.

The AWIRS team contacted a sample of AWIRS90 respondents to see whether they would permit release of their name to a researcher. Some 44 managers agreed, 42 refused and 24 could not be contacted or did not reply. Of the 43 in-scope managers who were then approached, 35 agreed to participate. Employer response rates varied by industry, and were lower amongst smaller and non-union workplaces, particularly the workplaces classified by the AWIRS team as 'informal': none of the nine non-union, predominantly small, private-sector workplaces with non-structured management, agreed to participate in SEMSE.

A sampling ratio was determined for each workplace that would lead to constant *variance* in the estimates for each workplace. Employees were selected using a process of systematic random sampling, and only *non-managerial* employees were selected. In most private-sector workplaces, it was convenient to define these as employees covered by awards. In public-sector workforces, it was necessary to identify and exclude senior management. References to 'employees' in SEMSE thus designate the non-managerial employees in the sampling frame. In this respect, the term 'employees' differs from its usage in LCS, AES and AWIRS95.

Since SEMSE also involved the collection of data from management and union delegates on matters relating to union-management relations, it was necessary in a number of workplaces to over-sample delegates; in analysing the data for employees generally, the data from delegates were weighted according to the inverse of their probability of selection. A 'Managers survey' was also undertaken at the same time as SEMSE, producing data from industrial relations managers or general managers in 30 of the 35 workplaces visited in SEMSE.

The employee response rate varied substantially between workplaces, from as low as 25 per cent to as high as 97 per cent; both these results were obtained in quite small workplaces. The median response rate was 57 per cent, and the overall response rate just over 50 per cent due to a lower response rate in a small number of larger workplaces. Employee response rates were higher in workplaces with a higher proportion of white-collar employees, where employees were able to complete the questionnaire in work time, and in workplaces where management gave active encouragement to employees to complete the questionnaire.

Employer response rates were low where there had been compulsory redundancies, where industrial conflict was *currently* under way (though there did not appear to be bias against workplaces that had *recently* experienced conflict) and where employee involvement in decision making was perceived by management to be low. However, on a number of important matters relating to industrial conflict, workplace bargaining, management, compulsory unionism and workplace reform there were no differences between SEMSE workplaces and AWIRS90 workplaces. SEMSE respondents included an under-representation of casual and part-time employees, due both to under-representation of workplaces with high casual employment (especially 'informals') and a lower response rate amongst casual employees themselves. Workplace-based surveys appear less effective at collecting data from casual employees than household-based surveys.

As the SEMSE sample cannot be said to be truly representative when compared with AWIRS, the most important issue is the impact that this had upon the information gleaned from the survey. Testing the impact of four alternative weighting systems upon estimates from SEMSE indicated that, for most questions, the difference between results from the simplest weighting system (which just accounted for the oversampling of union delegates) and the most complex weighting system (which also accounted for workplace size, the frequency of workplace size bands, and the actual industry composition of employment) were of no practical significance. Accordingly, the estimates reported in this book use a simple weighting procedure that only adjusts for the differential sampling of union delegates.

All differences between groups from survey data reported in the text are significant at least at the 5 per cent level, unless otherwise indicated. Relationships significant at the 10 per cent probability level are described as 'weak' or 'marginal' relationships. To be described as 'strong', a relationship has to be significant at the 1 per cent probability level, though to avoid verbal clutter this adjective is usually not added. In bivariate comparisons, the significance test usually used is the log-likelihood chi-squared test. In multivariate comparisons, the significance test used is the appropriate one for the relevant regression technique. Results from SEMSE are generally reported as referring to 'respondents with an opinion'. This excludes respondents whose response to the relevant question was 'no opinion', or who did not put any mark next to the question. This procedure does *not* exclude respondents whose answer was of the class 'neither agree nor disagree' or 'neither satisfied nor dissatisfied'. Such respondents are taken to have expressed an opinion that falls midway between the extreme options. Further details can be found in Peetz (1995) or obtained from the author.

Shift-share Analysis

Typically, analyses of the impact of structural change in the labour market upon unionism have relied on 'shift-share' analysis to model the impact of compositional or structural change (e.g. Visser 1988, 1991; Meltz 1985, 1990a; Freeman & Pelletier 1990). This is a precise means of estimation, to whatever level of disaggregation the data and software permit. There are several reasons for preferring this technique of analysis of structural change to the more common (in Australia) practice of including proxy variables for structural change in time-series regressions. Shift-share analysis makes maximum use of all information and no assumptions about functional form. It produces estimates that do not vary according to other explanatory variables involved and are not subject to the sampling error of the type that increases as the number of years being observed declines.

In essence, shift-share analysis of time-series data enables the separate identification of those changes in union membership that are due to:

(i)   changes in the composition of employment between groups (for example, industries, occupations) with high union membership and groups with low union membership;
(ii)   changes in the composition of employment between groups in which union membership is growing and those in which union membership is falling; and
(iii)   changes in union membership within the groups themselves.

To identify the impact of structural changes, the question asked is 'what would have happened to overall union density if union density within each group had remained unchanged over period x – would it have still risen/fallen as a result of changes in the employment shares of groups with high and low union density?' That is, the impact of structural change *between* groups is tested by simulating what union density would be if there had been no *within*-group changes in union density.

Similarly, the concepts underlying shift-share analysis can be used to analyse the importance of certain structural factors at a given point of time. For example, whether gender has an important, independent influence upon union membership can be tested by asking 'what would have been the difference between male and female unionisation rates if males and females had the same occupations and the same likelihood of being in casual employment?' That is, by assuming that male and female employees had the same distribution of employment by occupation and employment status, it is possible to test whether major differences in male and female unionisation rates would persist.

Notes

1 Patterns and Issues in Union Decline

1 The Accord was first negotiated when the ALP was in Federal Opposition in 1983 and was renegotiated several times, Accord 'Mark VII' taking effect for the period 1993–96.

2 The members series is subject to sampling error, and until recently has not been conducted annually, but the union census is subject to non-sampling error if union records are inaccurate, and its density estimates are also subject to sampling error because the denominator (the number of employees) is estimated from a survey. The union census collected data on 'financial' members of unions only from 1985; prior to that, only data on 'all' members are available and this may have been defined differently by different unions; hence, there is a break in the union census series in 1985. Estimates of union density from the union census are complicated by the fact that the ABS changed the basis for measuring the denominator (the number of employees) in the density ratio for estimates from 1990 onwards. For earlier data, the denominator in the census was based on employee estimates from the employer-based Survey of Employees and Earnings; for the later data, the denominator is based (like in the members series) on estimates from the Labour Force Survey. There are also conceptual differences between the series, for example the members series only takes account of whether employees are union members in their main job and ignores membership in their second job, whereas the census will count twice those employees who belong to more than one union. The data are presented in figures 1.1 and 1.2 and tables 1.1 and 1.2.

3 The G7 nations are: US, UK, Germany, France, Italy, Canada, Japan.

4 See Wheeler (1985); Wheeler & McClendon (1991).

5 There are some caveats on these estimates. Evidence from a database on Australian trade unions suggests that the ABS union census may underestimate union density in the 1890s by a factor of two or three. Estimates for the early 20th century may also be understated, by an as yet unknown amount (Quinlan & Gardner 1994).

6 As Rawson (1978:27) suggests, the decline may have been even greater than union officials cared to admit in their census return: many 'members' had paid no fees for years.

7 The employment data used here are from Keating (1973), and exclude the defence forces.

2 Joining and Leaving Unions

1 The original AWIRS95 data (N = 18,863) had 39 per cent agreeing and 33 per cent disagreeing that they would rather be in a union; restricting the sample to industries covered in SEMSE changes these figures to 39 and 31 (N = 8775); excluding non-union unstructured workplaces brings them to 40 and 30 (N = 8400); and excluding the ASCO group managers brings them to 41 and 29 (N = 7578). The combined proportion of neutrals and undecideds remains unchanged at 30 per cent.

2 In AES, some 63 per cent of all employees said they were free to choose whether to join a union, but this would have included an unknown proportion who were in non-union workplaces. LCS-96 showed that the majority of employees in non-union workplaces considered that their employer would not like them to join a union.

3 Data were missing on union workplace presence for 3 per cent of employees.

4 Figures do not add to 100 per cent due to rounding.

5 Amongst respondents to the union instrumentality question, by mathematical necessity the union exit rate was the converse of the rate of union density.

6 If anything, sample bias in SEMSE might have led to overstatement rather than understatement of union satisfaction.

7 Responses to each of the three questions were scored from 1 (strongly agree) to 5 (strongly disagree). To produce the index they were combined into a single additive scale, the scores on which ranged from 3 (most positive) to 15 (most negative).

8 See chapter seven for a discussion of union strength.

9 This table is based on cross-tabulations that do not control for other variables. However, regression analysis (Peetz 1998) shows the persistence of these relationships in multivariate analysis.

10 For responsiveness $\times$ instrumentality r = .31; responsiveness $\times$ union sympathy r = .15; protection $\times$ instrumentality r = .35; protection $\times$ union sympathy r = .19.

3 Sympathy for Unions

1 The variable was not included because the resultant index would not have had a sufficiently high α, and therefore would not be sufficiently reliable.

2 Responses to this question should not be directly compared with the other question on union power cited earlier, as the earlier question tends to systematically produce fewer negative responses.

4 Structural Change in the Labour Market

1 The level of aggregation is the one-digit International Standard Industrial Classification (ISIC) level.

2 These are the 12 one-digit Australian Standard Industry Classification (ASIC) industries, listed in note 3 below.
3 Low-density industries were agriculture, recreation and personal services, wholesale and retail trade, and finance, property and business services. Medium-density industries were construction, manufacturing, community services and mining. High-density industries were transport and storage, public administration and defence, communications, and electricity, gas and water.
4 The ABS changed from ASIC to the Australian and New Zealand Standard Industry Classification (ANZSIC) system, increased the number of industries from 12 to 17 and altered the relative size of the 'high' and 'low' density industries.
5 Analysis of the monthly labour force survey employment data (ABS Cat. No. 6303.0) shows that the long benign period, dating back to the war, during which changes in the industrial (but not necessarily occupational) composition of employment favoured unions, peaked in 1983–84; from then on changes in the industrial composition of employment have gone against unions. There are no members survey data for 1983–84.
6 For example, in the 1982–92 period, public-sector employment grew in community services and transport and storage by less than 30 per cent while private-sector employment grew by over 60 per cent. In communications and finance, property and business services, public-sector employment fell while private-sector employment grew by 40 per cent or more.
7 In electoral studies, swing is expressed as a proportion of total voters ('normal swing') rather than as a proportion of voters for the party experiencing the swing against it ('partial swing'), as the use of partial swing would imply that, with recurrent swings oscillating between parties, the differences in voting patterns between electorates would eventually disappear. Normal swing is more easily predicted than partial swing, and vote switchers do not come from a pool of electors who vote for only one party but from a pool of 'soft' voters who could previously have voted for any party (Peetz 1989:472).
8 Longer-term data on firm size suggest that the size effect might be a recent phenomenon, though it is difficult to be certain. The Survey of Employees and Earnings (SEE) has collected data on enterprise size since 1985–86. (The data relate to the size of an enterprise within a State. Each operation in each State counts as a separate enterprise.) They show that there was little in the way of change in the share of different size groups between 1985–86 and 1990–91. Then, in May 1991, a sharp drop in the share of large enterprises and rise in the share of small enterprises was observed. After a small, seasonal reversal, this shift has continued. It is unlikely, however, that the shift in the composition of employment was as severe as the SEE data suggest. More likely, the May 1991 data reflected an updating of the business register by the ABS and the catching up with earlier trends. The December 1990 SEE employee data had fallen behind the LFS data.
9 This is measured at the one-digit International Standard Industries Classification (ISIC) level.

5 The Institutional Break in Union Membership

1 It would be wrong to think that there is a consistent employer 'push' for closer cooperation with their employees. For every employee who thinks

that their employer is cooperating better with them, there is at least another employee who thinks that things are getting worse – as would be expected, given the inherent conflicts that exist in the employment relationship (Peetz 1996).

2 The terms 'closed shops' and 'compulsory unionism' are used more or less interchangeably here, to refer to situations where an employee is required to belong to a union in order to obtain and/or retain his or her job. No distinction is made between pre-entry and post-entry closed shops, as this distinction is not important for understanding the overall trends, and time-series data making this distinction are almost unobtainable.

3 An estimate of 33 per cent is used for August 1995, based on interpolation of the trend from 54 per cent in mid-1990 to 29 per cent in early 1996.

4 (r = .74). Wooden estimated the proportion of union members who were covered by closed shops. This has been adjusted to an estimate of the proportion of employees who were covered by closed shops by using data in Callus et al. (1991). Wooden underestimated the incidence of closed shops by not taking full account of the data from union delegates about the existence of closed shops (Peetz 1995), but this does not make a major difference to the grouping of industries by their incidence of closed shops.

5 In 1988, 337 non-randomly selected workplace managers participated in the survey using a self-administered questionnaire (BCA 1989); the 1988 survey was reviewed by Frenkel and Peetz (1990a, b). The sample size and selection process for the 1992 survey is not reported in the BCA's main publication of findings (Hilmer et al. 1993).

6 The chief executive officer (CEO) data come from a separate survey of 61 BCA CEOs undertaken in 1992, which is compared to a survey of 54 CEOs in 1988, and is reported (without frequencies or any description of the questions) in Hilmer et al. (1993:73). According to Hilmer et al., 'voluntary unionism' was the third 'most preferred change to Australian industrial relations' in 1992, whereas 'end closed shop agreements' was the sixth 'most preferred' change in 1988.

7 This relationship persisted after controlling for industry and occupation. AWIRS95 does not provide data on union-related questions for non-members in open jobs, except for same-workplace union leavers.

8 This is the sum of estimates in column 5 of table 5.4 over the four years concerned.

9 Firm size, as defined by the ABS, refers to the size of the enterprise within a State/Territory, not Australia-wide.

10 The higher level of overall dissonance between union membership and status in the two LCS data sets partly reflects the lower proportion of 'neutrals' identified through the question as a result of the way potential responses were framed to discourage respondents from sitting on the fence.

6 Within the Workplace

1 AWIRS panel density estimates were implied from questions regarding whether 'some', 'none', 'most' or 'all' employees in each occupational group belonged to a union. It was assumed that if the respondent said 'most' then 67 per cent of the relevant occupational group belonged to a union, 'some' indicated 33 per cent, and so on. Hence the distribution of density estimates has a multi-modal distribution, peaking around 33 and

67 per cent, whereas estimates from the main survey based on a direct question do not.

2   Some workplaces only had data for one year. Hence the difference in the averages for 1989–90 and 1995–96 (65 – 54) is not the same as the average difference (9).

3   This was done through ordinary least squares regression.

4   While Callus et al. (1991) called this category 'workplace bargainers', Morehead et al. (1997:327) renamed it as 'delegate negotiations', perhaps to avoid confusion with the post-AWIRS90 development of 'enterprise bargaining' in the wage system and to emphasise that it does not encompass non-union bargaining or bargaining beyond the workplace. However, for our purposes it is adequate to retain the original nomenclature.

5   An early indication of this was found in the AWIRS90 data: in work-places where management saw no need to change any awards at the workplace, unionisation had been perceived as falling (by management) in less than 5 per cent of cases and as rising in 12 per cent. But amongst workplaces where management wanted to make changes to awards, unionisation fell in 9 per cent and rose in just 10 per cent.

6   To be precise, during the year prior to the survey undertaken in 1995–96.

7   This pattern occurred regardless of whether over-award payments were observed at the start or at the end of the period. The data presented here are based on whether over-awards were paid in 1989–90.

8   $3.3 \times 0.37 = 1.2$. The actual figure will be slightly greater than this because of higher deunionisation rates in workplaces with less than 20 employees.

9   This was significant only at the 10 per cent level on the weighted data, but the estimates were identical using unweighted data and here the difference was significant at the 0.1 per cent level because of the larger sample size.

10 Even in a workplace with only 20 union members where the probability of any individual leaving a union is 50 per cent, the probability of it deunionising is less than 0.0000001, and for larger numbers the probability is exponentially smaller, whereas the observed proportion of workplaces with under 100 employees deunionising was 0.09.

11 The pattern in workplaces that remained non-union was less stark: 25 per cent of employees said they were more dissatisfied, and 25 per cent were more satisfied. There is no information on workplaces that switched from non-union to union status prior to WBS94; on the basis of figures discussed above, we might not expect some with high levels of dissatisfaction to remain non-union for long.

12 Wooden and Balchin estimated, from AWIRS90 data, that where the major workplace union had 35,000 to 75,000 members, average workplace union density was 9 percentage points less than where the major union had less than 5000 members; unions with more than 75,000 members were no less successful than those with 5000 or fewer members. Presumably the discrepancy with Harris arose from use of different control variables.

13 Union strength was also perceived to be higher amongst employees who belonged to unions with over 75,000 members, and union strength was seen to be least likely to be increasing by members in unions with under 40,000 members. For an explanation of these variables, see chapter seven.

14 In another 1 per cent of multi-union workplaces in the main survey, the number of unions had changed because of employees switching unions, but in half of these cases the number of unions had increased, rather than decreased, as a result.

7 The Accord and the Post-Accord Industrial Relations Order

1   Earlier, measured real wages rose sharply in late 1983 and early 1984 following the end of the wages pause and the Medicare effect on the CPI.
2   For further details see Peetz and Groot (forthcoming).
3   These issues were: staffing or manning levels; working conditions; occupational health and safety; introduction of new technology; dismissals and disciplinary action; and changes to work practices.
4   See the glossary for explanation of these terms.
5   This provided, in effect, that a new union could not be registered if the potential members could already conveniently belong to an existing registered union.
6   The 'no disadvantage' test essentially provided that an agreement would not be certified or approved if it reduced employees' overall entitlements below the benefits provided in the relevant award and it was against the public interest for their benefits to be so reduced.

Glossary

Accord A bilateral prices and incomes policy, agreed between the Federal Australian Labor Party (ALP) Government and the Australian Council of Trade Unions, involving agreement on wage increases and/or wage-fixing arrangements and varying elements of economic, social and industrial policy. The Accord was first negotiated when the ALP was in Federal Opposition in 1983 and was renegotiated several times, Accord 'Mark VII' taking effect for the period 1993–96.

active union workplace A workplace with active union delegate(s). A workplace was classified as having active unions if (a) the senior delegate of the largest union spent one hour or more per week on union activities and carried out tasks beyond recruiting members and (b) it satisfied at least one of the following: a general meeting of members had been held at least every six months in the year preceding the survey; a union committee existed and met with management at least three times in the previous year; or the senior delegate of the largest union met with management at least once a month.

aggregate union exit rate Union leavers as a proportion of the total number of union members and leavers.

apathy See **union apathy**.

attitudinal union propensity An attitudinal measure of whether employees, free to choose, would prefer to belong or not belong to a union. This measures a general predisposition towards union membership. This is measured in SEMSE by responses to the statement 'If I were totally free to choose, I would rather be in a union than not in one.'

availability See **union reach**.

award restructuring A process of internal restructuring of awards, formally commenced as a result of the AIRC's August 1988 National Wage Case decision, aimed principally at reducing the number of classifications in awards, promoting broadbanding and multiskilling, improving career paths and removing inefficiencies in awards.

bargaining workplace A workplace in which bargaining with a union takes place. In AWIRS, this was defined as existing where the management respondent indicated that negotiation with the union with the most members at the workplace had taken place on any issue in the previous year, and that

209

delegates had been involved in negotiations on at least one out of the following: staffing levels, wage increases, working conditions, occupational health and safety, discipline, change to work practices, or the introduction of new technology.

blue-collar workers   Workers employed in manual occupations (such as tradespersons, plant and machine operators, labourers and related workers).

Coalition   The Liberal and National Party (conservative) political coalition (Australia).

closed shop   A workplace or work area in which union membership is, in effect, compulsory.

compulsory unionism   A requirement that employees in particular jobs belong to a union.

computer-integrated manufacturing   Advanced factory automation in which all aspects of manufacturing, including design, production, inspection and packing, are coordinated and controlled by computers (Lamming & Bessant 1988:42–3).

critical juncture   A major watershed in political life that establishes certain directions of change and forecloses others in a way that shapes politics for years to come.

delegates   See **union delegates**.

deunionisation rate   The number of workplaces that were both unionised in 1989–90 and union-free in 1992–93, divided by the total number of workplaces that were unionised in 1989–90.

enterprise bargaining   See **single-employer bargaining**.

enterprise bargaining principle   A wage principle of the AIRC, introduced in the October 1991 National Wage Case decision, that allowed for wage increases to be negotiated between unions and individual employers provided that certain conditions were met.

enterprise union   A union that recruits its members from a single enterprise, rather than on the basis of their trade or occupation (Callus & Sutcliffe 1994:61).

free-riding   Obtaining the benefits (e.g. of union membership) without incurring the costs involved in securing those benefits (e.g. paying union dues).

ideology   See **union sympathy**.

indexation   See **wage indexation**.

informal workplace   A non-union, non-bargaining workplace without **structured management**.

institutional break   A fundamental change (or 'paradigm shift') in the relationships governing union membership.

instrumental incentive to unionise   The extent to which the benefits of trade union membership provide an incentive for employees to join a union.

instrumentality   See **union instrumentality**.

just-in-time   A production system that aims to provide component parts and materials only as they are required at a particular stage of the production process. This relieves firms of the need to maintain stockpiles or inventories and is designed to reduce waste and improve efficiency (Sutcliffe & Callus 1994:103).

leaders   See **union officials and leaders**.

leavers   See **union leavers**.

managers survey   A survey of managers associated with SEMSE (see Appendix).

members' survey   The ABS survey, *Trade Union Members, Australia* (Cat. No. 6325.0) (see chapter two).

member-driven union   A union whose principal orientation is towards securing maximum coverage and retention of members through interactions with employees. It is generally alert to and responds to members' wishes and interests and gives high priority to the workplace, internal democracy, merit principles and circulation of leadership. See also **territory-driven union**.

negative propensity   A preference by employees not to be in a union.

non-bargaining workplace   A workplace in which bargaining does not take place. For measurement see **bargaining workplace**.

non-union job   A form of **restricted job** in which the occupant does not belong to a union, irrespective of employee preference.

observed union propensity   A behavioural measure of union propensity, based on observations of whether employees who are free to choose actually join a union. In SEMSE, this is measured by union status in open jobs.

officials   See **union officials and leaders**.

open job   A job in which the union status of the occupant is primarily determined by the choice of the occupant, that is by **union propensity**, rather than by **union reach**.

open neutrals   Employees in **open jobs** who do not show a preference either to belong, or not to belong, to a union (i.e. have neutral **union propensity**).

panel survey   A longitudinal survey in which a part of the original sample is reinterviewed at a later point in time, to control for the effects of compositional change in the sample and identify factors influencing change within the respondent unit (e.g. the workplace). In the case of AWIRS, the panel survey comprised 698 workplaces in which managers (and, where available, union delegates) were interviewed in 1989–90 and again in 1995–96, using a similar questionnaire.

paradigm shift   An 'institutional break' or fundamental change in the relationships governing union membership.

pattern bargaining   Bargaining that is based upon the outcome of agreements in other firms, industries or sectors. The initial agreements are used as models for others' agreements (Callus & Sutcliffe 1994:139).

positive propensity   A preference by employees to belong to a union.

prices and incomes Accord   See **Accord**.

propensity   See **union propensity**.

protection   See **union protection**.

quality circle   A work team given responsibility for advising management in regard to possible efficiencies, improved production methods and quality control. Work teams generally consist of managers or supervisors and the relevant work group, and tend to focus on the need for continuous improvement in relation to the part of the production process for which they are responsible (Sutcliffe & Callus 1994:150).

reach   See **union reach**.

responsiveness   See **union responsiveness**.

restricted jobs   Jobs where the union status of an employee is determined by the characteristics of the job rather than the choice of the employee. There are two types: *restricted union jobs*, arising usually from decisions by unions, management and/or tribunals that those jobs should be unionised; and *restricted non-union jobs*, arising from either employer attempts to prevent unionisation or union failure to contact and recruit employees.

retention ratio   After employees leave a closed shop (either because it is withdrawn or the members change jobs), the proportion of formerly compulsorily unionised employees who remain as union members.

same-workplace exit rate   The number of employees who have left a union at their current workplace, divided by the sum of this group plus current members at the workplace.

satisfaction   See **union satisfaction**.

second tier   An aspect of the 'Restructuring and Efficiency Principle' under the ACAC's 1987 wage principles. Under the second tier of wage fixing, employees were entitled to an increase of up to 4 per cent based on efficiency gains (often in the form of cost offsets) negotiated at the enterprise or workplace level.

shift-share analysis   A method of disaggregating labour force (and other) data which separately identifies the effect of structural change in employment shares *between* groups and the effect of *within*-group changes in, for example, union density (see Appendix).

single-employer bargaining   Bargaining between a union (or employees) and a single employer. Typically single-employer bargaining occurs at the level of either the location ('workplace bargaining') or the organisation ('enterprise bargaining'). In common parlance the terms 'workplace bargaining' and 'enterprise bargaining' are used interchangeably.

single unionism   Having only one union within a workplace.

structured management   A workplace in which management's approach to managing employees is predominantly structured. In AWIRS, structured management was defined as existing where at least four of the following were present: a formal grievance procedure that is used by managers at least some of the time; a formal disciplinary procedure; monitoring of employees by the use of any two of performance appraisal, work study or measurement of labour productivity; employee relations training for most first-line managers; a committee or employee representative for occupational health and safety; either a joint consultative council or quality circle that meets more than four times a year; and a manager at the workplace whose job included responsibility for equal employment opportunities.

sympathy   See **union sympathy**.

territory-driven union   A union whose principal orientation is towards securing maximum coverage of members through interactions with employers, tribunals and/or the state. The principal tools of territory-driven unions are compulsory membership agreements or determinations and union preference clauses, and they are characterised by a focus on extending territorial boundaries, inertia in internal structures, defending incumbency of existing officers, and factional alignments based around internal territories, while lower priority is given to developing workplace communication structures.

total quality management   An approach to the management of an organisation, based on consideration for the clients of the organisation, that emphasises the need to maintain the quality of the services provided to them. It is associated with advanced production and process techniques (such as **just-in-time**) and with participative work practices and a means of delivering quality (such as **quality circles**) (Sutcliffe & Callus 1994:187).

union apathy   A disinterest in union matters and a consequent lack of opinion on union-related issues. In SEMSE, this is measured in terms of the number, out of 13 union-related questions, that are answered with neutral ('neither agree nor disagree', 'neither satisfied nor dissatisfied') or 'no opinion' responses. A union apathetic is defined as one who answers more than half those questions in this way.

union cohesion The extent to which unions appeared to be working together rather than fighting with each other. This is measured in SEMSE by responses to the statement 'unions at this workplace spend a lot of time fighting each other'.

union competencies A group of characteristics referring to whether unions are seen by their members as being responsive to their priorities, protecting their interests, having influence at the workplace and behaving in a cohesive manner.

union commitment A measure of identity with a union.

union delegates Shop stewards or other delegates or representatives of the union who are employed at the workplace.

union exit Leaving a union: see also **aggregate union exit rate** and **same-workplace union exit rate**.

union instrumentality The extent to which employees consider that they have benefited or will benefit from union membership. In SEMSE this is measured by responses to the question 'Have you benefited from belonging to a union, or been made worse off by it?'

union job A form of **restricted job** in which the occupant must belong to a union, irrespective of employee preference, as a result of union compulsion.

union joiners Employees who have recently joined a union. In SEMSE, this is measured as the number of employees who have been a union member for one year or less.

union joining rate The number of employees who have been a union member for one year or less as a proportion of the sum of that number and the number of non-members.

union leavers Employees who have previously belonged to a union but are now non-members.

union officials and leaders In SEMSE, refers to full-time officers and leaders of the trade union that represents 'employees like' the respondent.

union propensity The willingness or unwillingness of employees to join a union. This can be measured as **attitudinal union propensity** or as a behavioural measure – **observed union propensity**. Unless otherwise specified, the term 'union propensity' when used in the text generally refers to attitudinal propensity.

union protection The extent to which employees consider they are protected in their employment by union membership. In SEMSE, this is measured by responses to questions on whether unions here make sure their members get a fair go and whether unions here do a good job in obtaining a safe and comfortable working environment.

union reach The extent to which a job is non-union, optionally unionised, or compulsorily unionised. When an employee is in a restricted job, his/her union status is determined by union reach. When an employee is in an open job, his/her membership status is not predetermined by union reach but instead is a result of their **union propensity**. Union reach determines the union status of a job when, for example: it is a condition of employment that an employee belong to a union (union compulsion); an employee belongs to a union because of peer pressure rather than his/her own preference; an employer prevents unions from gaining access to employees or otherwise avoids unionisation by making jobs non-union; an employee does not join a union because there has been no information provided to him/her about the union and the union has not attempted to organise the job or workplace.

union responsiveness   The extent to which employees consider that unions are able to reflect accurately and respond to employee preferences on desired conditions. In SEMSE, this is measured by responses to questions on whether unions here generally do what their members want, whether unions who have members here really take notice of their members' problems and complaints and satisfaction with the way unions here keep in contact with employees.

union satisfaction   The extent to which employees are satisfied with their union. In SEMSE, two measures of union satisfaction are used: satisfaction with union delegates at the workplace and satisfaction with the officials and leaders of the union that represents employees 'like' them.

union sympathy   A general ideology regarding unionism. This is quite distinct from the organisational values and culture that may be possessed by unions themselves. Union sympathy is measured in SEMSE by responses to questions on whether Australia would be better off without unions and whether Australian unions have too much power.

union tenure   The length of time a member has been in a union.

union voice   The extent to which employees consider unions can represent and protect their interests. In SEMSE, union voice is measured through those items measuring union responsiveness and union protection.

union wage   The wage rate achieved from bargaining between unions and employers, as distinct from the going wage rate in non-union areas. The gap between these two wages, holding other variables constant, is the 'union wage differential'.

unwilling conscripts   Employees who belong to a union but would prefer not to be in one. They usually belong because of some form of union compulsion.

unwillingly excluded   Employees who do not belong to a union but would prefer to be in one if free to choose.

volunteers   Employees who join a union by choice.

wage indexation   The tying of wage increases to increases in the consumer price index (CPI). In the period 1983–85, a series of National Wage Case decisions awarded rises in award wages approximately every six months in line with rises in the CPI.

white-collar workers   Workers employed in non-manual occupations (such as administrators and managers, professionals, para-professionals, clerks, sales and personal service workers).

work study   A form of job appraisal concerned with improving efficiency, for example, through the application of time and motion studies (Sutcliffe & Callus 1994:207).

workplace bargaining   See **single-employer bargaining**.

Bibliography

ABS (Australian Bureau of Statistics) Cat. No. 6303.0, *Labour Force, Australia.*
ABS Cat. No. 6310.0, *Weekly Earnings of Employees (Distribution), Australia.*
ABS Cat. No. 6319.0, *Superannuation, Australia.*
ABS Cat. No. 6323.0, *Trade Union Statistics, Australia.*
ABS Cat. No. 6325.0, *Trade Union Members, Australia.*
ABS Cat. No. 6342.0, *Working Arrangements, Australia.*
ACTU (Australian Council of Trade Unions) (1987) *Future Strategies for the Trade Union Movement*, Melbourne.
ACTU (1991) *Together for Tomorrow*, Melbourne.
ACTU/TDC (Australian Council of Trade Unions and Trade Development Council) (1987) *Australian Reconstructed*, AGPS, Canberra.
Adams, M. (1994) 'Tassie Union's Winning Formula', *Workplace*, Winter, 27–9.
Adams, R.J. (1977) 'Bain's Theory of White-Collar Union Growth: A Conceptual Critique', *British Journal of Industrial Relations*, 15(3), November, 317–21.
Age Poll (1971) 'Villains in the Power Game', *Age*, 25 March.
Age Poll (1974) 'Unions Too Powerful, Say Voters', *Age*, 12 August.
Age Poll (1988) 'Poll Puts Libs Ahead on Immigration', *Age* (and *Sydney Morning Herald*), 9 September.
AIRC (Australian Industrial Relations Commission) (1994) *Aluminium Industry (Comalco Bell Bay Companies) Award 1983: Decision*, Print L7449, Melbourne, 8 December.
Aitkin, D. (1977) *Stability and Change in Australian Politics*, 1st edn, ANU Press, Canberra.
ALP/ACTU (Australian Labor Party and Australian Council of Trade Unions) (1983) 'Statement of Accord by the Australian Labor Party and the Australian Council of Trade Unions Regarding Economic Policy', February, reprinted in Advisory Committee on Prices and Incomes (1984) *Prices and Incomes Policy: The Third Progress Report on Government Initiatives*, AGPS, Canberra, December, 120–44.
ANOP (Australian Nationwide Opinion Polls) (1989) 'The Image of the Trade Union Movement in Australia', Research Project for the Development of the ACTU's Communications Campaign, Sydney, February.

ANOP (1992) 'The Middle Ground View of Industrial Relations Issues: A Qualitative Research Analysis Prepared for the ACTU', October, Sydney.

Antos, J.R., Chandler, M. & Mellow, W. (1980) 'Sex Differences in Union Membership', *Industrial and Labor Relations Review*, 33(2), January, 162–9.

APAS (Australian Political Attitudes Survey) (1979), frequencies code book and computer file, School of History, Politics and Philosophy, Macquarie University, Sydney.

APOP (Australian Public Opinion Polls) (1942) 'Public's Attitude to Enforced Unionism', Poll 63, July.

APOP (1943a) 'Opinion Divided on Enforced Unionism', Poll 107, February.

APOP (1943b) 'Public Opposed to Compulsory Unionism', Poll 143, August.

APOP (1946) 'Arbitration Court as Wage-Fixer', Poll 339, April–May.

APOP (1948) 'No Arbitration While Men are on Strike', Poll 487, February–March.

APOP (1949) 'Public Puts Arbitration Before Right to Strike', Poll 638, November–December.

APOP (1951) 'Trade Unions Have Done Good Work', Poll 761, February.

APOP (1953a) 'Vary Margins With Basic Wage', Poll 932, June–July.

APOP (1953b) 'Compulsory Unionism Not Too Popular', Poll 949, August.

APOP (1955) 'Leave Hours, Wages to the Court', Poll 1131, November–December.

APOP (1959) 'Preference for Voluntary Unions', Poll 1369, December.

APOP (1960) 'Arbitration More Value than Strikes', Poll 1478, June–August 1960.

APOP (1962) 'Court Better than Strikes', Poll 1640, November–December.

APOP (1966) 'Unions Approved if Voluntary', Poll 1952, November.

APOP (1970) 'Fix Wages by Arbitration', Poll 2172, January–March.

APOP (1971) 'Forced Unionism Opposed', *Advertiser*, 17 August.

APOP (1979) 'Wage Indexation System Should be Modified', Poll No. 02/07/79, 1 August.

APOP (1984), 'Wage System gets a Strong "Yes"', Poll No. 04/11/84, November.

APOP (1986), 'Conflicting Views on Deregulation and Privatisation', Gallup Poll No. 03/12/85, 2 January.

Archer, R. (1995) 'Organising: An International Perspective', in *Unions 2000*, Evatt Foundation, Sydney, July.

Arthur Andersen/Holding Redlich (1993) 'Results of the 1993 Enterprise Bargaining Survey', Sydney.

Ashenfelter, O. & Pencavel, J.H. (1969) 'American Trade Union Growth: 1900–1960', *Quarterly Journal of Economics*, 83(3), August, 434–48.

Bachrach, P. & Baratz, M.S. (1962) 'The Two Faces of Power', *American Political Science Review*, 56(4), December, 947–52.

Bachrach, P. & Baratz, M.S. (1963) 'Decisions and Nondecisions: an Analytical Framework', *American Political Science Review*, 57(3), September, 632–42.

Bachrach, P. & Baratz, M.S. (1970) *Power and Poverty: Theory and Practice*, Oxford University Press, New York.

Badcock, B. (1982) 'Was the South Australian Labor Party Struck Down by a Bus?', *Politics*, 17(1), May, 77–83.

Bain, G.S. (1970) *The Growth of White Collar Unionism*, Oxford University Press, London.

Bain, G.S. & Elsheikh, F. (1976) *Union Growth and the Business Cycle: an Econometric Analysis*, Blackwell, Oxford.

Bain, G.S. & Price, R. (1983) 'Union Growth: Dimensions, Determinants and Destiny', in G.S. Bain (ed) *Industrial Relations in Britain*, Blackwell, Oxford, 3–34.

Barbash, J. (1985) 'Do We Really Want Labor on the Ropes?', *Harvard Business Review*, July–August, 20.

Barling, J., Fullagar, C. & Kelloway, E.K. (1992) *The Union and Its Members: A Psychological Approach*, Oxford University Press, New York.

Barling, J., Kelloway, E.K. & Bremermann, E.H. (1991) 'Pre-employment Predictors of Union Attitudes: The Role of Family Socialization and Work Beliefs', *Journal of Applied Psychology*, 76, 725–31.

Batstone, E., Boraston, & Frenkel, S.J. (1977) *Shop Stewards in Action*, Blackwell, Oxford.

Baupain, T. (1992) 'Trade Union Membership: Further Probing of Explanatory Factors with Special Reference to Belgium', communication to Ninth World Congress, International Industrial Relations Association, Sydney, September.

BCA (Business Council of Australia) (1987) 'Towards an Enterprise-based Industrial Relations System', *Business Council Bulletin*, 32, March, 6–10.

BCA (1989) *Enterprise-based Bargaining Units: A Better Way Of Working*, BCA, Melbourne.

BCA (1993) 'The *Employment Contracts Act* and the Reform of Industrial Relations in New Zealand', *Business Council Bulletin*, 94, supplement, January/February, 1–19.

Beaumont, P. (1983) 'Statutory Recognition Provisions in Britain, 1976–1980', *Relations Industrielles*, 38(4).

Beaumont, P. (1987) *The Decline of Trade Union Organisation*, Croom Helm, London.

Beaumont, P. & Elliot, J. (1992) 'Employee Choice Among Unions: the Case of Nurses in the NHS', *Industrial Relations Journal*, 23(2), Summer, 130–43.

Beaumont, P. & Harris, R. (1991) 'Trade Union Recognition and Employment Contraction, Britain 1980–1984', *British Journal of Industrial Relations*, 29(1), March, 49–58.

Beaumont, P. & Harris, R. (1993) 'Opposition to Unions in the Non-union Sector in Britain', mimeo, Department of Social and Economic Research, University of Glasgow.

Beaumont, P. & Rennie, I. (1986) 'Organisational Culture and Non-union Status of Small Businesses', *Industrial Relations Journal*, 17(3), Autumn, 214–24.

Beaumont, P., Thomson, A.W.J. & Gregory, M.B. (1980) 'Bargaining Structure', *Management Decision*, 18(3), 103–69.

Ben-Israel, G. & Fisher, H. (1992) 'Trade Unions in the Future: Organizational Strategies in a Changing Environment', in *Trade Unionism in the Future*, Ninth World Congress of International Industrial Relations Association, Proceedings Volume 2, 30 August–3 September, 85–97.

Bernstein, A. (1994) 'Why America Needs Unions – But Not the Kind it has Now', *Business Week*, 23 May, 70–82.

Berry, P. & Kitchener, G. (1989) *Can Unions Survive?*, Building Workers Industrial Union (ACT Branch), Canberra, September.

Beynon, H. & Blackburn, R.M. (1972) *Perceptions of Work*, Cambridge University Press, Cambridge, UK.

Beynon, H. & McMylor, P. (1985) 'Decisive Power: The New Tory State Against the Miners' in H. Beynon (ed.), *Digging Deeper*, Verso, 29–46.

Bigoness, W.J. & Tosi, H.L. (1984) 'Correlates of Voting Behaviour in a Union Decertification Election', *Academy of Management Journal*, 27(3), September, 654–9.

Blanchflower, D.G. & Freeman, R.B. (1992) 'Unionism in the US and Other Advanced OECD Countries', *Industrial Relations*, 31(1), Winter, 56–79.

Bodman, P.M. (1996) 'Explaining the Decline in Australian Trade Union Membership', paper presented to Australian Conference of Economists, Canberra, September.

Booth, A.L. (1983) 'A Reconsideration of Trade Union Growth in the United Kingdom', *British Journal of Industrial Relations*, 21(3), November, 377–91.

Booth, A.L. (1986) 'Estimating the Probability of Trade Union Membership: A Study of Men and Women in Britain', *Economica*, 53, February, 41–61.

Booth, A.L. (1991) 'What Do Unions Do Now? A Study of the Provision by British Trade Unions of Benefits and Services to their Members', *Labour Studies Journal*, Summer, 50–64.

Borland, J. & Ouliaris, S. (1989) 'The Determinants of Australian Trade Union Membership', Working Paper 163, Department of Economics and Commerce, University of Melbourne.

Boxall, P. & Haynes, P. (1992), 'Unions and Non-union Bargaining Agents Under the *Employment Contracts Act 1991*: An Assessment After 12 months', *New Zealand Journal of Industrial Relations*, Vol. 17 No. 2, August.

Bradbury, B., Doyle, J. & Whiteford, P. (1990) 'Trends in the Disposable Incomes of Australian Families, 1982–83 to 1989–90', *Discussion Paper No. 16*, Social Policy Research Centre, University of New South Wales, Sydney, January.

Bray, M. & Walsh, P. (1994) 'Accord and Discord: The Differing Fates of Corporatism under Labour Governments in Australia and New Zealand', *Labour and Industry*, 6(3), October, 1–26.

Brett, J.M. (1980) 'Why Employees Want Unions', *Organizational Dynamics*, 8(4), Spring, 47–59.

Brooks, B. (1978) *The Practice of Industrial Relations in New Zealand*, CCH, Auckland.

Brooks, G.W. & Gamm, S. (1976) 'The Causes and Effects of Union Mergers with Special Reference to Selected Cases in the '60s and '70s', Labour Management Services Administration, Department of Labor, Washington DC, September.

Brotslaw, I. (1967) 'Attitudes of Retail Workers Towards Union Organisation', *Labor Law Journal*, 18(3), March, 149–71.

Bruce, P.G. (1989) 'Political Parties and Labour Legislation in Canada and the US', *Industrial Relations*, 28(2), Spring, 115–41.

Callus, R., Morehead, A., Cully, M. & Buchanan, J. (1991) *Industrial Relations at Work*, Department of Industrial Relations, AGPS, Canberra.

Cameron, C. (1982) *Unions in Crisis*, Hill of Content, Melbourne.

Cameron, D. (1984) 'Social Democracy, Corporatism, Labour Quiescence and the Representation of Economic Interests in Advanced Capitalist Society', in J.H. Goldthorpe (ed.), *Order and Conflict in Contemporary Capitalism*, Clarendon, Oxford, 143–78.

Carney, S. (1988) *Australia in Accord: Politics and Industrial Relations Under the Hawke Government*, Sun, Melbourne.

Carruth, A. & Disney, R. (1988), 'Where Have Two Million Trade Union Members Gone?' *Economica*, 55(217), February, 1–19.

Castles, F. (ed.) (1993) *Families of Nations*, Dartmouth.

Chaison, G.N. (1986) *When Unions Merge*, Lexington Books, Lexington MA.

Chaison, G.N. & Rose, J.B. (1990) 'Continental Divide: The Direction and State of North American Unions', in D. Lewis, D. Lipsky & D. Sockell (eds), *Advances in Industrial and Labour Relations*, JAI Press, Greenwich CN, 169–205.

Chaison, G.N. & Rose, J.B. (1991) 'The Macrodeterminants of Union Growth and Decline', in G. Strauss, G.D. Gallagher & J. Fiorito (eds), *The State of the Unions*, Industrial Relations Research Association, Madison WI, 3–46.

Chaples, E.A., et al. (1977) *A Survey of Members of the Amalgamated Metal Workers Union in the Sydney Metropolitan Area*, 1976 Field Studies Class, Department of Government, University of Sydney, Sydney.

Chapman, B.J., Dowrick, S., & Junanker, P.N. (1991) 'Perspectives on Australian Unemployment: The Impact on Wage Setting Institutions in the 1980s', in F.H. Gruen (ed.), *Australian Economic Policy: Conference Proceedings*, Centre for Economic Policy Research, Australian National University, Canberra, 21–57.

Chapman, B.J. & Gruen, F. (1990) 'An Analysis of the Australian Incomes Policy: The Prices and Incomes Accord' in C. de Neubourg (ed.), *The Art of Full Employment*, Elsevier/North Holland, Amsterdam.

Christie, V. (1992) 'Union Wage Effects and the Probability of Union Membership', *Economic Record*, 68(200), 43–56.

Christie, V. & Miller, P. (1989) 'Attitudes towards Trade Unions and Union Membership', *Economics Letters*, 30(3), September, 263–8.

Clegg, H. (1970) *The System of Industrial Relations in Great Britain*, Blackwell, Oxford.

Clegg, H. (1976) *Trade Unionism Under Collective Bargaining*, Blackwell, Oxford.

Coghill, K. (1987) 'Regrouping to Win Hearts and Minds', in K. Coghill (ed.), *The New Right's Australian Fantasy*, Penguin, Ringwood, 116–44.

Collier, R.B. & Collier, J.D. (1991) *Shaping the Political Arena: Critical Junctures, the Labour Movement and Regional Dynamics in Latin America*, Princeton University Press, Princeton NJ.

Cook, F.G., Clark, S.G., Roberts, K. & Semenoff, E. (1975) 'White and Blue Collar Workers' Attitudes to Trade Unionism and Social Class', *Industrial Relations Journal*, 6(4), Winter, 47–58.

Cornfield, D. (1986) 'Declining Union Membership in the Post-World War II Era: The United Furniture Workers Union of America 1939–1982' *American Journal of Sociology*, 91(5), March, 1112–53.

Costa, M. (1997) 'Union Reform: Union Strategy and the Third Wave', in M. Costa & M. Hearn (eds), *Reforming Australia's Unions: Insights from Southland Magazine*, Federation Press, Sydney, 12–25.

Costa, M. & Duffy, M. (1991) *Labor, Prosperity and the Nineties: Beyond the Bonsai Economy*, Federation Press, Sydney.

Cregan, C. & Johnston, S. (1990) 'An Industrial Relations Approach to the Free Rider Problem: Young People and Trade Union Membership in the UK', *British Journal of Industrial Relations*, 28(1), March, 84–104.

Creighton, B. (1987) 'Trade Unions, the Law and the New Right', in K. Coghill (ed.), *The New Right's Australian Fantasy*, Penguin, Ringwood, 74–92.

Crockett, G. & Hall, K. (1987) 'Salaried Professionals and Union Membership: An Australian Perspective', *Journal of Industrial Relations*, 29(1), March, 49–65.

Crouch, C. (1982) *Trade Unions: The Logic of Collective Action*, Fontana, London.

Cully, M. & Fraser, R. (1993) *The Australian Workplace Industrial Relations Survey (AWIRS): The State Dimension*, Industrial Relations Research Monograph No. 4, Department of Industrial Relations, Canberra, September.

Cunnison, S. (1983) 'Participation in Local Union Organisation – School Meals Staff: A Case Study', in E. Gamarnikow, D. Morgan, J. Purvis and D. Taylorson (eds), *Gender, Class and Work*, British Sociological Association/Gower, Aldershot, 77–95.

Curtain, R. & Mathews, J. (1992) 'Two Models of Award Restructuring', in B. Dabscheck, G. Griffin & J. Teicher (eds), *Contemporary Australian Industrial Relations*, Longman Cheshire, Melbourne.

Dabscheck, B. (1990) 'Industrial Relations and the Irresistible Magic Wand: The BCA's Plans to Americanise Australian Industrial Relations', in M. Easson & J. Shaw (eds), *Transforming Industrial Relations*, Pluto Press & Lloyd Ross Forum, Sydney, 117–30.

de Witte, H. (1989) 'Why Do Youngsters Join a Trade Union', paper presented to Fourth Western European Conference on the Psychology of Work and Organisation, Cambridge UK, April.

Deery, S. & De Cieri, H. (1991) 'Determinants of Trade Union Membership in Australia', *British Journal of Industrial Relations*, 29(1), March, 59–73.

DEET (Department of Employment, Education and Training) (1991) *1989 Australian Youth Survey: First Results*, Monograph Series No. 9, Economic and Policy Analysis Branch, DEET/AGPS, September.

Deshpande, S.P. & Fiorito, J. (1989) 'Specific and General Beliefs in Union Voting Models', *Academy of Management Journal*, 32, 883–97.

Dickens, W.T. & Leonard, J.S. (1985) 'Accounting for the Decline in Union Membership 1950–1980', *Industrial and Labor Relations Review*, 38(3), April, 323–34.

DIR (Department of Industrial Relations) (1995) *Enterprise Bargaining in Australia: Annual Report 1995*, AGPS, Canberra.

DIR (1996) *Enterprise Bargaining in Australia: Annual Report 1994*, AGPS, Canberra.

Doyle, P.M. (1985) 'Area Wage Surveys Shed Light on Decline in Unionization', *Monthly Labor Review*, 108(9), September, 13–20.

Dufty, N. (1972) *Industrial Relations in the Australian Metals Industry*, West Publishing Corporation, Sydney.

Dufty, N. (1979) *Industrial Relations in the Public Sector: The Firemen*, University of Queensland Press, Brisbane.

Dworkin, J.B. & Extejt, M. (1979) 'Why Workers Decertify Their Unions', *Proceedings of 39th Annual Meeting, Academy of Management*, Georgia, August, 241–5.

Edwards, R. & Podgursky, M. (1986) 'The Unravelling Accord: American Unions in Crisis', in R. Edwards, P. Caronna & F. Todtling (eds), *Unions in Crisis and Beyond*, Auburn House, Boston, 14–60.

Elias, P. (1990) 'Growth and Decline in Trade Union Membership in Great Britain: Evidence from Work Histories', Working Paper 16, Social Change and Economic Life Initiative, Economic and Social Research Council, Oxford.

Ellwood, D.T. & Fine, G. (1987) 'The Impact of Right-to-Work Laws on Union Organising', *Journal of Political Economy*, 95(2), 250–73.

Elton, J. (1997) 'Making Democratic Unions: From Policy to Practice', in B. Pocock (ed.), *Strife: Sex and Politics in Labour Unions*, Allen & Unwin, Sydney.

Evans, M.D.R. (1996) 'Public Opinion on Trade Unions in Australia: Continuity and Change', *Worldwide Attitudes*, 1996–03–25, March.

Evatt Foundation (1995) *Unions 2001*, Sydney.

Ewer, P., Hampson, S., Lloyd, C., Rainford, J., Rix, S. & Smith, M. (1991) *The Politics of the Accord*, Pluto, Sydney.

Farber, H.S. (1985) 'The Extent of Unionization in the US', in T. Kochan (ed.), *Challenges and Choices Facing American Labor*, MIT Press, Cambridge, 15–43.

Farber, H.S. (1990) 'The Decline of Unionisation in the United States: What Can Be Learned from Recent Experience?', *Journal of Labor Economics*, 8(1), Part 2, January, s75–s105.

Feuille, P. (1991) 'Unions as Antagonists, not Partners', in G. Strauss, D.G. Gallagher & J. Fiorito (eds), *The State of the Unions*, Industrial Relations Research Association, Madison WI, 85–92.

Fiorito, J. (1992) 'Unionism and Altruism', *Labor Studies Journal*, 17(3), Fall, 19–34.

Fiorito, J., Gallagher, D.G. & Fukami, C.V. (1988) 'Satisfaction with Union Representation', *Industrial and Labor Relations Review*, 41(2), January, 294–307.

Fiorito J., Gallagher, D.G. & Greer, C.R. (1986) 'Determinants of Unionism: A Review of the Literature', in K.M. Rowland & G.R. Ferris (eds), *Research in Personnel and Human Resource Management*, 4, JAI Press, Greenwich CT, 269–306.

Fiorito, J. & Greer, C.R. (1982) 'Determinants of US Unionism: Past Research and Future Needs', *Industrial Relations*, 21(1), Winter, 1–19.

Fiorito, J. & Greer, C.R. (1986) 'Gender Differences in Union Membership, Preferences and Beliefs', *Journal of Labor Research*, 7(2), Spring, 145–64.

Fisher, C. (1998) 'Unions, industry and bargaining,' unpublished MS. Canberra.

Flatau, P., Lewis, P. & Rushton, A. (1991) 'The Macroeconomic Consequences of Long-Term Unemployment', *Australian Economic Review*, 4th quarter, 106, 48–56.

Freedman, A. (1985) *The New Look in Wage Policy and Employee Relations*, The Conference Board, New York.

Freeman, R.B. (1985) 'Why are Unions Faring Poorly in NLRB Elections?', in T. Kochan (ed.), *Challenges and Choices Facing American Labor*, MIT Press, Cambridge, 45–88.

Freeman, R.B. (1990) 'On the Divergence in Unionism Among Developed Countries', in R. Brunetta & C. Dell'Aringa (eds), *Labour Relations and Economic Performance*, Macmillan, London, 304–23.

Freeman, R.B. & Kleiner, M.M. (1990) 'Employer Behavior in the Face of Union Organizing Drives', *Industrial and Labor Relations Review*, 43(4), April, 351–65.

Freeman, R.B. & Medoff, J.L. (1984), *What Do Unions Do?*, Basic Books, New York.

Freeman, R.B. & Pelletier, J. (1990) 'The Impact of Industrial Relations Legislation on Union Density in the UK and Ireland', *British Journal of Industrial Relations*, 28(2), June, 141–64.

Frenkel, S.J. (1988) 'Australian Employers in the Shadow of the Labor Accords', *Industrial Relations*, 27(2), Spring, 166–79.

Frenkel, S.J. (1990) 'Industrial Relations in Eight Advanced Countries: A Comparative Overview', *Bulletin of Comparative Labour Relations*, (20), 191–217.

Frenkel, S.J. (ed.) (1993) *Organized Labor in the Asia–Pacific Region: A Comparative Study of Trade Unionism in Nine Countries*, ILR Press, Cornell.

Frenkel, S.J. & Peetz, D. (1990a) 'Enterprise Bargaining: The BCA's Report on Industrial Relations Reform', *Journal of Industrial Relations*, 32(1), March, 69–99.

Frenkel, S.J. & Peetz, D. (1990b) 'The BCA Report: A Rejoinder', *Journal of Industrial Relations*, 32(3), September, 419–30.

Fundacion Largo Caballero (1988) *Perfil, Actitudes Y Demandas del Delegado y Afiliado a UGT*, Madrid.

Gale, F. (1990) 'A Comfortable Kind of Union?', *Australian Quarterly*, 62(1), Autumn, 15–20.

Gallagher, D.G. & Strauss, G. (1991) 'Union Membership Attitudes and Participation', in G. Strauss, D.G. Gallagher & J. Fiorito (eds), *The State of the Unions*, Industrial Relations Research Association, Madison, 139–74.

Gallie, D. (1989) 'Trade Union Allegiance and Decline in British Urban Labour Markets', Working Paper 9, Social Change and Economic Life Initiative, Economic and Social Research Council, Oxford.

Geare, A.J. (1990) 'Do Bosses Still Love the Closed Shop?', *Employee Relations*, 12(6), 17–23.

Getman, J.G., Goldberg, S.B. & Herman, J.B. (1976) *Union Representation Elections: Law and Reality*, Russell Sage, New York.

Gevers, P. (1992) 'Trade Unions, the Belgian Model of Industrial Relations and the Developments in the European Community', communication to Ninth World Congress, International Industrial Relations Association, September, Sydney.

Gilson, C.H.T. & Wagar, T. (1992) 'Accounting for Union Success in Representation Elections: Some Canadian Evidence', communication to Ninth World Congress, International Industrial Relations Association, Sydney, September.

Glick, W., Mirvis, P. & Harder, D. (1977), 'Union Satisfaction and Participation', *Industrial Relations*, 16(2), May, 145–51.

Godbout, T.M. (1993) 'Employment Change and Sectoral Distribution in 10 Countries, 1970–90', *Monthly Labor Review*, 116(10), October, 2–30.

Goldfield, M. (1987) *The Decline of Organized Labor in the United States*, University of Chicago Press, Chicago.

Goldthorpe, J.H., Lockwood, D., Bechhofer, F. & Platt, J. (1968) *The Affluent Worker: Industrial Attitudes and Behaviour*, Cambridge University Press, Cambridge, UK.

Gollan, R.A. (1960) *Radical and Working Class Politics: A Study of Eastern Australia 1850–1910*, Melbourne University Press, Melbourne.

Goot, M. (1990) 'The Forests, the Trees and the Polls', in C. Bean, I. McAllister & J. Warhurst (eds), *The Greening of Australian Politics*, Longman Cheshire, Melbourne, 114–33.

Goot, M. & Peetz, D. (forthcoming) 'To Have and To Hold', Australian Centre for Industrial Relations Research and Training, University of Sydney, Sydney.

Green, F. (1990) 'Trade Union Availability and Trade Union Membership in Britain', *Manchester School*, 58(4), December, 378–94.

Green, R. (1996) 'Reconnecting with the Workplace', *Australian Quarterly*, 68(4), Summer, 73–83.

Griffin, G. (1983) 'White Collar Unionism 1969 to 1981: Some Determinants of Growth', *Journal of Industrial Relations*, 25(1), March, 26–37.

Griffin, G. & de Rozairo, S. (1993) 'Trade Union Finances in the 1970s and 1980s', *Journal of Industrial Relations*, 33(3), September, 424–35.

Grimes, P.F.M. (1994) 'The Determinants of Trade Union Membership: Evidence from Two Australian Surveys', PhD thesis, Research School of Social Sciences, Australian National University, Canberra.

Guest, D.E. & Dewe, P. (1991) 'Company or Trade Union: Which Wins Workers' Allegiance? A Study of Commitment in the UK Electronics Industry', *British Journal of Industrial Relations*, 29(1), March, 75–96.

Guille, H. (1985) 'Industrial Relations in Queensland', *Journal of Industrial Relations*, 27(3), September, 383–96.

Hammarström, O. (1992) 'Local and Global: Trade Unions in the Future', in *Trade Unionism in the Future*, Ninth World Congress of International Industrial Relations Association, Proceedings Vol. 2, 30 August – 3 September, 116–24.

Hammer, T.H. & Berman, M. (1981) 'The Role of Noneconomic Factors in Faculty Union Voting', *Journal of Applied Psychology*, 66(4), 415–21.

Hancké, R. (1993) 'Trade Union Membership in Europe, 1960–1990: Rediscovering Local Unions', *British Journal of Industrial Relations*, 31(4), December, 593–613.

Hancock, K. & Rawson, D. (1993) 'The Metamorphosis of Australian Industrial Relations', *British Journal of Industrial Relations*, 31(4), December, 489–513.

Hanson, C.G., Jackson, S.M. & Miller, D. (1982) *The Closed Shop: A Comparative Study in Public Policy and Trade Union Security in Britain, the USA and West Germany*, Gower, Aldershot.

Harbridge, R. & Crawford, A. (1997) 'External Legitimacy of Unions in New Zealand: An Update', paper presented to Third International Conference on Emerging Union Structures, Australian National University, Canberra.

Harbridge, R. & Moulder, J. (1992) 'Collective Bargaining and the Employment Contracts Act 1991: One Year On', Industrial Relations Centre, Victoria University of Wellington, 15 May.

Harding, A. & Landt, J. (1992) 'Policy and Poverty: Trends in Disposable Incomes March 1983 to September 1991', *Australian Quarterly*, 64(1), Autumn, 19–48.

Harding, A. & Mitchell, D. (1992) 'The Efficiency and Effectiveness of the Tax-Transfer System in the 1980s', *Australian Tax Forum*, 9(3), 277–304.

Harris, R. (1993) 'Variations in Union Presence and Density in Australia: Evidence from AWIRS, 1989', *Journal of Industrial Relations*, 35(4), December, 571–84.

Hartley, J.F. (1992) 'Joining a Trade Union', in J.F. Hartley & G.M. Stephenson (eds), *Employment Relations: the Psychology of Influence and Control at Work*, Blackwell, Oxford, 163–83.

Hills, S.J. (1985) 'The Attitudes of Union and Non-union Male Workers Toward Union Representation', *Industrial and Labor Relations Review*, 38(2), January, 179–94.

Hilmer, F., Angwin, M., Layt, J.E., Dudley, G., Barratt, P. & McLaughlin, P.A. (1993) *Working Relations: A Fresh Start for Australian Enterprises*, Employee Relations Study Commission, Business Council of Australia, Melbourne.

Hirsch, B.T. (1980) 'The Determinants of Unionization: An Analysis of Inter-area Differences, *Industrial and Labor Relations Review*, 33(2), January, 147–61.

Hirsch, B.T. & Addison, J.T. (1986) *The Economic Analysis of Unions*, Allen & Unwin, Boston.

Hirsch, B.T. & Berger, M.C. (1984) 'Union Membership Determination and Industry Characteristics, *Southern Economic Journal*, 50(3), January 1984, 665–79.

Hirschman, A.O. (1971) *Exit, Voice and Loyalty*, Harvard University Press, Cambridge MA.

Hofstede, G. & Bond, G.H. (1988) 'The Confucian Connection: From Cultural Roots to Economic Growth', *Organizational Dynamics*, 16(4), Spring, 5–21.

HTM (Heylen Research Centre and Teesdale Mueli and Co.) (1992) *A Survey of Labour Market Adjustment Under the Employment Contracts Act 1991*, Report prepared for Industrial Relations Service, Department of Labour, Wellington, October.

Hundley, G. (1989) 'Things Unions Do, Job Attributes and Union Membership', *Industrial Relations*, 28(3), Fall, 335–55.

Jackson, M.P. (1982) *Trade Unions*, Longman, London.

Jarley, P., Kuruvilla, S.C. & Casteel, D. (1990) 'Member-Union Relations and Union Satisfaction', *Industrial Relations*, 29(1), Winter, 128–34.

Johnson, K.R. & Golembiewski, R.T. (1992) 'National Culture in Organization Development: A Conceptual and Empirical Analysis', *International Journal of Human Resource Management*, 3(1), May, 71–84.

Johnston, R. (1977) 'The Immigrant Worker' in A. Bordow (ed.), *The Worker in Australia: Contributions from Research*, University of Queensland Press, Brisbane, 68–112.

Jones, R., McAllister, I., Denemark, D. & Gow, D. (1993) *Australian Election Study 1993*, computer file, Social Science Data Archives, Australian National University, Canberra.

Jones, R., McAllister, I. & Gow, D. (1996) *Australian Election Study 1996*, computer file, Social Science Data Archives, Australian National University, Canberra.

Karmel T. & MacLachlan, M. (1986) 'Sex Segregation: Increasing or Decreasing?', Technical Paper No. 40, Bureau of Labour Market Research, Canberra, September 1986.

Kassalow, E.M. (1969) *Trade Unions and Industrial Relations: An International Comparison*, Random House, New York.

Kelley, J., Cushing, R.G. & Headey, B. (1984) *Australian National Social Science Survey 1984*, User's guide and data file, Social Science Data Archives, Australian National University, Canberra.

Kelly, J. (1990) 'British Trade Unionism 1979–89: Change, Continuity and Contradictions', *Work, Employment and Society*, Special Issue, May, 29–60.

Kelly, J. & Heery, E. (1989) 'Full-time Officials and Trade Union Recruitment', *British Journal of Industrial Relations*, 27(2), July, 196–213.

Kelly, P. (1985) *The Hawke Ascendancy*, Angus and Robertson, Sydney.

Kenyon, P.D. & Lewis, P.E.T. (1991) 'Trade Union Membership and the Accord', paper presented to Australian Labour Market Research Workshop, Centre for Economic Policy Research, Australian National University, February (also presented as paper to Conference of Economists, Sydney, 1990).

Kenyon, P.D. & Lewis, P.E.T. (1992) 'Trade Union Membership and the Accord', *Australian Economic Papers*, 31(59), December, 325–45.

Kenyon, P.D. & Lewis, P.E.T. (1996) 'The Decline in Trade Union Membership: What Role Did the Accord Play', paper presented to conference on The End of the Accord, Victoria University of Technology, Melbourne, November.

Klandermans, B. (1986) 'Psychology and Trade Union Participation: Joining, Acting, Quitting', *Journal of Occupational Psychology*, 59(3), September, 189–204.

Kochan, T.A. (1979) 'How American Workers View Labor Unions', *Monthly Labor Review*, 102, April, 23–31.

Kochan, T.A. & Dyer, L. (1992) 'Managing Transformational Change: The Role of Human Resource Professionals', in Ninth World Congress of International Industrial Relations Association, Proceedings Vol. 3, 30 August – 3 September, 71–86.

Kochan, T., Katz, H. & McKersie, R. (1986) *The Transformation of American Industrial Relations*, Basic, New York.

Kumar, P. (1993) *From Uniformity to Divergence: Industrial Relations in Canada and the US*, IRC Press, Kingston.

Lamming, R. & Bessant, J. (1988) *Macmillan Dictionary of Business and Management*, Macmillan, London.

Lansbury, R.D. (1978) *Professionals and Management*, University of Queensland Press, Brisbane.

Leicht, K.T. (1989) 'Unions, Plants, Jobs and Workers: An Analysis of Union Satisfaction and Participation', *Sociological Quarterly*, 30(2), Summer, 331–62.

Leigh, D.E. (1986) 'Union Preferences, Job Satisfaction and the Union-Voice Hypothesis', *Industrial Relations*, 25(1), Winter, 65–71.

Lewis, D.E. (1983) 'The Measurement and Interpretation of the Segregation of Women in the Workforce', *Journal of Industrial Relations*, 25(3), September, 347–52.

Lewis, P.E.T. & Kirby, M.G. (1987) 'The Impact of Incomes Policy on Wage Determination in Australia', *Economic Record*, 63(181), June, 156–61.

Light, D. & Pollak, A. (1986) 'Business Backs Robe River Stand', *Sydney Morning Herald*, 29 August.

Lipset, S.M. (1986) 'North American Labor Movements: A Comparative Perspective', in S.M. Lipset (ed.), *Unions in Transition: Entering the Second Century*, ICS Press, San Francisco, 421–54.

Lipset, S.M. & Rokkan, S. (1967) 'Cleavage Structures, Party Systems and Voter Alignments: An Introduction', in S.M. Lipset & S. Rokkan (eds), *Party Systems and Voter Alignments: Cross-National Perspectives*, Free Press, New York, 1–63.

Lipset, S.M., Trow, M. & Coleman, J. (1956) *Union Democracy: The Inside Politics of the International Typographical Union*, Free Press, New York.

LO (Swedish Trade Union Confederation) (1991) *Trade Union Organisation in the Future*, Summary of a Report to the 1991 LO Congress, Stockholm.

Lumley, R. (1973) *White Collar Unionism in Britain*, Methuen, London.

Lumsden, K. & Petersen, C. (1975) 'The Effects of Right-to-Work Laws on Unionization in the United States', *Journal of Political Economy*, 83(6), 1237–48.

McAllister, I. & Mughan, A. (1987) *Australian Election Survey 1987*, machine-readable data file, Social Science Data Archives, Australian National University, Canberra.

McCarthy, P. (1985) 'Power Without Glory: The Queensland Electricity Dispute', *Journal of Industrial Relations*, 27(3), September, 364–82.

McDonald, J. & Timo, N. (1996), 'Killing the Union? Individualised Contracts and CRA', in G. Griffin (ed.), *Contemporary Research on Unions: Membership,*

Organisation, Marginalisation and Non-standard Employment, Monograph No. 8, National Key Centre in Industrial Relations, Monash University, Melbourne.

Macintyre, S.F. (1983) 'Labour, Capital and Arbitration', in B.W. Head (ed.), *State and Economy in Australia*, Oxford University Press, Melbourne, 55–78.

MacKinnon, B.H. (1996) 'The Struggle for Managerial Prerogative: Ramifications of the CRA Weipa Dispute', in R. Fells & T. Todd (eds), *Current Research in Industrial Relations: Proceedings of the 10th AIRAANZ Conference*, Association of Industrial Relations Academics of Australia and New Zealand, Perth, February, 287–95.

McNair Anderson Associates & Layton, R. (1980) *Managers and Workers at the Crossroads*, Sentry Holdings, Sydney.

McNair, I.W. (ed.) (1988) *Australian Public Opinion Polls (The Gallup Method) 1973–1987*, Quadrant Research Services, Sydney.

Manning, H. (1990) 'Union Membership Decline: Women and Unionism in Australia', paper presented to conference on Labour Movement Strategies for the 21st Century, Evatt Foundation, Sydney, September.

Maranto, C.L. & Fiorito, J. (1987) 'The Effect of Union Characteristics on the Outcome of NLRB Certification Elections', *Industrial and Labor Relations Review*, 40(2), January, 225–40.

Martin, R.M. (1975) *Trade Unions in Australia*, Penguin, Ringwood.

Mason, R. & Bain, P. (1993) 'The Determinants of Trade Union Membership in Britain: A Survey of the Literature', *Industrial and Labor Relations Review*, 46(2), January, 332–51.

Meltz, N.H. (1985) 'Labour Movements in Canada and the US' in T.A. Kochan (ed.), *Challenges and Choices Facing American Labor*, MIT Press, Cambridge MA, 315–34.

Meltz, N.H. (1989) 'Interstate vs Interprovisional Differences in Union Density', *Industrial Relations*, 28(2), Spring, 142–58.

Meltz, N.H. (1990a) 'Unionism in the Private Services Sector: A Canada–US Comparison', in J. Jensen (ed.), *Canadian–American Labor Responses: Economic Restructuring and Union Strategies*, Temple University Press, Philadelphia.

Meltz, N.H. (1990b) 'Unionisation in Canada and the US: On Parallel Treadmills?', *Forum for Applied Research and Public Policy*, Winter, 46–52.

Mercer, D.E. & Weir, D.T.H. (1972) 'Attitudes to Work and Unionism Among White-Collar Employees', *Industrial Relations Journal*, 3, 49–60.

Millward, N. (1990) 'The State of the Unions', in R. Jowell, S. Witherspoon & L. Brook with B. Taylor (eds), *British Social Attitudes: the Seventh Report*, Gower, Aldershot, 27–50.

Millward, N. (1994) *The New Industrial Relations?*, Based on the ED/ESRC/PSI/ACAS Surveys, Policy Studies Institute, London.

Millward, N. & Stevens, M. (1986) *British Workplace Industrial Relations 1980–1984*, Gower, Aldershot.

Millward, N., Stevens, M., Smart, D. & Hawes, W.R. (1994) *Workplace Industrial Relations in Transition: The ED/ESRC/PSI/ACAS Surveys*, Dartmouth, Aldershot.

Mitchell, D.J.B. (1983) 'Is Union Wage Determination at a Turning Point?' *Proceedings of the 35th Annual Meeting of the Industrial Relations Research Association*, Madison WI, 1354–61.

Montgomery, R.B. (1989) 'The Influence of Attitudes and Normative Pressures on Voting Decisions in a Union Certification Election', *Industrial and Labor Relations Review*, 42(2), January, 262–79.

Moore, W.J. & Newman, R.J. (1975) 'On the Prospects for American Trade Union Growth: A Cross-Section Analysis', *Review of Economics and Statistics*, 57, November, 435–45.

Morehead, A., Steele, M., Alexander, M., Stephen, K. & Duffin, L. (1997) *Changes at Work: The 1995 Australian Workplace Industrial Relations Survey*, Longman, Melbourne.

Morgan Gallup Poll (1974) 'Trade Unions', Computer Printout Poll 48, Melbourne, August–September.

Morgan Gallup Poll (1976) 'What Australians Think About Trade Unions', Poll 361A, May.

Morgan Gallup Poll (1977) 'Use the Arbitration Commission for Wage Negotiations', special poll for Channel 9, 10 May.

Morgan Gallup Poll (1978) 'Most Against Compulsory Unionism', Finding 594, Melbourne, November.

Morgan Poll (1992a) 'Fewer Believe Trade Unions in Australia a Good Thing and Most Believe Trade Unions Have Too Much Power', Finding No. 2354, 14 December.

Morgan Poll (1992b) 'Pharmacists, Doctors and Dentists Get Top Billing for Ethics and Honesty', Finding No. 2252, 18 May.

New South Wales Anti-Discrimination Board (1983) *Trade Unions: Membership and Non-membership*, NSW ADB, Sydney.

Newspoll (1989) 'ALP Polls Well on Environmental Issue', *Australian*, 15 September.

Newspoll (1991) 'Voters Rate Jobs the Big Concern', *Australian*, 29 October.

Newspoll (1992) 'Coalition Best to Handle Crucial Jobs Issue', *Australian*, 20 May.

Niland, J. & Turner, D. (1985) *Control, Consensus or Chaos? Managers and Industrial Relations Reform*, George Allen and Unwin/Industrial Relations Research Centre (University of New South Wales), Sydney.

O'Neill, H. (1971) 'The Growth of Municipal Employee Unions' in R.H. Connery & W.V. Farr (eds), *Unionisation of Municipal Employees*, Proceedings of Academy of Political Science, 30(2), New York, 1–13.

Organisation for Economic Cooperation and Development (OECD) (1991) *Employment Outlook*, Paris, July.

Organisation for Economic Cooperation and Development (1994) 'Collective Bargaining Levels and Coverage', in *Employment Outlook*, Paris, July.

Palmer, I. & McGraw, P. (1990) 'Union Diversification and the Battle for Recognition in the Travel Agency Industry', *Journal of Industrial Relations*, 32(1), March, 3–18.

Pankert, A. (1992) 'Adjustment Problems of Trade Unions in Selected Industrialised Market Economy Countries: The Union's Own View', in *Trade Unionism in the Future*, Ninth World Congress of International Industrial Relations Association, Proceedings Volume 2, 30 August – 3 September, 147–57.

Payne, J. (1989) 'Trade Union Membership and Activism Among Young People in Great Britain', *British Journal of Industrial Relations*, 27(1), March, 111–32.

Peetz, D. (1989) 'Donkeys, Deserters and Targets: Causes of Swing in the 1987 Federal Election', *Australian Quarterly*, 61(4), Summer, 468–80.

Peetz, D. (1995) 'Union Membership, Labour, Management and the Accord', PhD thesis, School of Industrial Relations and Organisational Behaviour, University of New South Wales, Sydney.

Peetz, D. (1996) 'Unions, Conflict and the Dilemma of Cooperation', *Journal of Industrial Relations*, 38(4), December.

Peetz, D. (1997a) 'Deunionisation and Union Establishment: The Impact of Workplace Change, HRM Strategies and Workplace Unionism', *Labour and Industry*, 8(1), August, 21–36.

Peetz, D. (1997b) 'The Accord, Compulsory Unionism and the Paradigm Shift in Union Membership', Discussion Paper No. 358, Centre for Economic Policy Research, Australian National University, January 1997.

Peetz, D. (1997c) 'Why Bother? Apathy and Union Membership', Discussion Paper No. 357, Centre for Economic Policy Research, Australian National University, January 1997.

Peetz, D. (1997d) 'Sympathy for the Devil? Ausralian Unionism and Public Opinion', seminar paper, University of Queensland, Brisbane.

Peetz, D. (1998) 'Why Join? Why Stay? The Individual Decision to Unionise', *Economic and Labour Relations Review*, 9(1), June.

Peetz, D. & Goot, M. (1998) 'Did Workers Really Reject the Accord?', Working paper, Centre for Research in Employment and Work, Griffith University, Brisbane.

Peetz, D., Preston, A. & Docherty J. (eds) (1993) *Workplace Bargaining in the International Context*, First Report of the Workplace Bargaining Research Project, Industrial Relations Research Monograph No. 2, Department of Industrial Relations, Canberra, January.

Peetz, D., Quinn, D., Edwards, L. & Riedel, P. (1993) 'Workplace Bargaining in New Zealand: Radical Change at Work', in Peetz, Preston & Docherty (1993), 195–328.

Piore, M.J. (1982) 'American Labor and the Industrial Crisis', *Challenge*, March–April, 5–11.

Piore, M.J. (1991) 'The Future of Unions' in G. Strauss, D.G. Gallagher & J. Fiorito (eds), *The State of the Unions*, Industrial Relations Research Association, Madison WI, 3–46.

Plowman, D. (1992) 'Arresting Union Decline: Membership Retention and Recruitment Strategies', in M. Crosby and M. Easson (eds), *What Should Unions Do?*, Lloyd Ross Forum/Pluto, Sydney, 266–88.

Plowman, D., Deery, S. & Fisher, C. (1981) *Australian Industrial Relations*, McGraw-Hill, Sydney.

Pocock, B. (1997) 'Institutional Sclerosis: Prospects for Trade Union Transformation', paper to Third International Conference on Emerging Union Structures, Australian National University, Canberra, December.

Prandy, K., Stewart, A. & Blackburn, R.M. (1974) 'Concepts and Measures: The Example of Unionateness', *Sociology*, 8(3), 427–46.

Prandy, K., Stewart, A. & Blackburn, R.M. (1982) *White Collar Work*, Macmillan, London.

Premack, S. & Hunter, J. (1988) 'Individual Unionisation Decisions', *Psychological Bulletin*, 103, 223–34.

Price, R. & Bain, G.S. (1989) 'The Comparative Analysis of Union Growth', in *Recent Trends in Industrial Relations Studies and Theory*, 8th World Congress, International Industrial Relations Association, Brussels, 99–110.

Princeton Survey Research Associates (1994) 'Worker Representation and Participation Survey: Top-Line Results', Princeton NJ.

Purcell, J. (1993) 'The End of Institutional Industrial Relations', *Political Quarterly*, 64(1).

Quiggin, J. (1996) *Great Expectations: Microeconomic Reform in Australia*, Allen & Unwin.

Quinlan, M. & Gardner, M. (1994) 'Researching Industrial Relations History: The Development of a Database on Australian Trade Unions 1825–1900', paper to Eighth Conference of Association of Industrial Relations Academics of Australia and New Zealand, Sydney, February.

Rawson, D. (1978) *Unions and Unionists in Australia*, George Allen and Unwin, Sydney.

Rawson, D. (1983) 'Is Unionism Everywhere in Decline?', paper to Australasian Political Studies Association annual conference, August.

Rawson, D. (1992) 'Has Unionism a Future?' in M. Crosby and M. Easson (eds), *What Should Unions Do?*, Lloyd Ross Forum/Pluto, Sydney, 2–15.

Rawson, D. & Wrightson, S. (1980) *A Handbook of Australian Trade Unions and Employees' Associations*, 4th edn, Occasional Paper No. 15, Department of Political Science, Research School of Social Sciences, Australian National University, Canberra.

Rawson, D. & Wrightson, S. (1985) *Australian Unions 1984*, Croom Helm, Sydney.

Regini, M. (1992) 'Human Resource Management and Industrial Relations in European Companies', in Ninth World Congress of International Industrial Relations Association, Proceedings Volume 3, 30 August – 3 September, 121–31.

RIALS (Research Institute for Advancement of Living Standards) (1993) 'Trade Unions – Present and Future', Report Issued by the Committee on Industrial Relations, Rengosoken, Tokyo, January.

Rose, J.B. & Chaison, G.N. (1985) 'The State of the Unions: United States and Canada', *Journal of Labor Research*, 6(1), Winter, 97–111.

Rose, J.B. & Chaison, G.N. (1992) 'Union Density and Union Effectiveness: The North American Experience', communication to Ninth World Congress, International Industrial Relations Association, Sydney.

Rose, J.B. & Chaison, G.N. (1993) 'Convergence in International Unionism, etc: The Case of Canada and the USA: A Comment', *British Journal of Industrial Relations*, 31(2), June, 293–7.

Russell, W. & Tease, W. (1988) 'Employment, Output and Real Wages', *Research Discussion Paper* RDP 8806, Reserve Bank of Australia, Sydney, September.

Ryan, E. & Prendergast, H. (1982) 'Unions are for Women, Too!' in K. Cole (ed.), *Power, Conflict and Control on Australian Trade Unions*, Penguin, Ringwood, 261–78.

Saltzman, G.M. (1985) 'Bargaining Laws as a Cause and Consequence of the Growth of Teacher Unionism', *Industrial and Labor Relations Review*, 38(3), April, 335–51.

Saunders, P. & Whiteford, P. (1987) 'Ending Child Poverty: An Assessment', paper to 16th Conference of Economists, Surfers Paradise, August.

Savery, L. & Soutar, G. (1993) 'Wage System Preferences: A Conjoint Analysis', *Australian Bulletin of Labour*, 19(4), December, 298–313.

Scherer, P. (1983) 'The Nature of the Australian Industrial Relations System: A Form of State Syndicalism', in K. Hancock, Y. Sono, B. Chapman & P. Foyle (eds), *Japanese and Australian Labour Markets: A Comparative Study*, Australia–Japan Research Centre, Canberra and Tokyo, 157–82.

Schriesheim, C.A. (1978) 'Job Satisfaction, Attitudes Towards Unions and Voting in a Union Representation Election', *Journal of Applied Psychology*, 68, 548–52.

Scoville, J. (1971) 'Inflation and Unionization in the US in 1966', *Industrial Relations*, 10(3), October, 354–61.

Sharpe, I.G. (1971) 'Growth of Australian Trade Unions 1907–1969', *Journal of Industrial Relations*, 13(2), June, 138–54.

Sharma, B. (1989) 'Union Growth in Malaysia and Singapore', *Industrial Relations*, 28, Fall, 446–58.

Shaw, J., Walton, M. & Walton, C. (1990) 'A Decline in Union Membership: Some Ideas for Trade Unions in the 1990s', paper to conference on Labour Movement Strategies for the 21st Century, Evatt Foundation, Sydney, September.

Sheldon, P. (1993) 'Arbitration and Union Growth and Behaviour in Australia: A Historical Re-evaluation', in N. Haworth, M. Hill & N. Wailes (eds), *Divergent Paths? Industrial Relations in Australia, New Zealand and the Asia–Pacific Region*, Proceedings of the 7th Conference, Association of Industrial Relations Academics of Australia and New Zealand, Auckland, February, 315–31.

Sheridan, T. (1975) *Mindful Militants: The Amalgamated Engineering Union in Australia 1920–1972*, Cambridge University Press, Cambridge.

Short, M., Preston, A. & Peetz, D. (1993) *The Spread and Impact of Workplace Bargaining: Evidence from the Workplace Bargaining Research Project*, Department of Industrial Relations, Canberra, August.

Short, M., Romeyn, J. & Callus, R. (1994) *Reform and Bargaining at the Workplace and Enterprise: Evidence from Two Surveys*, Industrial Relations Research Series No. 12, Workplace Bargaining Research Project, Department of Industrial Relations, Canberra, November.

Simey, T.S. (ed.) (1956) *The Dock Worker: An Analysis of Conditions of Employment in the Port of Manchester*, Liverpool University Press, Liverpool.

Singleton, G. (1992) *The Accord and the Australian Labour Movement*, Melbourne University Press, Melbourne.

Smith, P. & Morton, G. (1994) 'Union Exclusion – Next Steps', *Industrial Relations Journal*, 25(1), March, 3–14.

Spillane, R. (1980) 'Attitudes of Business Executives and Union Leaders to Industrial Relations: 23 Years Later', *Journal of Industrial Relations*, 22(3), September, 317–25.

Stilwell, F. (1986) *The Accord and Beyond*, Pluto, Sydney.

Storer, D. & Hargreaves, K. (1976) 'Migrant Women in Industry', in S. Staats (ed.), *Social Policy and Problems of the Workforce*, Vol. 1, Social Welfare Unit, Australian Council of Trade Unions, Melbourne, 39–104.

Strauss, G. (1991) 'Comment on: State Policies and Workplace Relations', in H. Katz (ed.), *The Future of Industrial Relations*, Proceedings of the Second Bargaining Group Conference, Institute of Collective Bargaining, New York State School of Industrial and Labour Relations, Cornell University, Ithaca.

Streeck, W. (1984) 'Neo-Corporatist Industrial Relations and the Economic Crisis in West Germany' in J.H. Goldthorpe (ed.), *Order and Conflict in Contemporary Capitalism*, Clarendon, Oxford, 291–314.

Sutcliffe, P. & Callus, R. (1994) *Glossary of Australian Industrial Relations Terms*, Australian Centre for Industrial Relations Research and Teaching and Australian Centre in Strategic Management, Sydney and Brisbane.

Thompson, M. (1993) 'Convergence in International Unionism, etc: The Case of Canada and the USA: A Comment', *British Journal of Industrial Relations*, 31(2), June, 299–303.

Thorpe, M. (1998) 'Members' perceived support from, and commitment to, their trade union: A measure of individual attitudes of members of the TWU Queensland Branch', draft PhD thesis, University of Queensland, Brisbane.

Troy, L. (1992) 'Convergence in International Unionism, etc: The Case of Canada and the USA' *British Journal of Industrial Relations*, 30(1), March, 1–43.

Troy, L. (1993) 'Convergence in International Unionism, etc: The Case of Canada and the USA: Reply', *British Journal of Industrial Relations*, 31(2), June, 305–8.

Turner, T. (1994) 'Unionisation and Human Resource Management in Irish Companies', *Industrial Relations Journal*, 25(1), March, 39–51.

Undy, R., Ellis, N., McCarthy, W.E.J. & Halmov, A.M. (1981) *Change in Trade Unions: The Development of UK Unions Since the 1960s*, Hutchinson, London.

Van de Vall, M. (1970) *Labor Organisations*, Cambridge University Press, Cambridge.

Visser, E.J. (1988) 'Trade Unionism in Western Europe: Present Situation and Prospects', *Labour and Society*, 13(2), April, 125–82.

Visser, E.J. (1991) 'Trends in Trade Union Membership', in Organisation for Economic Cooperation and Development, *Employment Outlook*, Paris, July, 97–134.

Visser, E.J. (1992) 'Union Organisation: Why Countries Differ?', in *Trade Unionism in the Future*, Ninth World Congress of International Industrial Relations Association, Proceedings Volume 2, 30 August – 3 September, 158–76.

Waddington, J. & Whitston, C. (1993) 'Why do White Collar Staff Join Unions? Some Evidence on the Tension Between Individual Activity and Collective Organisation', paper to conference on Unions on the Brink: The Future of the Trade Union Movement, Cardiff Business School, September.

Walton, R.E. (1985) 'From Control to Commitment in the Workplace', *Harvard Business Review*, 2, March–April.

Wedderburn, D. & Crompton, R. (1972) *Workers' Attitudes and Technology*, Cambridge Papers in Sociology 2, Cambridge University Press, Cambridge.

Western, B. (1993a) 'Postwar Unionisation in Eighteen Advanced Capitalist Countries', *American Sociological Review*, 58, April, 266–82.

Western, B. (1993b) 'A Comparative Study of Working Class Disorganisation: Union Decline in 18 Advanced Capitalist Countries', mimeo, Department of Sociology, Princeton University.

Western, B. (1994) 'Institutional Mechanisms for Unionisation in Sixteen OECD Countries: An Analysis of Social Survey Data', *Social Forces*, 73(2), December, 497–519.

Wheeler, H.M. (1985) *Industrial Conflict: An Integrative Theory*, University of South Carolina Press, Columbia SC.

Wheeler, H.M. & McClendon, J.A. (1991) 'The Individual Decision to Unionize', in G. Strauss, D.G. Gallagher & J. Fiorito (eds), *The State of the Unions*, Industrial Relations Research Association, Madison WI.

Williams, L. (1985) 'Discussion: Labour Movements in Canada and the US', in T.A. Kochan (ed.), *Challenges and Choices Facing American Labor*, MIT Press, Cambridge, 335–6.

Willman, P. (1989) 'The Logic of Market Share Unionism', *Industrial Relations Journal*, 20(4), Winter, 260–70.

Wooden, M. (1992) 'Compulsory Unionism and the AWIRS: Redrawing the Map', *Economic and Labour Relations Review*, 3(2), December, 180–99.

Wooden, M. & Balchin, J. (1992) 'Unionisation in Australia: Evidence from the AWIRS', Working Paper Series No. 122, National Institute of Labour Studies Inc, April.

Wooden, M. & Balchin, J. (1993) 'Unionisation in Australia: Evidence from the AWIRS', *Economic Record*, 69(206), September, 305–13.

Wright, K. (1983) 'Union Demarcation Disputes', in G.W. Ford & D. Plowman (eds), *Australian Unions: An Industrial Relations Perspective*, Macmillan, Melbourne, 325–43.

Wright, M. (1983) 'Union Preference and the Closed Shop', in G.W. Ford & D. Plowman (eds), *Australian Unions: An Industrial Relations Perspective*, Macmillan, Melbourne, 241–57.

Youngblood, S., De Nisi, A., Molleston, J. & Mobley, W. (1984) 'The Impact of Work Environment, Instrumentality Beliefs, Perceived Labor Union Image and Subjective Norms on Union Voting Intentions', *Academy of Management Journal*, 27(3), September, 576–90.

Zappala, G. (1992) 'Should Unions Support the Closed Shop?' in M. Crosby & M. Easson (eds), *What Should Unions Do?*, Lloyd Ross Forum/Pluto, Sydney, 296–315.

Index